I and Tao

Jonathan R. Herman

I and Tao

Martin Buber's Encounter with Chuang Tzu

STATE UNIVERSITY OF NEW YORK PRESS

Production by Ruth Fisher
Marketing by Bernadette LaManna

Published by
State University of New York Press, Albany

© 1996 State University of New York

For information, address the State University of New York Press,
State University Plaza, Albany, NY 12246

Library of Congress Cataloging-in-Publication Data

Herman, Jonathan R., 1957–
    I and Tao : Martin Buber's encounter with Chuang Tzu / Jonathan R.
Herman.
        p. cm.
    Includes a translation into English of Martin Buber's German
translation of selections from the Nan-hua ching of Chuang-tzu.
    Includes bibliographical references and index.
    ISBN 0-7914-2923-7 (ch : alk. paper). — ISBN 0-7914-2924-5 (pb :
alk. paper)
    1. Chuang-tzu. Nan-hua ching. 2. Buber, Martin, 1878–1965—
Contributions in Taoism. 3. Buber, Martin, 1878–1965. Ich und du.
4. Mysticism—Comparative studies. I. Buber, Martin, 1878–1965.
II. Chuang-tzu. Nan-hua ching. German. Selections. III. Chuang-
tzu. Nan-hua ching. English. Selections. IV. Title
BL1900.C576B8334 1996
299'.51482—dc20   95-20801
                                                               CIP

10 9 8 7 6 5 4 3 2

For my father,
Joseph Lewis Herman
(July 6, 1924–April 3, 1991)

❧-CONTENTS-❧

❧·PREFACE·❧

When I inform colleagues that the subject of this book is Martin Buber's 1910 translation of and commentary on the Taoist classic, *Chuang Tzu,* the vast majority of them—sinologists, Buber scholars, and comparative religionists alike—are astonished to learn that such a work even exists. "When," they ask, "did Buber learn Chinese?" "Did he really publish *Reden und Gleichnisse des Tschuang-tse* more than a decade before he wrote *I and Thou?*" "What is the significance of this work in the development of Buber's dialogical philosophy?" But once my associates realize that Buber's actual sinological skills were minimal and that he based his work chiefly on English translations, their initial astonishment invariably mingles with some skepticism about the merit of evaluating a dated study by a nonspecialist. "Didn't Buber simply pass along the misinterpretations and erroneous translations of his sources?" "How could such an obviously unscholarly document offer any substantial contributions to the sinological discourse?" "Does it even really matter that Buber briefly became a Taoist dilettante?"

I sometimes counter these concerns with a handful of standard, marginally convincing defenses. I might argue that how and why any major Western thinker seriously approached a Chinese classic is, in and of itself, an important historical question. Or, I might point out that Buber's work had some significant social and political impact, particularly with the German Jewish Youth Movement. However, my *real* justification for this project is that I had detected a thematic resonance between *Chuang Tzu* and *I and Thou* years before I had ever heard of Buber's Taoist studies. In fact, a seminar paper written shortly before my initial exposure to Buber already seemed to anticipate a dialogical interpretation of *Chuang Tzu,* as I argued that Taoist enlightenment is characterized by "an intense personal freedom, where individuality and integrity are maintained

without the threat of egoism" (Herman 1985:14). Shortly after my
initial encounter with *I and Thou,* as well as the corpus of Hasidic
and Kabbalistic mysticism, I presented a paper that challenged the
historical particularism dominating Jewish studies and related the
dialogical principle to various typologies of mystical experience put
forth by modern theorists and methodologists. With the brashness
of an aspiring scholar, I wrote in the introduction, "This approach
is admittedly experimental, but perhaps it is the germination of a
project directed both to broaden the bases of contemporary Jewish
scholarship, and to demonstrate the imperative of Jewish contributions to the newly-emerging discipline of inter-faith dialogue"
(Herman 1986:4). In the body of the paper, I drew direct connections between Buber and Chuang Tzu and concluded by asking,
"Can typological similarities bring Jews to discover a kinship with
diverse cultures originally thought to be foreign and unrelated"
(16)?

But while I grew increasingly interested in developing some type
of project dealing with both thinkers, I was at first unable to find
the spark, the rigorous methodological basis or historical foundation that would inform a meaningful juxtaposition and distinguish
it from the kinds of romantically drawn parallels that have so often
undermined the credibility of comparative religion as a discipline.
Ironically, it was when I had all but abandoned any hope for proving this study feasible, that my wife-to-be Ellen Rae Gallow, then
a student at the Episcopal Divinity School, called to my attention
Buber's German translation of *Chuang Tzu.* As it turns out, this
romantic, impressionistic, and astonishingly perceptive volume
hardly represents a "lost" work—the *Encyclopedia of Religion* does
list it as one of Buber's early "studies in mysticism" (Silberstein
1987:317), and the commentary portion has been available in English translation for quite some time—but it has certainly occupied
a relatively obscure position next to Buber's Hasidic and dialogical
writings, and it is never mentioned in mainstream sinological discourse. Needless to say, this "discovery" provided the crucial pivot
I had been seeking. The resonance I had previously detected between Buber and Chuang Tzu was no longer an imagined simili-
tude, but a very real affinity between the two thinkers, the embryo
of which was fortuitously chronicled in one often forgotten document. And as the focus of my preliminary research became more

clearly defined, I learned that the Taoist work represented not only a transitional stage between Buber's very early Hasidic studies and the first edition of *I and Thou,* but also the onset of his ongoing involvement with Chinese philosophy and religion. Most notably, Buber followed *Reden und Gleichnisse des Tschuang-tse* the very next year with a translation of Chinese folk tales and in 1924 with an unpublished commentary on the *Tao Te Ching.*[1] Although Buber would eventually turn his attention almost exclusively to the revitalization of the Jewish tradition, he nevertheless continued to quote his favorite Taoist texts in a number of interesting contexts, even when he could no longer stand by the philosophies expressed.[2]

Once it became clear that my study of Buber and *Chuang Tzu* would take *Reden und Gleichnisse* as its central point of departure, I began my own English retranslation of both the text translation and commentary, but soon learned that Humanities Press International, the publishing company housing several translations of other Buber materials, had only recently invited another scholar to provide renderings of the two early Chinese volumes (see Buber 1991). After much initial alarm that this "competition" would undermine the relevance of my own project, I discovered that the translator, Alex Page, was not particularly familiar with either Chuang Tzu or Buber and had a general disinterest in mysticism, and thus much technical detail became lost to an aesthetically appealing, but fairly free rendering.[3] More importantly, I found in Chinese historian Irene Eber, the author of the insightful introduction to the volume, an invaluable scholarly ally in my research. Eber, who had previously written a brief prologue to Richard Wilhelm's *Lectures on the I Ching* (1979), was quite receptive to open exchanges of information, furnishing me with considerable background data on the history of German sinology and offering an approach to the subject that complemented my own.

The more deeply I moved into my research, the more clear it became that I was less interested in the fairly prosaic task of establishing Chuang Tzu's influence on Buber than in the more unpredictable sinological enterprise of evaluating the significance of this much overlooked work for interpreting the text of *Chuang Tzu.* This was due partially to my hope that the translation and commentary together could somehow provide a legitimate vehicle for bringing the I-Thou relation to *Chuang Tzu,* but also to my investment in the thorny hermeneutic challenges that such an approach might bring to light. While Buber knew little of the Chinese text's interpretive history, he inadvertently entered (and made bold contributions to) a complex and longstanding discourse that had already produced and continues to produce a tremendously variegated range of readings. To this day, modern sinologists, not unlike more than two millennia of Chinese thinkers, have been unable to agree upon a coherent or consistent interpretive strategy for unraveling the meanings to be found amid the pages of *Chuang Tzu*. And while I am loath to lapse into the kind of interpretive nihilism that consumes deconstructionists and their kindred spirits, I would nevertheless suggest that it may be the sheer richness and diversity of historical applications of the text that portends the most eloquent warning against too soon dismissing peripheral or iconoclastic contributions.

❧-ACKNOWLEDGMENTS-❧

This single page of acknowledgments can only begin to express my indebtedness to the many people and institutions who in various ways made it possible for me to produce this work. I am especially grateful to Tu Wei-ming, Dick Niebuhr, and Jim Engell, for their helpful advice and guidance at every stage along the way. Special thanks also to Maurice Friedman, for his tremendous ongoing support for this project, and to Irene Eber, for sharing the fruits of her research during my own preliminary stages of work. Bill Graham offered constructive advice to help me formulate an appropriate focus, and Chad Hansen offered encouragement when I seemed to need it. Roger Ames and David Hall were instrumental in helping me find the right audience for the book.

A number of people provided information or helped me to locate important source material. My thanks to Michael Appell, Nila Baker, Kay Evans, Francis Schussler Fiorenza, Aleene Friedman, Robert Gimello, D. Jonathan Grieser, Lewis Jacobs, Michael LaFargue, Steven Kepnes, Masatoshi Nagatomi, Alex Page, Laurence Silberstein, Katherine Steinburger, Wilfred Cantwell Smith, Jay Wexler, and Lee Yearley. Some materials were provided with the cooperation of the Martin Buber Archive, the Leo Baeck Institute, and Humanities Press International.

Various activities associated with the research for this book were partially funded by grants from the Center for the Study of World Religions (Harvard University), Lewis & Clark College, and St. Lawrence University.

And of course, this book would not be, were it not for the continuing inspiration and support from my family, friends, and cats. My parents never seemed to lose hope, and my wife Ellen continues to provide me with good cause for it.

Introduction:
Chuang Tzu, Martin Buber, and Reden und Gleichnisse des Tschuang-tse

Martin Buber's *Reden und Gleichnisse des Tschuang-tse (Talks and Parables of Chuang Tzu)* is more than just an antiquated study of a Taoist text. It is the chronicle of a creative and exciting encounter between Buber and *Chuang Tzu*, between one of the modern West's most influential thinkers and one of ancient China's most inspiring literary documents. The volume represents a fresh voice in the longstanding sinological task of interpreting *Chuang Tzu*, it represents a turning point in Buber's philosophical development, and it represents a concrete example of what we in the academy call "comparative mysticism." It is the first of these subjects with which this book is primarily concerned, though the sinological inquiry cannot really be isolated from the other two issues; how Buber transformed Taoist philosophy and how he was transformed by it are simply complementary perspectives on the same comparative question. This study includes annotated English translations of the text translation and commentary portions of Buber's volume, as well as critical analyses integrating Buber's work into the sinological discourse. The point of departure is the complex interpretive history of *Chuang Tzu* itself, and how Buber's unique interpretive perspective brings crucial hermeneutic challenges to light.

Background: The Text of Chuang Tzu as a Source of Perplexity

It is widely accepted that the philosopher named Chuang Chou lived during the fourth and early third centuries B.C.E., roughly two hundred years after Confucius, and midway through the formative "Hundred Schools" Period that produced many of China's most profound thinkers. He wrote against a background of political instability, ongoing debates over moral criteria (principally between the followers of Confucius, who defended the ancient cultural legacy of classical learning and ritualized social interaction, and the followers of Mo Tzu, who advocated mutual benefit as an objective utilitarian standard), and an intriguing "language crisis" over the relationship between names and actualities. Chuang Tzu evidently left behind an uncoordinated body of writings—alternately couched in the vehicles of poetry, paradox, and satire—which coalesced with other assorted documents into a single book about a century after his death. Shortly thereafter, Han dynasty doxographers classified it with many other works under the fairly interchangeable bibliographic headings of "School of Tao" (Tao-chia) and "Huang-Lao," the latter referring to the teachings of Lao Tzu (the reputed author of the Tao Te Ching) and the legendary Yellow Emperor. The exact contours of the text remained quite fluid for several centuries—the search for fragments of up to twenty "lost" chapters continues to be an exciting and intermittently rewarding enterprise[1]—and it eventually reached its standard thirty-three chapter form in the hands of Kuo Hsiang, a third century C.E. philosopher and participant in the hsüan-hsüeh ("Profound Learning") movement which first categorized "Lao-Chuang" as a singular mystical tradition.[2]

From the beginning of this process of compilation through the modern era, the identity and purport of Chuang Tzu have been debated vigorously. And while it would certainly be a daunting task to reconstruct the entire interpretive history, its breadth can be well illustrated through a summary of some key and interesting moments in the life of the text. Over the years, Chuang Tzu has been variously identified as a mystic's chronicle, a work of radical individualism, a philosophical statement of freedom, and even a linguistic and epistemological treatise. It has indirectly informed the legacies of Taoist asceticism, landscape painting, and romantic poetry, while also contributing to the ancestries of traditions as diverse as Ch'an Buddhism and shamanistic immortality cults. The text has been viewed as both brilliant pastoral literature and the abject remnant of a moribund slave-owning class, and it continues to be employed by a Taiwanese monastic community as a manual for meditation.³ Given the complexity of the text's history within China, it is not surprising that the task of translating it into Western languages, a project that is barely a century old, has produced a number of disparate documents. The finest of the early translations—those of Herbert A. Giles (1889) and James Legge (1891)—often bear only a superficial resemblance to modern renderings. Even more puzzling is that the rigorous and technically dazzling translations by two excellent contemporary sinologists, Wu Kuang-ming (1990) and the late Angus Charles Graham (1981), at times hardly appear to be addressing the same text.⁴

Nevertheless, it is Graham's landmark translation—the most thorough and ambitious historical-critical analysis of a classical Chinese text ever attempted—that provides an elemental framework to which most new sinological scholarship on *Chuang Tzu* invariably refers, just as Julius Wellhausen's documentary hypothesis defined Biblical study for subsequent generations. Building on the work of Kuan Feng and others, Graham identifies and dates five coherent voices within the text, including those of the historical Chuang Tzu (the seven "Inner Chapters" and textually misplaced fragments), later followers of Chuang Tzu addressing related themes ("School of Chuang Tzu"), a single idiosyncratic critic of civilization (the "Primitivist"), a group concerned with the nurture of the body (the "Yangists"), and an eclectic contingent emphasizing government and the establishment of social order (the "Syncretists"). Built into this textual arrangement is some exquisite historical detail on the origins and development of the text itself. For example, Graham attributes the original redaction of the text to "Syncretist" authors of the second century B.C.E.; Harold Roth takes this one step further by postulating a single compiler writing in the court of Liu An around 130 B.C.E. (Roth 1991:123). And while Graham's work hardly represents the final word on *Chuang Tzu*, it does bring into focus some crucial issues relating to translation and interpretation and provide sober scholarship to check the text's less disciplined readers. It is in the light of this watershed study, as well as the text's fascinating history, that one may begin to evaluate responsibly the possible contributions of Buber's Taoist studies.⁵

Buber's Taoist Volume

Buber's *Reden und Gleichnisse des Tschuang-tse*, which includes a
partial text translation followed by an interpretive "Nachwort,"
contains in its very structure a self-conscious hermeneutic framework. The first section, like Buber's translations of Hasidic texts,
departs considerably from its original source in a number of significant ways. Most immediately apparent is that it includes only fifty-
four essays and dialogues (which are selected from the first
twenty-five chapters), unreferenced to the original text but provided with concise thematic titles. Many of the episodes are themselves incomplete. Some entire concluding or intermediate
paragraphs are omitted, or the included portions are actually fragments taken out of context from larger essays. Even more important, if somewhat less obvious at first glance, is that Buber's
limitations with the Chinese language prevented him from producing what today would be considered rigorous scholarship. As indicated only in the postscript to the original edition, Buber's work is
based almost entirely on the available English versions by Giles
and Legge, with particularly liberal use of the former. Buber's language may also suggest some familiarity with Frederic Henry
Balfour's version (1881), the first complete English rendering. Virtually every line of Buber's translation can be traced to one of these
sources, though he occasionally (and very significantly) paraphrases
loosely, combines sources, and splices editorial comments from the
various translators directly into the text. In addition, Buber evidently availed himself of uncredited, unspecified advice from Shanghai native Wang Chingdao, a visiting lecturer at the Berlin Seminar
for Oriental Languages from 1907 to 1911.[6]

Though Buber was indeed aware that the original text included
the writings of several different authors, Western language works
addressing this theme were not in abundance during the early
twentieth century, and he admittedly ignored the limited historical
and philological data in his determination of the authenticity of the
various passages and choice of translated material. In this regard,
the extent of Wang Chingdao's influence is questionable at best, as
correspondence from Wang to Buber (preserved in the Buber Archive)
does not explicitly refer to the translation of *Chuang Tzu,* and
Wang's only published writings demonstrate no interest in or

familiarity with the Taoist classical legacy.[7] In the final edition of *Reden und Gleichnisse*, Buber does acknowledge "comparing (available English versions) to the original with the help of Chinese collaborators" (15), but he mentions none by name and gives no suggestion that they aided him in any way beyond this technical capacity. He instead maintains that he selected material to support and illustrate the themes discussed in his interpretive essay. But regardless of how or by whom the passages were chosen, Graham's subsequent critical scholarship demonstrates that a sensitive and uniform vision did indeed inform Buber's selection of material. Buber's first twenty-two passages are all taken from the seven "Inner Chapters," while twenty-six more selections are from the section identified by Graham as "School of Chuang Tzu." Only a small minority, Buber's remaining six passages, are from authors who have more tenuous philosophical connections with the historical Chuang Tzu; three selections are from the "Primitivist," two are from the "Syncretists," and one, taken by Graham to be from a body of "easily translatable episodes which do not seem to add to the philosophical or literary value of the book" (1981:32), is not associated with any specific source. Parenthetically, Buber does not include any writings by the "Yangists."

Buber's interpretive "afterword," which also incorporates a number of quotations from primary sources, is a treatise in nine untitled chapters that begins with a phenomenological introduction, moves through a discussion of the thought of Lao Tzu, and concludes with a discussion of the thought of Chuang Tzu and its relation to that of Lao Tzu. Despite this presentation, it is not a conventional commentary on translated passages of *Chuang Tzu*; rather, it is an independently standing essay on *Die Tao-Lehre* ("The Tao-Teaching"), which may actually be a fusion of two originally separate documents.[8] As noted earlier, it is supposedly the content of this completed essay that has determined the choice of illustrative selections in the translation. Though Buber did not vary the format of *Reden und Gleichnisse* in any of its subsequent editions, he nevertheless continued to treat this essay as an autonomous, prior work, including it as one of a trilogy of essays in *Die Rede, Die Lehre, und Das Lied: Drei Beispiele* (1917) and as part of a longer anthology in *Hinweise* (1953). When it was finally translated into English by Maurice Friedman in 1957 as "The

Teaching of the Tao," Buber characterized it as "the treatise which introduced my 1909 [sic] translation of selected *Talks and Parables of Chuang-tzu*" (ix).

The passages from *Chuang Tzu* that Buber cites in his afterword are, for the most part, not among those included in the body of the text translation. Buber refers by title to only four chapters from the translation, and of the thirty-two direct or indirect citations (some of which are as short as two words), only four also appear in the translation. Nevertheless, it should be noted that here, as with the text translation, Buber tends to select passages that later scholarship would demonstrate to be authentic or thematically related to the authentic passages. The "Inner Chapters" are cited fifteen times, and the "School of Chuang Tzu" section nine times, while the "Primitivist" is represented only five times and the "Syncretists" three times. Again, he does not cite any passages from the "Yangists." Also in the afterword, Buber nonchalantly quotes a number of other texts, which creates the illusion that he is drawing material from a rather wide range of Chinese sources, though he actually does not stretch very far beyond the texts used for the translation. The only significant addition is a dated rendering by Victor von Strauss of the *Tao Te Ching*, from which Buber coincidentally also includes thirty-two citations.[9] For much of the other cited material, however, Buber simply employs the translations of *Chuang Tzu* by Giles and Legge in a number of creative ways. First, he includes four snips of biographical information from Ssu-ma Ch'ien's *Shih Chi (Records of the Historian)*, which are merely culled from the introductions to the two translations, evident from identical glosses and ellipses. Secondly, he includes three citations from other Taoist texts (one from *The Classic of Purity and Rest*, two from *Lieh Tzu*), both to which he was directed by Legge's translation.[10] While the former had been available in German translation for quite some time (Neumann 1836), Buber was familiar with it only because Legge included it as an appendix to his *The Texts of Taoism*. Similarly, Buber evidently learned of Ernst Faber's translation of *Lieh Tzu* (1877) from Legge's references; in his brief glossary of characters appearing in the text, Buber's mention of Faber's work is simply a paraphrase of Legge. The afterword also includes one citation from the Buddhist *Maha-Parinibbana-Sutta* and one from the New Testament.

Buber's *Reden und Gleichnisse* enjoyed several printings over a period of four decades, undergoing two major revisions. For the 1918 edition, Buber made more than two hundred changes in the text translation, many of which were not particularly consequential. These included the standardization of the romanization of Chinese names, corrections of typographical errors, replacement of words or short phrases with more appropriate language, and various changes in mood, case, tense, compound words, grammatical particles, and paragraph divisions. Others were more substantial, as they involved translations of key philosophical terms, titles of chapters, whole sentences, or paragraphs. For a number of these corrections, Buber simply switched sources, replacing his translations or paraphrases of Giles with those of Legge, which, in these particular cases, tended to be closer to the original Chinese. Similarly, Buber made nearly one hundred more changes for the 1951 edition, most of which occurred in the first half of the book.[11] On the other hand, Buber made very few changes over the years in his afterword, and most of those that did appear in the later editions were inconsequential deletions. In addition, Friedman's English version included several more deletions, but these seem not to have been at Buber's suggestion, but instead to have resulted from errors in transcription or typesetting.[12]

The Hermeneutic Challenge

Given both the interpretive history of *Chuang Tzu* and the complex position of Buber's Taoist volume, the task of evaluating possible contributions to a sinological discourse becomes particularly difficult. On the one hand, because the scholarly community still has not produced a significant consensus on the Chinese text itself, there is no single standard by which Buber's positions might be judged. That is to say, each specific interpretive lens—whether that of Taiwanese monastic Taoists or of analytical historians like A. C. Graham—would produce its own appraisal of Buber's work. On the other hand, Buber's translation and commentary arise from an intellectual milieu so tangential to traditional sinology that one must consider Buber's own philosophical agenda as well as the subtleties inherent in this kind of linguistic and cultural cross-fertilization. In essence, the entire enterprise calls into question a range of hermeneutic issues concerning the nature of meaning and interpretation, such as whether one can responsibly reconstruct authorial intent without the benefit of historical-philological expertise, or, more importantly, whether *true textual meaning* is even to be found through this kind of reconstruction. In order to address the pressing sinological questions regarding Buber's encounter with *Chuang Tzu*, it also becomes necessary simultaneously to confront the hermeneutic problems that are implicit in such an investigation.

What I therefore undertake in this book is to evaluate Buber's Taoist volume with respect to different models of meaning, where each model is justified through a combination of established work in hermeneutic theory and the intentions suggested by Buber's work itself. In other words, I approach *Reden und Gleichnisse* not with an a priori definition of textual meaning or a single method of interpretation, but with a receptivity to the gamut of hermeneutic debate and a willingness to adapt to the demands of the document at hand. Thus, this project serves dual sinological purposes, as it examines sympathetically the possible contributions of one specific work toward an understanding of *Chuang Tzu*, while also broadening the larger question of what is actually meant by "understanding" a text such as *Chuang Tzu*. The hermeneutic challenge posed by this study is both to consider new answers to the customary questions and to rethink the questions themselves. It is also worth noting that the sinological foundation established by such a comprehensive study is crucial for Buber scholars wishing fully to determine the role of Taoist thought in Buber's later philosophical development. Moreover, any demonstrated relationship between Buber and Chuang Tzu, or even between the respective sinological and Buberian concerns, most certainly has significant ramifications for the current methodological debate in the comparative study of mysticism.

The body of this book is divided into two sections. The first consists of annotated retranslations of Buber's text translation and commentary (as well as his preface, postscript, and glossary), while the second consists of three hermeneutic chapters and a brief conclusion. For the text translation, each segment is referenced to its location (page, chapter, and line numbers) in the standard concordance to *Chuang Tzu* (1956), with all rearrangements or omissions noted accordingly. Because of the implications of A. C. Graham's historical-critical work for any study of *Chuang Tzu,* each segment also includes a reference indicating to which hypothetical source it belongs (i.e., "Inner Chapters," "School of Chuang Tzu," etc.), as well as Graham's suggestions for textual rearrangement. Unless otherwise noted, the retranslation follows the 1951 edition; explanations are provided in places where important or interesting changes have been made since the first edition.

Since this portion is now three or more translative layers removed from the original Chinese, I follow Buber's German as precisely as possible, while keeping an eye toward his sources. When there is some ambiguity as to how a particular word or phrase should be translated, I choose the language that most closely approximates that of Buber's apparent source. For cases where the intent is less readily apparent, such as the many instances where Buber liberally paraphrases his sources, I choose the language that seems most appropriate to the context, though not without considering how the word or phrase has been conventionally translated or how Buber employs it in other works. And because most of Buber's renderings are actually composites, I indicate their sources only where there is a particularly interesting evolution to the translation, and in the few important instances where the gloss appears to be entirely Buber's own.

Despite the multiple layers of translation and the occasional laxity of both Buber and his source translators, there is a good deal of relevant Taoist jargon—particularly terms referring to the sagely person or to the qualities of that person—that is rendered somewhat consistently into German. The chart shown on the next page is a key to how these terms are translated by Buber and retranslated here; all exceptions are indicated in the annotations to the chapter.

For the translation of the commentary, all citations from *Chuang Tzu* within the body of the afterword are referenced to the standard concordance, identified by Graham's theoretical sources, and, when applicable, cross-referenced to the text translation (the page number in parenthesis next to the passage refers to its location in this book). All citations from the *Tao Te Ching* are referenced chapter and verse to D. C. Lau's translation (Lao Tzu 1963),

RETRANSLATION	BUBER'S GERMAN	ORIGINAL CHINESE
Virtue	*Tugend*	*te* (virtue/power)
Humanheartedness	*Menschenliebe*	*jen* (humanheartedness)
Righteousness	*Gerechtigkeit*	*yi* (rightness)
Sage	*Weise*	*sheng* (sage)
		sheng-jen (sagely man)
Accomplished man	*Vollendete*	*chih-jen* (utmost man)
Pure man	*Reine Mensch*	*chen-jen* (true man)
Superior Man	*Überlegene*	*chün-tzu* (gentleman)
	Überlegene Mensch	
Man of virtue	*Mann der Tugend*	*te-jen* (man of virtue)

abbreviated in the notes simply as LT. Unless otherwise noted, the translation of the commentary portion follows the *original* edition, restoring it to its form prior to the publisher's accidental omissions in Maurice Friedman's translation; explanations are provided in places where changes occurred in later editions, or where my translation challenges in some important way that of Friedman's edition.

In addition to the issues mentioned above, the central purpose for most of the notes to the first two chapters is to juxtapose Buber's translated segments with the original Chinese, in order to illustrate exactly what "incarnation" of *Chuang Tzu* Buber was encountering. Annotating every place where the German departs considerably from the Chinese would be a prohibitive task, especially since Buber's main source, though described by Graham as having "a place on the margins of literary history" (1981:30), is, as Wing-tsit Ch'an simply states, "complete but not good" (1964:794). Were I to devote space to the analysis of each instance of questionable translation, this book would quickly be transmuted into a study of the works of Giles, Legge, and Balfour. Fortunately, Buber avoids most of the places where Chuang Tzu employs sophisticated technical repartee or complex epistemological argument, and he instead concentrates on parables, tales of sages, and the like; thus, much of his translation amounts to liberal, but serviceable paraphrase. With this in mind, I provide annotations with more current translations of the original Chinese for the following: cosmological or metaphysical propositions, apparent descriptions of mystical experience, allusions to esoteric practice or training, passages making extensive use of the philosophical jargon of the "Hundred Schools" Period, language relevant to Buber's dialogical philosophy, and language laden with obvious theological overtones. Because the afterword includes brief citations rather than complete stories, the quoted material tends to consist of provocative chunks that are severely decontextualized and pregnant with layers of ambiguity. When necessary, I provide the broader context for such citations. The translations from the Chinese are, unless otherwise specified, my own. I make no claim to be offering definitive translations; rather, I am attempting to produce—for the purpose of comparison—informed, plausible readings of the text that reflect my own interpretations in light of current translations, linguistic studies of literary Chinese, and Chinese dictionaries.

Each of the three hermeneutic chapters evaluates aspects of the text translation and commentary in light of a different model of meaning, although the connections among the apparently disjoint models are made clear as the book progresses. The first of these chapters addresses the historical question of reconstructing authorial intent, an enterprise that for many would be the first and only significant aim of textual study. Building on conclusions from this chapter, the next chapter questions whether *Chuang Tzu* itself demands a unique hermeneutic, and it expands the methodological discourse to consider the role of the reader and the various possibilities for interpretation. The third chapter, in many ways the culmination of this study, completes the process begun in both of the previous sections, as it employs hermeneutic reception theory in order to bring Buber's I-Thou principle into direct dialogue with *Chuang Tzu*. In the conclusion, I briefly consider some of the broader implications of this project for textual studies in sinology, Buber studies, and the comparative study of mysticism.

PART I

Text and Commentary

The Text Translation
"Talks and Parables of Chuang Tzu"

Preface to the 1951 Edition:
"Prefatory Note"

This little book, an early work, the first edition of which had been published in 1910 by Insel-Verlag in Leipzig, consists of two parts. The one appearing within as the second, the "Afterword," was originally composed independently as an attempt to represent summarily the Taoist teaching, to which I am indebted for a great deal; in order to complement it—first only for a circle of friends—through a series of clear and characteristic texts, I produced from the thirty-three chapters of Chuang Tzu, which at that time had not yet been taken up into German publication (a nearly complete rendering by Richard Wilhelm has been available since 1912), first going out from English works, then comparing to the original with the help of Chinese collaborators, the small selection which at this time forms the principal part of the book, and now suitably revised the presentation as well. For the new edition of 1918, the translation was greatly improved, and for the present one newly revised once more. On the other hand, the "Afterword" has remained almost unchanged since the first edition; I believed that it should not be altered, though my view of much of the subject treated therein has changed substantially.

That I presently despatch this small volume again into the world, after it was presumed dead since the Hitler era, is done above all in the remembrance of Hofmannsthal,[1] who counted it among his favorite little books.

For the useful revision of Chinese names in this edition, W. J. Tonn has assisted me in a praiseworthy way.

I. The Inactive Man

Chien Wu said to Lien Shu, "I heard Chieh Yü expressing something immoderate, which had neither sense nor continuity.[1] What
he said surprised me very much, for it seemed to me as limitless
as the Milky Way, but at the same time without coherence and far
from the experiences of men."

"What was it?" asked Lien Shu.

Chien Wu answered, "He explained that on Mount Ku-she lives
a spirit-like man,[2] whose flesh is like ice or snow, whose comportment is like that of a virgin; he eats no fruits of the Earth, he feeds
on air and dew; and riding the clouds, flying dragons his team, he
wanders beyond the four seas.[3] This being is perfectly inactive.[4]
Nevertheless, he wards off decay of all things and makes the seeds
thrive. Now then, I call this nonsense and I do not believe it."

Lien Shu spoke, "Indeed, one does not question a blind man
about a painting, and does not invite a deaf man to a festival of
song. But blindness and deafness are not merely of the body; there
are also souls that are blind and deaf.[5] You, it thus seems to me,
are afflicted by this infirmity.

"In reality, the good influence of that man fills all of Creation.[6]
And yet you want him to condescend to the details of a state while
a miserable species cries for transformation![7]

"The world of things cannot wear on him. In a flood that reached
to Heaven, he would not even be moistened. In a fire that melted
the metals of the Earth and scorched the mountains, he would not
become hot. From his dust and siftings, one could make two famous
men of yours. And you desire that he should occupy himself with
things!" ("Inner Chapters" 2/1/26–34)

II. The Useless Tree

Hui Tzu said to Chuang Tzu, "Sir, I have a great tree of a worthless
kind. Its trunk is so uneven and gnarled that it is no good for
boards; and its branches are so tortuous that it admits for no useful distribution. It stands at the main road, but no carpenter considers it. Your words, sir, are like this tree; big and useless, of no
employ."

Chuang Tzu answered, "Sir, have you never seen a wild cat that lies crouching in wait for its prey? To the right, to the left, it springs from branch to branch, up, down—until it by chance falls into a trap or dies in a snare. Then there is the buffalo with its massive body, like a cloud that darkens Heaven. He can rightly and wisely be called big. But he does not really understand mouse-catching.

"Now then, you have a big tree and do not know what you should undertake with it—why don't you plant it in the secluded and shapeless wilderness? You can idly saunter to its base or sleep in its shade in undisturbed harmony for your enjoyment. There one would think of using no axe or hatchet; there you would be beyond use or damage with it." ("Inner Chapters" 3/1/42–47)

III. The Organ-Playing of Heaven[1]

Tzu-ch'i of Nan-kuo sat leaning over his table. He looked toward Heaven, breathed deeply and easily, and appeared enraptured, as though body and soul had separated.[2] Yen Ch'eng Tzu-yu, who stood by him, called, "What happened to you that your body is like a withered tree and your mind is like dead ashes? Truly, the man who now leans over the table is not he who was once here."

Tzu-ch'i spoke, "You are in the right to ask. I have buried myself today. Can you understand that? You may have heard the organ-playing of man, but not the organ-playing of the Earth. You may have heard the organ-playing of the Earth, but not the organ-playing of Heaven."

"Explain to me what you mean," said Tzu-yu.

Tzu-ch'i continued, "The breath of nature is known as wind.[3] At times it is motionless. When it is in motion, each aperture resounds to its breath. Have you never listened to the swelling roar? Pits and valleys at mountains and woods, the caverns of the gigantic, incomprehensible trees, they are like nostrils, like mouths, like ears, like goblets, like mortars, like furrows. When the wind thrashes through them, there come the sounds of bubbling waters, of whirring arrows, of strict orders, of breath, of shouts, of harsh speech, of profound complaint, of mournful and hissing voices. The first sounds are weak, those that follow them deeper, yet in unison.

Gentle winds beget a small answer, mighty ones a big one. Finally, the storm subsides, and the openings are empty and calm. Have you never watched such confusion under the trees?"

"Indeed," said Tzu-yu, "since the organ-playing of the Earth comes only from holes and the organ-playing of man from fifes and flutes, whence comes the organ-playing of Heaven?"

Tzu-ch'i spoke: "The working of the wind on the different holes is not of a uniform quality. But what is it that gives each its particularity, that gives to all the faculties of sound?[4]

"Great knowledge spans the whole; petty knowledge spans components. Great speech is universal; petty speech is particular."

"Whether the mind is banished into slumber, whether free in the waking hours, we are ever in confusion, irresolution, unclarity, defensiveness, fear, and trembling anguish.[5] Soon, the mind flies along like a javelin, judge over good and evil; soon, it stands like a monument, watchman over rights. Then comes the growing decline in Autumn and Winter frost, a disappearance like running water that does not return. Finally, when all is blocked up as if in an old drainage ditch, a stoppage, and the mind falters and will not again see the light.[6] Joy and vexation, sorrow and good fortune, caution and contrition arrive to us one after another in restless change. They come like music from the hollows, like mushrooms from moisture. Day in and day out, they replace one another within us; but, we cannot say whence they originated. Will we be permitted to hope for a moment in which we will touch upon the cause?" ("Inner Chapters" 3/2/1–14)

IV. The Conditioned and the Unconditioned

Nieh Ch'üeh asked Wang Ni, "Do you know what it is on which all beings are of the same mind?"

Wang Ni answered, "How can I know this?[1] When a man sleeps in a damp spot, he will fall down from loin-pains and die. But how is it with an eel? To dwell in a tree is unsafe and enraging. But how is it with monkeys? Of these three—man, eel, monkey—whose abode is the right, absolute way? Human beings feed themselves on meat, deer on grass. Whose taste is the right, absolute way? Monkeys pair themselves with monkeys; the doe-buck with the hind; fish keep company with fish; and men adore beautiful women, at whose view fish dive into the water, birds fly in the air, deer run away. Who will say what is the standard of measure for beauty? I think the standards of measure for good and bad, of yes and no, are so intricate that it is not possible to separate them."[2]

Nieh Ch'üeh asked, "If you yourself do not know what is evil, does the accomplished man also lack this knowledge?"

Wang Ni Answered, "The accomplished man is a spiritual being. If the ocean evaporated, he would feel no heat. If the great rivers froze,[3] he would feel no cold. If the thunder tore up the mountain and the storm catapulted up the great depth, he would not tremble. He would climb the clouds of Heaven, drive himself forth to the sun and moon, and stride to the boundaries of the four seas, where death and life have no more authority over man—let alone what is evil to him. ("Inner Chapters" 6/2/64–73)

V. Antitheses and Infinity

Ch'ü Ch'üeh-tzu said to Ch'ang Wu-tzu, "Confucius[1] spoke in my presence: 'I have heard it said that the appointed man[2] pays no attention to worldly things. He does not seek profit and does not avoid injury. He desires nothing from the hands of man. He adheres to Tao without questioning.[3] He can speak without talking; he can talk and yet tells nothing. Thus he rambles beyond the dust. These,' Confucius spoke further, 'are rash words.' But they appear to me as expert representations of Tao. Which is your opinion, sir?"

Ch'ang Wu-tzu answered, "How should Confucius understand that which was not apparent to the Yellow Emperor?[4] You go too fast. You look at one egg and expect already to hear it crow. You look at your crossbow and expect already to have for yourself a roast duck. I will say some words to you at random, and have you listen to them at random.

"How is it that the appointed man[5] sits down on the moon and sun and carries space and time in his arms? He has resolved all things in themselves to the oneness, he has rejected the confusion of 'this' and 'that.' Without rank and order, unified he stands before the crowd like a fool. The rolling of ten millennia does not touch his oneness. The world of things may come and go, the sage will endure.

"Is love of life at base not a delusion? Is one who is afraid to die not like a child who has gone astray and cannot find the way home?

"Lady Li was the daughter of the border-keeper of Ai. When the Prince took her to Chin, she wept until the bosom of her clothes was saturated with tears. But when she came to the court couch, lived with the prince and fed on riches, she regretted her crying. Perhaps the dead regret that they once clung to life?

"Those who dream of a banquet wake up to complaint and sorrow. Those who dream of complaint and sorrow wake up to frolicsome hunting. While they dream, they do not know that they are dreaming. Many even wish to interpret the dream when they are dreaming; and only when they awake do they realize that it was a dream. Soon, soon, comes the great awakening, and then we will discover that this life was a great dream. Fools suppose that they are now awake and believe to know whether they, in truth, are princes or servants. Confucius and you, you both are dreamers; and I, who say this, I myself am in a dream. This is a contradiction. Tomorrow, a sage will appear and explain this; tomorrow, when ten thousand generations will be gone.[6]

"Now, consider that we are quarreling with one another over opinions. If you beat me and I do not beat you, are you unequivocally right and I wrong? Or if I beat you and you do not beat me, am I unequivocally right and you wrong? Or are we both in one part right and in the other wrong? Or are we both totally right and totally wrong? You and I, we cannot know this, and so the world is in want of truth.

"Whom should I employ as arbiter between us? If I establish one who is of a mind with you, he will hold to you. How can such a one decide between us? If I establish one who is of a mind with me, he will hold to me. How can such a one decide between us? And if I establish one who either deviates from us both or agrees with us both, he will be incapable of impartially deciding between us. Since you now cannot decide, and I cannot, and no one can, then must we not depend on another? Such a dependence is as if it were no dependence. We will embrace in the all-quenching oneness of Heaven.[7] There is perfect adaptation for whatever may happen, and so we complete our allotted span[8]—do not attend to time, and do not attend to rightness and wrongness.[9] Step into the realm of the boundless, and seize therein your state of repose."[10] ("Inner Chapters" 6/2/73–92, with much of 90–92 omitted or rearranged)

VI. The Butterfly

I, Chuang Tzu, once dreamed that I was a butterfly, one fluttering here and there, without worries and desires, unconscious of my humanity.[1] Suddenly, I awoke; and there I lay, again "myself." Now I did not know if I was thus a man who dreamed he was a butterfly, or am I now a butterfly who is dreaming that he is a man. Between man and butterfly is a boundary. The crossing over is called transformation.[2] ("Inner Chapters 7/2/94–96)

VII. The Cook

Prince Wen-hui's cook was employed to cut up an ox. With each blow of his hand, each hoist of his shoulders, each step of his foot, each thrust of his knee, each hiss of cleaved flesh, each howl of the axe, all were in perfect harmony—arranged like the dance of mulberry groves, sounding together like the music of Ching-shou.

"Well done!" called the prince. "This is truly skillfulness."

"Your servant," answered the cook, "has surrendered to the Tao. This is better than skillfulness. When I first began to cut up oxen, I saw before me the whole ox. After three years of practice, I no longer saw the whole animal. And now, I work with my spirit and no longer with my eyes. If my senses bid me to pause, but my spirit moves further, I find my support in the eternal principles.[1] I follow the openings and holes that must be in accord with the natural qualities of the beast. I do not try to cut across joints and ligaments, let alone the large bones.

"A good cook changes his axe once a year—because he cuts. An ordinary cook changes it once a month—because he hacks. But I have conducted this axe for nineteen years, and although I have cut up several thousand oxen with it, its edge is as new as if it came from the whetstone. In the joints is always space, and since the edge is without thickness, all that is necessary is to fit it in each space. Through here the gap has widened, and the blade finds enough space. So I have had my axe nineteen years long, as though it came from the whetstone.

"Yet, when I turn to a hard part, where the blade meets with a hindrance, I collect myself in caution. I fix my eyes therein. I hold back my hand. Gently, I aim my blade until the piece yields with a hollow sound, like clumps of earth that sink down. Then, I take out my axe and lift myself up, and look around, and stand still, until finally, contentedly, I dry my axe and carefully set it aside."

"Well spoken!" called the prince. "From the words of this cook I have learned how to care for my life."[2] ("Inner Chapters" 12/3/ 2–12)

VIII. The Death of Lao Tzu

When Lao Tzu died, Ch'in Shih went to mourn for him. He sighed three times and turned back.

A student asked him, "Were you our master's friend or were you not?"

"I was," he answered.

The student asked further, "Since you were, do you consider this as a proper expression of grief?"

"Yes," said Ch'in Shih. "I had thought he was a man of men, and now I see that he was not. When I came to mourn for him, I found old people who wept for him as for a child, and young people who lamented for him as for a mother. To obtain such great love, he must have spoken words that should not have been spoken, and must have wept tears that should not have been wept, violating the eternal principle, multiplying the amount of human excitement, and leaving behind the source from which his life was received. The old ones called such excitement the trammels of mortality.

"The master came, because it was his time to be born; he went, because it was his time to die. For one who thus accepts the phenomena of birth and death, there is no complaint and sorrow. The old ones said of death, that God cut loose a man who hung in the air.[1] The fuel is consumed, but the fire is passed on; and we do not know that it ever ends." ("Inner Chapters" 8/3/14–19)

IX. With Men

Yen Hui came to Confucius to take leave.[1]

"Where will you go?" asked the master.

"I am going to the state of Wei," answered the former.

"And what do you intend to do there?" asked Confucius further.

"I have learned," said Yen Hui, "that the prince of Wei is indeed mature in years, but is of an untamed disposition. He behaves as though the state were without importance, and does not want to see his weaknesses. So the people are ruined, and the corpses are scattered all around like underwood in the swamp. The people are at extremes. But I have heard you say, Master, when a state is well ruled, we are permitted to neglect it; when it is poorly ruled, we should frequent it. At the door of the doctor are many sick people.[2] I would like to put my knowledge to the test that I may perhaps demonstrate some good to this state."

"Alas," called Confucius, "that will only succeed in bringing evil upon yourself. For Tao may not be distributed. If it is distributed, it loses its oneness. If it loses its oneness, it becomes uncertain. And so it brings to pass a disturbance of the mind[3]—from which there is no escape.

"The high ones of antiquity first obtained Tao for themselves, only then did they obtain it for others.[4] Before you possess it yourself, what business do you have to concern yourself with the doings of tyrants?

"Moreover, do you know how virtue flows in and how cleverness[5] goes out? Virtue flows in searching after glory; cleverness goes out in quarreling. In combat over glory, men fight one another, and all of their cleverness only abets the conflict. Virtue and cleverness are dangerous implements and may not be carelessly employed.

"Besides, those who, before they have exercised influence through their own firm virtue and unimpeachable veracity, before they have reached the hearts[6] through the example of their own contempt for fame and reputation, go out and preach humanheartedness and righteousness to tyrants, they will only bring one result, that the men to whom they preach will learn to hate them by virtue of their goodness. Such people will be known as evil-speakers. And those who speak evil of others, it comes to them that evil is spoken of them. This will be, alas, your end.[7]

"But of course you have a plan. Tell it to me."

"Serious comportment," answered Yen Hui, "and calmness, energy, and perseverance—is that not enough?"

"Alas," said Confucius, "that is not enough. This man makes a show of perfection and is full of conceit. His being cannot be revealed by his comportment.[8] The common man will not oppose him, and so it has become for him a pleasure that others bow. If he has thus failed at the practice of ordinary virtue, can you expect that he willingly surrender to the higher ones? You may insist, but without result. Outwardly, he will perhaps yield to you truly, but inwardly not truly. How will you then bring it about so that he will change his ways?"

"In the same way," answered Yen Hui. "I am inwardly upright and outwardly bent, accomplished after the examples of antiquity.

"Whoever is inwardly upright, he is a servant of Heaven.[9] And whoever is a servant of Heaven knows that the emperor and he are in the same way sons of Heaven. Does such a one need to torment himself over whether men agree with him or contradict him? Men regard him as a child. This is called being a servant of Heaven.

"Whoever is outwardly bent, he is a servant of man. He bows, he kneels, he folds his hands; this is the customary form of state officials. What all men do, should I dare not to do? What all men do, nobody will blame me for it. This is called being a servant of man.

"Whoever is accomplished after the example of antiquity, he is a servant of antiquity.[10] Though I may also remind him and correct his speech, it is antiquity that speaks, not I. Thus, my uprightness, as the servant of the sages of antiquity, will not bring me to danger. Is this not enough?"

"Alas," answered Confucius, "it is not enough. Your plans are too multifarious and they are lacking in common sense. After all, your solidness protects you from harm; but that is all. You will not be able to influence the prince to such a degree that it would seem to him that he is following only the precepts of his own heart."

"Then," said Yen Hui, "I am without all help, and I dare ask about a way."

Confucius spoke, "Fast!

"I will explain it to you.

"You have a way, but it is hard to follow it. The easy ones are not of Heaven."

"I have," said Yen Hui, "for many months tasted neither wine nor meat. Is that not fasting?"

"The fasting of sacrifice indeed," answered Confucius, "but not the fasting of the heart."[11]

"And is it permitted of me to ask," said Yen Hui, "wherein lies the fasting of the heart?"

"Cultivate oneness," answered Confucius. "You hear not with the ears, but with the understanding; not with the understanding, but with your soul.[12] But let the hearing stop with the ears. Let the work of understanding stop with itself. Then, the soul will be a detached being, that answers things with its oneness that is separated from no action. In such a detached being alone can Tao dwell. And this state of detachment is the fasting of the heart."[13]

"Then," said Yen Hui, "the cause that I could not go this way is my own particularity. If I could get to it, my particularity would go away from me. Is this what you mean by the state of detachment?"

"It is," answered the master. "I will give you information. If you can enter into this man's realm without injuring his self-love, your manner singing when he hears you, silent when he does not, without invasion, without medicine, simply living within the state of perfect equanimity—then you will be near success.[14] It is easy to take steps by walking; the difficulty is to go without touching the ground. As counsel of man it is easy to win the spirit; but not as counsel of Heaven.[15] You know of the winged creatures that fly. Yet you do not know how one flies without wings. You know of men who are wise in knowledge. Yet you do not know how one is wise without knowledge.

"Look at that window. It makes it such that an empty space is animated by scenery; but the landscape remains outside. Were this not so, we would have a contradiction for ourselves, as if one thing at the same time could stand still and run away.

"So you may use your ears and eyes that they communicate the world to you, but you should banish all false knowledge out of your mind.

"Then the supernatural will come to you and dwell near you;[16] how should man thus deny you?

"This is the way to regenerate creation."[17] ("Inner Chapters" 8/
4/1–33, with portions omitted)

X. Training of Princes

Yen Ho was appointed tutor to the oldest son of Ling, the prince of
Wei. He said to Ch'ü Po-yü, the chancellor of Wei, of his pupil,
"This is a man whose natural disposition is of an inferior kind. To
allow his pernicious way would endanger the state. To try to re-
strain him would endanger my personal security. He has exactly
enough intellect to see the defects of others, but not enough to see
his own. I do not know what I should do."

"Truly, a good question," said Ch'ü Po-yü. "You must be careful
and proceed with self-discipline. Externally, you may adapt, but
internally you must stand firm by your own standard of rightness.[1]
There are two things against which you must guard. You may not
let the outer adaptation be forced inward, nor let the inner standard of rightness go outwardly public. If you do the first, you will
decline, will be wiped out, will collapse.[2] If you do the other, you
will become a sound, a name, a bogie, an oddity. If he is like a boy,
then you meet him as a boy too. If he steps on traditional propriety,
so you do likewise.[3] As widely as he goes, you go also. Thus you can
lead him without injuring him.[4]

"Do you not know the story of the praying mantis?[5] In their fury
they stretched out their limbs to block the movement of a carriage,
without considering that it exceeded their strength; so arrogant
was their zealous might. Be circumspect. When you injure others
through your superiority, you will certainly come to grief.

"Do you not know that those who hold tigers captive do not dare
to give them live animals as food, for fear that the killing of the
booty could excite their passion? And that they give the tigers no
entire animal for fear that the tearing of the booty could excite its
anger. They watch carefully the times of hunger and of satiation.
Tigers are of another species than man; nevertheless, you must
bear in mind that they indeed cling to those who feed them, but
that they sometimes kill them when they act contrary to their
being.

"Many love horses so much that they take up their dung in baskets and their urine in jugs.[6] Sometimes a horse is bothered by gnats or flies; if then the groom suddenly, without the animal expecting it, removes them, it indeed comes to pass that the horse breaks the reins and hurts itself in the head and chest. The intention was good, but it did damage to the true welfare. Be on your guard against this." ("Inner Chapters" 10/4/53–64)

XI. The Holy Tree

Carpenter Shih traveled to the state of Ch'i. As he came upon Ch'u-yüan, he saw a holy oak tree,[1] that was so big that a bull could conceal itself behind it; it had a circumference of a hundred spans, towered high over the summits of the hills, and carried branches, several of which if hollowed out could be suitable for boats. A crowd of people stood before it and stared up at it, but the carpenter did not pay attention to it and went further on his way, without looking around. His companion, on the other hand, looked at it for a while and, when he caught up with his master, he said, "Since I have handled an axe in your employ, I have never seen such a magnificent piece of timber as this. How is it, sir, that you did not remain to look at it?"

"It is not worth talking about," answered the Master. "The timber is good for nothing. Make a boat out of it—it will sink. A coffin—it will rot. Household furnishings—it will soon fall to pieces. A door—it will sweat. A pillar—it will be gnawed by worms. It is a piece of timber without class and without utility. That is how it has gotten so old."

When the carpenter came home, he dreamed that the oak tree appeared to him and spoke to him, "What is it with which you compare me? Is it the elegant trees? The whitethorn, the peartree, the orange tree, and other fruit-carriers, as soon as their fruits have ripened, are plundered and insultingly handled. Large branches are cracked, small ones broken off. These trees thus harm their own lives through their worth. They cannot complete their allotted spans, but perish prematurely in the midst of their journeys, since they are entangled in the surrounding world. So it is with all things.

For a long time it was my goal to become useless. Several times I was in danger, but finally I have succeeded, and so it came that I now am rich in use. But were I to have been of utility at those times, I would not have the great abundance of uses that I do now.

"Besides, we both belong, you and I, to the same class of things. Do away with this passion for blame. Is a worthless man the right person to talk about a worthless tree?"[2] ("Inner Chapters" 11/4/64–73)

XII. The Mutilated Man

In the state of Lu lived a man named Wang T'ai who had his toes cut off. His students were as numerous as those of Confucius.

Ch'ang Chi asked Confucius, "This Wang T'ai has been mutilated and nevertheless he shares with you, Master, the teaching authority in the state of Lu. He never preaches and never debates; yet they go, coming to him empty, leaving him fulfilled. He obviously teaches information that finds no expression in words; and although his stature is imperfect, perhaps his mind is perfect. What kind of man is this?"

"He is an appointed man,"[1] answered Confucius. "I have neglected until now to seek his instruction. I will go to him and learn from him. And if I do this, why not those who are not my equals? I will take not only the state of Lu with me, but the whole world with me."

"The man has been mutilated," said Ch'ang Chi, "and yet the people call him Master. He must be very different from the common people. But in what manner does he employ his mind?"

Confucius answered, "Life and death are all-powerful, but they are unable to get the better of his mind.[2] Heaven and Earth may tumble down together, but he will remain. He has found that which is without error; so he will not divide the lot of things.[3] He can bring about the transformation of things, yet he preserves himself untouched in primordial being."[4]

"How is that?" asked Ch'ang Chi.

Confucius answered," From the point of view of difference, we separate between liver and gall, between the state of Ch'u and the state of Yüeh. From the point of view of sameness, all things are one. This is the station of Wang T'ai. He does not worry about that which reaches through the senses of sight and hearing, but points his whole mind to the summit point of virtue.[5] He views all things as one, without noticing their deviations. And so it is to him that the loss of his foot is nothing more than a loss of the same amount of dirt."

"He concerns himself with action," said Ch'ang Chi, "and uses his cognition to complete his mind.[6] But how is it then that the people make so much of him?"

Confucius answered, "A man searches not in flowing, but in still water to catch sight of his image. So only what is itself firm can make others firm.

"The grace of earth has touched pines and cypress. In winter and summer they stay equally green. The grace of god[7] touched Yao and Shun, the exemplars.[8] It was given to them to rule their own lives and so to rule the life of humankind.

"Through proof of the original courage,[9] the sensation of fear can be so easily switched off that one single person is able to trample an army. If such an action can be reached in the search for glory, how much more must one reach who stretches his might over Heaven and Earth and embraces all things;[10] who, remaining in these boundaries of human life with his two channels, sight and hearing, moves to discern that all things are one and that the mind endures eternally.[11]

"He waits for the originally intended hour to raise himself from there,[12] and the people voluntarily follow him, the one who moves no finger to draw them to him." ("Inner Chapters" 12/5/1–13)

XIII. Shu-shan No-Toes

In the state of Lu lived a man who had his toes cut off. He was known as Shu-shan No-Toes. He came, walking on his heels, to see Confucius. But Confucius said to him, "You have not paid attention to yourself, and so have brought this misfortune upon yourself. What advantage is it now for you to come to me?"

"In my ignorance," answered No-Toes, "I let my body go and so I have lost my toes. But I come with one thing that is as valuable as toes and that I now seek to preserve. There are no people whom

Heaven did not secure; there are no people whom the Earth did not bear; and I thought that you, sir, would be like Heaven and Earth. I did not expect to hear these words from you."

"I am only one poor creature," said Confucius. "Step in and let me teach you."

But No-Toes then went away.

"See," said Confucius to his students, "here is a criminal without toes, who wishes to learn to practice penance for his misdeed. If he has such a wish, how much more should those who have committed no misdeed for which they must atone?"[1]

No-Toes came to Lao Tzu and spoke, "Confucius has not yet attained to wisdom. What has he to do with a crowd of his many students![2] He strives to be a fine spokesman and does not know that such a reputation will be regarded by the true sages as hand fetters."[3]

"Why do you not step towards him with the continuity of life and death, and the oneness of can and cannot," asked Lao Tzu, "and free him from his fetters?"

"He has been punished by Heaven in this way," answered No-Toes. "He cannot be freed."[4] ("Inner Chapters" 13/5/24–31)

XIV. The Leper

Ai, the prince of the state of Lu, said to Confucius, "In the state of Wei is a leper named Ai T'ai-t'o. The men who live with him love him and they cannot be without him. As for the women, those who have seen him said often to their elders, 'I would rather be this man's concubine than another one's wife.'

"He never preaches to the people, but settles in inner harmony among them. He possesses no strength through which he could protect the people from death. He has no possessions to give away through which he could satisfy their greed.[1] His appearance is, to a certain extent, strikingly ugly. He sympathizes, but does not give advice.[2] His knowledge is limited to his home territory. Yet men and women gather around him.

"Because I thought he must indeed be different from the common man, I sent for him and saw that his appearance was, in reality, strikingly ugly. And although we were not yet together a few months, I indeed had to turn my whole attention to his guidance. A year had not yet passed, when he had my complete trust. And when my state needed a chancellor, I offered him the post. He accepted it unenthusiastically, as if he would rather have declined. I was ashamed of myself for him.[3] Nevertheless, he accepted it. But after a very short time, he left me and went away. I grieved over him as for a lost friend, and as if no one remained in whom I could take pleasure. What kind of man is that?"

Confucius answered, "When I was underway on a mission to the state of Ch'u, I saw a brood of young pigs who were suckling on their dead mother. After a while, they looked at her and then all of them left the corpse and ran away. For their mother no longer looked at them and no longer appeared to them to be of the same type. What they had loved was their mother; not the body that contained her, but that which caused the body to be what it was.[4]

"Ai T'ai-t'o says nothing and is trusted. He does nothing and is loved. He makes it so that a man offered him the rulership of his state and feared only that he would decline. Truly, his talents are complete and his virtue without external form."[5]

"What do you mean, that his talents are complete?" asked the prince.

"Life and death," answered Confucius, "preservation and decay, success and failure, poverty and wealth, virtue and vice, good and bad reputation, hunger and thirst, warm and cold—they are all resonances in the lot of humanity.[6] Day time, night time, they follow one another and no one can say where each begins. Thus, they must not be permitted to disturb the harmony of the living, and must not be permitted to enter the realm of spirit.[7] To let flow the harmony of the living, bringing all souls to joy; to do this day after day without omission, that there be Springtime between one and the world of things; to be prepared for all times and possibilities—these are the signs of one whose talents are complete."[8]

"And virtue without external form, what is that?" asked the prince.

"In a water-balance," said Confucius, "the water is in a perfect condition of rest. Let this be a model for you. The water remains peaceful within and does not overflow. From this practice, virtue goes forth in such symmetry. And when virtue supposes no outer form, things will not be capable of breaking off from it."

Some days later, Prince Ai said to Min Tzu, "Once I thought, when I was bearing anxiety for the life of my people, to have fulfilled my work as ruler. But now that I have heard what a perfect man is,[9] it seems to me that I was straying; I have neglected my being and damaged my state. But Confucius and I, we are not prince and subject, but friends wishing for virtue." ("Inner Chapters" 13/5/31–40, 42–49)

XV. Pure Men

He who knows of the Heavenly, who knows of the human, has reached the goal. Knowing of the Heavenly, he knows whence he came. Knowing of the human, he rests in the knowledge of the known, he waits for the knowledge of the unknown. To complete the allotted life, not to perish along the way, this is the fullness of knowledge.

But there is a deficiency. Knowledge awaits fulfillment. Fulfillment is uncertain. How can I then know that my "Heavenly" is not, in reality, the human, or that my "human" is not, in reality, Heavenly?

We must first have pure men, only then will we have pure knowledge. But which is the pure man?

The pure men of antiquity acted without calculation, did not seek to secure results, did not concern themselves with plans. In failure, they had no cause for contrition, in success no cause for self-congratulation. Thus they could scale heights and feel no anxiety; plunge into water and feel no wetness, step through fire and feel no heat. So close did their knowledge bring them to Tao.

The pure men of antiquity slept without dreams, woke without angst. They ate without eager consumption. They breathed deeply. For the breath of the pure men comes out of the inner depths, the common man's breath only out of the throat.[1]

The pure men of antiquity did not love life, did not hate death. The beginning roused no joy, the end no struggle. To come composed, to go composed, that was enough.[2] They did not forget whence they sprung forth, they did not take pains over where they should go. They willingly accepted what was apportioned, they peacefully awaited being recalled. This is what was known as not striving against the Tao and not wanting to replace the Heavenly through the human.[3] This is the manner of pure men.

Such men are free in mind,[4] calm in manner, and of serene visage. Their coldness is that of autumn, their warmth that of spring. The vicissitude of their instincts carries them in a particular way as do those of the seasons. They are in harmony with all things and none knows of their boundaries.

So the appointed man may destroy a kingdom and not lose the hearts of the people; without practicing humanheartedness, he makes happy ten thousand generations.[5]

Whoever takes pleasure in men is not the appointed man. Whoever has affection is not one who loves.[6] Whoever pays attention to the ages is not a great man.[7] Whoever does not wisely take up good and evil is not a superior man.[8] Whoever does not stand on the other side of value is not an exemplar. Whoever does not relinquish himself in an unconditional manner cannot be a ruler. ("Inner Chapters" 15/6/1–12, with much of 6/7 omitted)

XVI. Steps

Nan-po Tzu-k'uei said to Nü-yü, "You are old and yet your countenance is like that of a child. How is that so?"

Nü-yü answered, "I have experienced Tao."[1]

"Can I obtain Tao through learning?" asked the other.

"You cannot," said Nü-yü. "You are not the right man for it. Now there was Pu-liang I. He had all the qualities of an appointed man,[2] but not Tao. Now I had Tao, although none of the qualities. But do you believe that I, however I wished, was capable of teaching Tao to him so that he would become an appointed man? In this case, it would truly be an easy thing to teach Tao to someone who has all the qualities of an appointed man. I imparted while I withheld. After three days, the separation of things ceased for him. When he had reached this, I withheld further. After seven more days, the external ceased for him. And after another nine days, he stepped out of his own existence. After that, his mind became radiant like daybreak and he beheld being, his I, countenance to countenance.[3] When he had seen this, he became without past and present. Finally, he entered the realm where death and life are no more, where one can kill without causing to die, and engender without causing to live. The one who is in Tao thus accompanies, thus finds, thus destroys, thus builds all things.[4] Its name is Shattered-Unbruised, and its path is completion."[5] ("Inner Chapters" 16/6/36–43)

XVII. The Four Friends

Four men, Tzu-Ssu, Tzu-Yü, Tzu-Li, and Tzu-Lai, were speaking with one another, and this is what they discussed: "Who can make 'nothing' as the head, life as the spine, death as the tail of his existence? Who knows how death and birth, life and lapse, form one being? That person should be permitted our friendship."[1] The four looked at one another and smiled; they quietly accepted the conditions and henceforth became friends.

After a while Tzu-Yü fell ill, and Tzu-Ssu visited him. "Truly, the creator is great!"[2] said the sick man. "See here how he has refashioned me. My back is curved and my bowels have turned upward. My chin is in the same hole as my navel. My shoulders tower over my head.[3] My hair stares toward Heaven. The whole arrangement of my composition is disordered. But the peace of my mind is not disturbed."[4] So speaking, he dragged himself laboriously to a spring, in which he could see himself, and yet said, "Ah, that the creator has so completely refashioned me!"

"Do you have reluctance?" asked Tzu-Ssu.

"I have none," answered Tzu-Yü. "How should I oppose this? If he carves me and makes a cock out of my left arm, I will call out in the night. If he makes a crossbow out of my right arm, I will chase down wild ducks.[5] If he transforms my hips into cartwheels and my soul[6] into a horse, I will travel in my own carriage. I received life because it was my time; I now depart from it by the same rule. Because I rest in the succession of these conditions, pleasure and sorrow cannot touch me. I am, as the old ones called it, suspended in the air, incapable of cutting myself loose, bound with the ropes of existence. But it always is man who yields to Heaven; so why should I oppose it?"

After a time, Tzu-Lai fell ill and lay at the end of breath, and so his wife and children gathered around him weeping. Tzu-Li visited him. "Go!" he called back to them, "you are disturbing his transition." Then he said, leaning on the door, "Truly, the creator is great![7] What will he next make out of you? Indeed, where will he dispatch you? Will he stick you in the liver of a rat or in the leg of an insect?"[8]

"A son," answered Tzu-Lai, "must go where his elders tell him to go. Yin and Yang are more than elders to man.[9] If they tell me to die imminently and I hesitate, then I am being an insubordinate son. They can do me no wrong. Tao gives me this form, this toil in manhood, this rest in old age, this loosening in death. And surely what has decided my life so kindly will decide my death for the best.[10]

"Suppose the seething ore bubbled up out of the crucible and said, 'Make a hero's sword out of me,' I think the founder would reject this ore as unsuitable. And if I said to the creator, 'Make a man out of me, make a man out of me,' I think he would reject me as unsuitable. The world is a crucible and the creator is a great founder. I will go where I am sent, to awaken peacefully as a man wakes out of dreamless sleep."[11] ("Inner Chapters" 17/6/45–60, with part of 57–58 omitted)

XVIII. The Death Song

Tzu Sang-hu, Meng-tzu Fan, and Tzu Ch'in-chang were speaking with one another. One of them asked, "Who can be and yet not be? Who can do and yet not do? Who can climb to Heaven, roam through the clouds, abandon space, forget existence, forever and ever without end?"

The three looked at one another and smiled; and since none of them stood in doubt, they became friends.

Shortly after this, Tzu Sang-hu died. Confucius sent his student Tzu-kung that he might take part in the mourning. As Tzu-kung arrived, one of the friends sang this tune, accompanied by the other on the lute:

> "When will you return to us, Sang-hu?
> When will you return to us, Sang-hu?
> You have gone home to your being,
> But we, alas, have remained in the lot of humanity."

Tzu-kung hastened ahead and called, "I dare ask whether it is in accord with the rules to sing next to a corpse?"

The two looked at each other, smiled, and spoke, "What does this man know of rules?"

Tzu-kung turned around, told this to Confucius, and asked him, "Why are men like this? They do not arrange anything and handle the body as if it were a stranger. They can sit by a corpse and yet sing unmoved. I know of no words by which I could describe them. What are they?"

"These men," answered Confucius, "wander beyond the rule of life.[1] I wander within it. Thus, our ways do not meet one another; and I dealt foolishly to send you to the mourning. They look upon themselves as companions of the creator and strolling in the indivisibility of Heaven and Earth.[2] They consider life as a tumor, from which death frees them. They do not know where they were before birth nor where they will be after death. Though they value the diversity of the elements, they prefer their station among the oneness of all things. They do not value their passions. They do not answer their senses. Backward and forward through all eternity, they know no beginning and no end. They wander beyond the dust, they wander in the realm of non-doing. How should such men trouble themselves over tradition or be troubled by what the masses think of them?"

"But if this is the case," said Tzu-kung, "why should we adhere to the rules?"

"Heaven has condemned me to that," answered Confucius. "Yet I am willing to share with you what I have reached."

"Upon which way is it reached?" asked Tzu-kung.

"Fish," said Confucius, "thrive in water. Man thrives in Tao.[3] If fish obtain a pond to live in, they find their nourishment. If a man obtains Tao to live in, he needs no doing and is secure.[4] Thus the saying, 'All a fish needs is water; all a man needs is Tao.'"[5]

"Is it permitted for me to ask, "said Tzu-kung, "how it is with the superior men?"

"The superior men," answered Confucius, "lay under Heaven.[6] Thus the saying, 'The pettiest creature in Heaven will be the most noble of Earth, and the most noble of Earth the pettiest in Heaven.'"[7]
("Inner Chapters" 17/6/60–74)

XIX. The Way

"I am advancing," said Yen Hui to Confucius.

"How is that?" he asked.

"I have forgotten humanheartedness and rightness," answered Yen Hui.

"Good," said Confucius, "but not enough."

On another day, Yen Hui met Confucius and said, "I am advancing."

"How is that?" asked Confucius.

"I have forgotten rites and music," answered Yen Hui.

"Good," said Confucius, "but not perfect."

A third time Yen Hui met Confucius and said, "I am advancing."

"How is that?" asked Confucius.

"I have forgotten everything,"[1] answered Yen Hui.

"Forgotten everything!" said Confucius, touched. "What do you mean by this?"

"I have made myself free of my body," answered Yen Hui. "I have dismissed my thought process. Since I became free of my body and mind, I have become one with the all-pervasive.[2] This is what I mean that I have forgotten everything."

"If you have become one," called Confucius, "there can be no more striving. Since you have thus transformed, you have been removed from all bounds.[3] You have exceeded me and I ask if you will permit me to tread in your footsteps."[4] ("Inner Chapters" 19/6/89–93)

XX. To Rule the State

T'ien Ken journeyed to the south of Yin Mountain. He came to the Liao River. There he met a nameless man. He said to him, "Permit me to ask what is there to do in ruling the State?"

"Away!" cried the nameless man. "You are a foolish man, and your question is inappropriate. I have become the companion of the creator. I swing on the light wings of emptiness beyond the six directions, in the kingdom of nothing, in the wilderness of spacelessness. And you ask how the kingdom is to be ruled!"

But T'ien Ken spoke his piece a second time.

The nameless man answered him, "Loosen the strength of your spirit to simplicity, the strength of your life to non-doing, surrender to the order of things, withdraw the selfness—and the kingdom will be ruled."[1] ("Inner Chapters" 20/7/7–11)

XXI. The Magician and the Accomplished Man[1]

In the state of Cheng lived a sorcerer named Chi Hsien.[2] He knew all about birth and death, preservation and destruction, luck and disaster, long life and short life, and foresaw the happenings of the day with spirit-like accuracy. The inhabitants of Cheng fled from his view; but Lieh Tzu sought him out and became so infatuated that after his return to Hu Tzu, he said, "I have looked on your Tao as the perfect one. Now I know something that is yet more perfect."

"Hitherto," answered Hu Tzu, "I have only taught you the garment, not the essence of the Tao;[3] and yet you suppose that you know all of it. If one has no cocks in the hen house, how will the hens lay eggs? If one wishes to force Tao upon the masses, he will only be abandoning himself. Bring that man to me, and I will show myself to him."

The next day, Lieh Tzu came with Chi Hsien to Hu Tzu. As they went out, Chi Hsien said, "Alas! Your teacher has neared death. He cannot live any longer than ten more days. I have seen something strange in him. I saw damp ashes."

Weeping, Lieh Tzu went inside and told this to Hu Tzu, who spoke, "I have shown myself to him as the Earth shows us its outer form, motionless and still, while the becoming is all the time carried out of itself. I only hindered him from seeing the pent-up energy.[4] Bring him here again."

The next day, they came again. When they left, Chi Hsien said to Lieh Tzu, "It is lucky for your teacher that he met with me. He is better. He has the signs of life. I saw a balance in equilibrium."

Lieh Tzu went in and reported this to Hu Tzu. He spoke, "I have shown myself to him as Heaven shows itself in its composed tranquility, and only let a little energy burst out from under my heels. So he could discover that I have it. Bring him here again."

The next day, they came again, and as they left, Chi Hsien said to Lieh Tzu, "Your teacher is never on one day as on the other.[5] I cannot say about his appearance. Cause him to be regular, and I will examine him anew."

As Lieh Tzu informed Hu Tzu of this, he spoke, "I have shown myself to him in a condition of undifferentiated, universal equilibrium.[6] Where the mermaid romps, there is the abyss. Where the water rests, there is the abyss.[7] Where the water circulates, there is the abyss. The abyss has nine names. These were three of them."

On the next day, the two came again to Hu Tzu. But Chi Hsien was not able to stand his ground, was confused, and fled.

"Follow him!" called Hu Tzu; and Lieh Tzu ran after him, but could not catch up with him. He returned and reported to Hu Tzu that the escapee had vanished.

"I have shown myself to him," said Hu Tzu, "as Tao appeared before the beginning was. I was to him like a great void that had continuity in and of itself.[8] He did not know whom he saw: soon it seemed a dwindling, soon it seemed a flowing.[9] So he fled."

Accordingly, Lieh Tzu understood that he had not yet begun to obtain cognition. He returned home and spent three years without leaving it. He helped his wife cook the family meal and fed his pigs as is if they were human beings. He put aside all the carving and painting and returned to pure simplicity. There he stood like a clump of earth.[10] In the midst of confusion he was unconfused. And so he remained until the end. ("Inner Chapters" 20/7/15–33)

XXII. The Boring[1]

The ruler of the Southern Sea was called Shu.

The ruler of the Northern Sea was call Hu.[2]

The ruler of the Middle Zone was call Hun-tun.[3]

Shu and Hu often met together at Hun-tun's territory. Since he always showed them kindness, they resolved to repay his goodwill.

They said, "All men have seven openings—for sight, hearing, eating, and breathing. Hun-tun alone has none. We will bore some into him."

So they bored one hole each day.

On the seventh day, Hun-Tun died. ("Inner Chapters" 21/7/33–35)

XXIII. The Strong Thief[1]

The precautions that are to be taken against thieves who open trunks, search through satchels, or plunder money-boxes consist of winding with string and fastening with bolts and locks the trunks, satchels, and boxes. This is what the world calls intelligence.

But a strong thief comes who carries the trunk on his shoulders and the satchel and box besides. And his only fear is that the bolts and locks may not be strong enough!

Accordingly, it follows that what the world knows as intelligence simply has given assistance to the strong thief.

And I dare to state that what the world knows as intelligence can be nothing other than subservient to the great thieves; and that what the world knows as wisdom means nothing other than protecting the great thieves.[2] ("Primitivist" 23/10/1–4)

XXIV. Over-Indulgence and Non-Doing[1]

Over-indulgence of sight leads to debauchery in colors; over-indulgence of hearing leads to debauchery in sounds; over-indulgence of humanheartedness leads to confusion in virtue; over-indulgence of righteousness leads to an inversion of principles; over-indulgence in the rites leads to deviation from genuine purpose; over-indulgence in music leads to a dissolution of the spirit; over-indulgence in knowledge leads to a prevalence of artifice; over-indulgence of keen intellect leads to an expansion of passion for blaming.

If men rest in the natural conditions of existence,[2] then it does not matter whether these eight elements will or will not be allowed. But if men do not rest in the natural conditions of existence, then these eight elements become hindrances and problem-makers, and they plunge the world into confusion.

Nevertheless, as the world honors and loves them, so much more do they go astray.[3] And this is not in a passing whim, but with instruction in words, with meekness in kneeling, and with the allure of a play and a song. What remains for me to do?

Therefore, there is for the superior man, who will be appointed ruler in inescapable wisdom, nothing other than non-doing. Through non-doing he will be capable of resting in the natural conditions of existence. And so it is that he who respects the state as his own self is, appropriately, to preserve it; and he who loves the state as his own self is, appropriately, to rule it.[4]

And if he can abstain from injuring his inner equilibrium and burdening the strength of his senses, if he is unmoved as a corpse while his dragon-power manifests itself roundabout, in profound silence while his thunder-voice resounds, and the might of Heaven answers each movement of his will,[5] and all things mature and thrive under the compliant influence of non-doing—what leisure does he have to go to the governing of the world? ("Primitivist" 25/11/8–16).

XXV. The Heart of Man

Ts'ui Chu asked Lao Tzu, "If the state should not be ruled, how are the hearts of men to be made good?"[1]

Lao Tzu answered, "Be careful not to disturb the natural state of men's hearts. The heart of man can be pressed down and it can be stirred up. Pressed down it is like a prisoner, stirred up it is like a madman.

Through gentleness the hardest heart can be made soft. But if you attempt to plane it and smooth it out—it will glow like fire or numb like ice. Before you turn your head, it will flee over the boundaries of the four seas. At rest, profoundly steadfast; in motion, flown out to Heaven; in resolute haughtiness all bonds refused—thus is the heart of man. ("Primitivist" 26/11/16–19)

XXVI. Immortality

For nineteen years the Yellow Emperor had ruled, and his laws governed the entire state. Then he heard that Kuang Ch'eng-tzu was living on Mount K'ung-t'ung. He visited him and spoke to him, "I have heard, master, that you possess the perfect Tao. Is it permitted of me to ask you wherein this perfect Tao consists? I wish

to avail myself of this good influence of Heaven and Earth, in order
to make the five grains thrive and nourish my people. I long to direct
Yin and Yang, to protect all living things. How can I fulfill this?"

Kuang Ch'eng-tzu answered, "What you wish to make use of is
the primordial wholeness of all things.[1] What you long to direct are
the powers that divide them up. But you, since you have governed
the state, the clouds have rained before they became heavy, the
leaves have fallen before they became faded, the brightness of the
sun and moon has paled. Your sense is like that of a clever-worded
flatterer. How might you wish to hear of the perfect Tao?"

The Yellow Emperor went away. He relinquished dominion. He
built for himself a secluded hut. He lay on a mat of white grass.
For three months he remained in seclusion. Then he sought out
Kuang Ch'eng-tzu a second time. He found him lying, his countenance toward the south. The Yellow Emperor approached him as
would a subordinate, on his knees. He threw himself down before
him and spoke, "I have heard, master, that you possess the perfect
Tao. Is it permitted of me to ask you how I can preserve my self so
that it will endure?"

Kuang Ch'eng-tzu sprung up. "A good question, for sure!" he
cried. "Come, I will tell you of the perfect Tao.

"The essence of the perfect Tao[2] is profoundly hidden; its highness is lost in obscurity.

"Gain footing where nothing is seen, where nothing is heard, let
your soul embrace tranquility; and the corporeal self will obtain its
own form.[3]

"Be still, be pure; do not tire your body; do not confuse your
vitality and you will endure. For when the eye sees nothing and the
ear hears nothing and the heart knows nothing, the soul will preserve the body, and the corporeal self will endure.[4]

"Guard what is in you and hold back what is outside, for false
knowledge is ruinous. Then I will put you at that height of great
light, where the wellspring of the driving primordial power is, and
I will lead you through the gate of profound mystery, where the
wellspring of the restraining primordial power is.[5] Here are the
rulers of Heaven and Earth, here is the dwelling of Yin and Yang.[6]

"Care for and preserve your self, and all others will prosper of
themselves. I preserve in myself the primordial one, I rest in harmony with all things. Because I have so preserved myself, for twelve
hundred years in the corporeal realm I have not perished."[7]

The Yellow Emperor threw himself down and spoke, "Surely, Kuang Ch'eng-tzu is a Heavenly being!"

But the former continued, "Come, I will explain it to you. This self that all men believe to be transitory is inexhaustible. This self that men believe to be finite is limitless.[8] Those possessing Tao are princes in this life and rulers in the next one. Those not possessing Tao gaze at the light of day in this life and are clumps of earth in the next one.

In the present existence, all beings spring out of the Earth and return to the Earth. But I will accompany you through the gates of eternity into the kingdom of the infinite.[9] My light is the light of the sun and moon. My life is the life of Heaven and Earth. I do not care who comes to me, who goes from me—all may die out, I will endure." ("School of Chuang Tzu" 26/11/28-44)

XXVII. The Cloud Prince and the Primordial Mist[1]

The prince of the clouds traveled eastward through the atmosphere, when he bumped into the primordial mist. He was occupying himself by skipping around, his arms folded. The cloud prince was amazed, he stepped reverently by his side and asked, "Who are you, old man, and what are you doing here?"

"Strolling!" answered the primordial mist, skipping farther.

"I would like to know something," continued the cloud prince.

The primordial mist lifted his gaze, looked at him, and said, "Bah!"[2]

"The power of Heaven has turned out from harmony, the power of Earth is fettered,"[3] said the cloud prince, "the six influences do not get on well with one another, and the four seasons follow no rule any longer. I want to mingle the six influences so that they nourish all living beings.[4] What should I do?"

"I do not know!" cried the primordial mist, shaking his head, without ceasing his hopping around; "I do not know!"

The cloud prince could not ask further. But three years later when he traveled eastward through the land of Yü Sung, he again bumped into the primordial mist. He was eminently pleased, hastened over to him, and said, "Have you forgotten me, O Heavenly one? Have you forgotten me, O Heavenly one?" He bowed twice to the ground and requested that it be granted of him to question the primordial mist. But he said, "I wander without knowing what I seek. I roam about without knowing where I go. I stroll along for myself, arms folded, and watch how all things go their way.[5] What should I know?"

"I also roam about," answered the cloud prince, "but men follow all my movements. So I cannot avoid being their director.[6] For that reason I would accept advice with pleasure."

"That the order of the world is troubled," spoke the primordial mist, "that the conditions of life are confused, that the will of Heaven does not come to pass, that the beasts of the fields are driven asunder, that the birds cry in the night, that mildew preys on trees and plants, that destruction widely creeps over all that is on Earth; this is the fault of *those who govern*."

"Certainly," said the cloud prince, "but what should I do?"

"This is indeed," cried the primordial mist, "whence the evil comes! Go back!"

"It does not happen often," objected the cloud prince, "that I encounter you, O Heavenly one! I would accept one bit of advice with pleasure."

"Then let," spoke the primordial mist, "your heart work.[7] Persist in non-doing, and the world will be good of itself. Relinquish your body. Spit out your mind-power. Forget things. Become one with the indivisible. Let loose your spirit. Make your soul free. Become empty. Become nothing. Let all beings return to their root.[8] When they return to the root without knowledge, from there will come a simple purity that they will never lose; but knowledge would only bring deviation. Do not seek the names and relations of things; and all things will flourish of themselves."

"You, Heavenly one," said the cloud prince, before he twice bowed to the ground and took leave, "have imbued me with power[9] and filled me with mystery. What I searched for I have now found." ("School of Chuang Tzu" 27/11/44–57)

XXVIII. The Pearl

The Yellow Emperor wandered northward from the Red Sea, climbed Mount K'un-lun and gazed toward the south. Upon his journey home, he lost his enchanted pearl. He sent Cognition out searching, but he did not find it. He sent Clear-sight out searching, but he did not find it. He sent Thought-power out searching, but he did not find it. Finally he sent Aimlessness[1] out, and he found it. "Strange but true," spoke the Emperor, "that Aimlessness had the capacity to find it." ("School of Chuang Tzu" 29/12/18–20)

XXIX. Cosmogony

In the primordial beginning was the nonbeing of nothing.[1] This was the nameless.

When the one stepped into existence, formlessly, from that things obtained what was known as their *virtue*. But that which was formless divided, nevertheless without differentiation, was known as *destiny*.[2]

Then came the motion that gave life, and the things that completed themselves in accord with the foundations of life, had what was known as *form*. When form surrounded the spiritual, each with its own characteristics, this was known as the *nature* of it. If we nurture the nature, so we are brought back to virtue; and when this is fulfilled, we become as all things were in the beginning. We become unlimited, and the limitless is great.[3] As birds unconsciously close their beaks while chirping, and without closing them they could not chirp—thus to be closed upon Heaven and Earth, without being conscious of it, this is god-like virtue, this is the great harmony.[4] ("School of Chuang Tzu" 30/12/37–41)

XXX. The Gardener

Tzu-kung once came, on his way back from Ch'u to Chin, to a region north of the Han River. There he saw an old man who was digging a ditch to connect a well with his vegetable garden. He drew a pail of water out of the well and poured it in the ditch—a great labor with a very small result.

"If you were to have a machine here," called Tzu-kung, "you could irrigate your tract of land a hundred times in one day with slight effort. Wouldn't you like to have one?"

"What is that," asked the gardener.

"It is a lever of wood," answered Tzu-kung, "that is hard behind and light in front. It draws water from the well as you do with your hands, but in a constantly overflowing torrent. It is known as a well-sweep."

The gardener looked at him angrily, laughed, and spoke, "This I have heard of from my teacher: those who have cunning implements are cunning in their affairs, and those who are cunning in their affairs have cunning in their hearts, and those who have cunning in their hearts could not remain pure and uncorrupted, and those who do not remain pure and uncorrupted are restless in the spirit,[1] and in those who are restless in the spirit Tao cannot dwell. It is not that I did not know of this thing; but I would shame myself to make use of it."

Tzu-kung was embarrassed, lowered his head, and said nothing.

After a while, the gardener asked him, "Who are you?"

"I am a student of Confucius," answered Tzu-kung.

"So you are," said the gardener, "one of those who distend their knowledge in order to appear wise; who talk big in order to set themselves over the multitude; who sing lonely, melancholy tunes in order to spread their reputation. If you could forget all the spirit-power and do away with the gestures[2]—only then would you be close. But you do not have the means to rule your own self and want to rule the world? Go on your way and do not disturb my work any longer."[3] ("School of Chuang Tzu" 31/12/52–60)

XXXI. Three Types

As Chün Mang went eastward toward the ocean, he met Yüan Feng by the eastern sea.[1]

"Whither the way?" he called to him.

"I am going to the ocean," answered Chün Mang.

"What will you do there!" asked Yüan Feng.

"Do?" said Chün Mang. "The ocean is no thing that one can fill through pouring in or empty through draining out. I am going there to take pleasure in it."

"But," continued Yüan Feng, "do you not have anything in mind about the beings who have eyes in front?[2] I wanted you to tell me how the sage rules."

"The sage?" said Chün Mang. "The officials limit themselves to their enjoined activity. All positions are divided up by qualifications. All circumstances are considered before one acts. Speaking and doing happen freely from within, and the world is transformed.[3] One nod, one glance is sufficient, and all rush to follow it. Thus rules the sage."

"But how," asked Yüan Feng further, "does the man of virtue rule?"[4]

"The man of virtue?" said Chün Mang. "There is no deliberation in rest and no apprehension in action. Then he does not place value on right and wrong, good and bad. When all within the four seas partake of what is theirs, this is his joy; when he distributes to all, this is his pleasure. The people cling to him as do children to their dying mother; they meet him as does a wanderer who has lost his way. He has property in excess and does not know how he came to it; he has food and drink in excess and does not know who is supporting him with them. Thus rules the man of virtue."

"But how," asked Yüan Feng further, "does the spirit-like man rule?"

"The spirit-like man," said Chün Mang, "rises up the light, and the bounds of the body are consumed. We call this to be absorbed into the light. He brings to the outermost the power with which he has been gifted, and does not leave a single quality unfulfilled. His joy is that of Heaven and Earth. All matters and obligations go away. All things return to their primordial nature.[5] We call this to cover oneself in darkness. ("School of Chuang Tzu" 31/12/69–77).

XXXII. The Prayer[1]

Chuang Tzu spoke, "Oh, my ideal![2] You who destroy all things and do not deem it cruel; you who give bounty to all time and do not deem it as generosity;[3] you who are older than antiquity[4] but do not deem this as permanence; you who carry the cosmos, who form the fullness of his power, and do not deem this as skill; this is the bliss of Heaven." ("Syncretists" 34/13/12–13).

XXXIII. Books[1]

Prince Huan was reading one day in his hall, when the wheel-wright P'ien, who worked downstairs, threw down his hammer and chisel, climbed up the steps and asked, "Is it permitted of me to ask what are the words that you, my prince, are exploring?"

"I am exploring the words of the sages," said the prince.

"Are the sages alive," asked the wheelwright.

"No," answered the prince, "they are dead."

"Then the words," said the wheelwright, "that you, my prince, explore are only the remnant of those men."

"How can you, a wheelwright," cried the prince, "speak an opinion on the book that I am reading? Explain your speech or you shall die."

"Your servant," said the wheelwright, "will explain it through his own profession. I wish to make a wheel; if I work too slowly, I cannot make it firm enough; if I work too hastily, the spokes will not be suitable. When the movements of my hand are not too slow and not too hasty, then what my mind intends will happen. Words could not say how this happens; it taps into a secret skill. I cannot teach this to my son; he cannot learn it from me. So I, though seventy years old, in my elder days still make wheels. The sages are dead and gone, and with them that which they could not teach, so what you, my prince, can explore is only their remnant. ("School of Chuang Tzu" 36/13/68–74).

XXXIV. The String-music of the Yellow Emperor[1]

Pei-men Ch'eng said to the Yellow Emperor, "When you, my emperor, played the Hsien-ch'ih in the wilds of Tung-t'ing Lake, I was at the first part shocked, at the second stunned, at the third enraptured, speechless, flabbergasted."

The Emperor said, "So it must be. I played in accord with humankind, but I allowed myself to drift toward Heaven. The playing was only precise in skill, but animated by the primordial purity.[2]

"Perfect music is first shaped after a human principle, then it follows the directions of Heaven; it comes in harmony with the five virtues and passes over in spontaneity.[3]

"The four seasons are coalescing in it, and all things unite in it. Alternating, the times emerge; in alternation all things arise. Now it is abundance, now decay; now soft, now vehement voices; now naked, now covered notes: the interplay of Yin and Yang.

"Like lightning was the sound that roused you, as the Spring rouses the insect community, and the blaring of the thunder followed, without end, without beginning, now dying, now living, now sinking, now climbing, on and on without fail. And so you would be shocked.

"As I played further, it was the harmony of Yin and Yang irradiated by the glory of the sun and moon; broken and stretched, tender and severe, in one indivisible, ungrounded, clanging power. Filling valleys and gorges, banishing the ears and overcoming the senses, adapted to the breadth of receptivity of all things, the sounds circled on all sides, with high and clear tones. The shadows of the deceased[4] remained in their places. The sun, moon, and stars remained in their courses. But when the melody wound itself down, I paused; and then all of its reverberation flowed without cessation. You would have considered, but you could not take hold. You would have viewed, but you could not see. You would have followed, but you could not obtain. You stood dazzled in the midst of the wilderness, you leaned on a decayed tree and hummed to yourself. The power of your glances was exhausted. Your strength failed your aspiration to reach me. Your body was but a hollow shell. But you took pains to preserve yourself. And so you were stunned.

"Then I played in sounds that are without stupor, out of the rules of spontaneity. There the melody impetuously broke forth like a proliferation from shoots out of a root, untamed and unformed as the roar in the forest. It shot itself out and left no footprint, it fell into the depth where no sound endures. It began in the nowhere and dwelled in the obscure; one might know it as dead, another as living, one as fruitful, another as a blossom-like, so it poured itself toward all sites in never foreseeable chords.

"The wondering world questions the appointed man.[5] He knows of the essence of this music, he who stands under the same law.

"Thus where no machinery is put in motion, and yet the music is perfect, this is the music of Heaven. The mind awakens to its bliss, without waiting for it to be called. This is the music that Yü-piao Shih thus praises: 'Listening you hear no sound; viewing you

see no form. It fills Heaven and Earth. It embraces the universe.'
You coveted to listen to it, but you were not able to seize its existence. And so you would be enraptured.

"My play first aroused fear, and you were afflicted as if by an
apparition. Then I joined stupor to that, and you were separated.
But finally came enrapture; for enrapture means turned-out-from-
sense,[6] turned-out-from-sense means Tao, and Tao means the great
absorption." ("School of Chuang Tzu" 37/14/13–30)

XXXV. The Ways of the World

To be self-confident and overbearing, to abandon community and to
go aloof ways, to follow haughty and supercilious talk—this is the
self-estimation affected by those who withdraw into the mountains,
condemn the world and stand like decayed trees in deep ravines.

To preach humanheartedness and righteousness, to proclaim
loyalty, sincerity, humility, moderation, selflessness, and friendly
behavior—this is the civility affected by peacemakers and instruc-
tors of the world who wish to travel far and wide after wisdom.[1]

To concern oneself with merit and reputation, to delimit the
boundaries between monarchs and ministers, to rectify the relation
between upper and under class—this is the dominion affected by
courtiers and land-savers who strive to expand the border of their
states and annex those of other states.

To shelter oneself in marshland and solitude, to spend one's days
angling and going after one's pleasure—this is non-doing like that
of the lovers of the river and sea, who turn their backs to the world
and take their leisure.

To breathe out and to breathe in with sincere mouth, to turn out
the old and take up the new breaths, to stretch oneself like a bear
and stretch one's neck like a bird—this is life-preservation,[2] as do
those who wish to remain healthy through breath-skill[3] and look
after their bodies skillfully, to reach the old-age of P'eng Tzu.

But self-awareness without self-confidence, civility without
humanheartedness and righteousness, dominion without class and
reputation, non-doing without leisure, life preservation without
skill—this means to forget all things and to possess all things,
limitless tranquility and unconditioned value. This is the Tao of

Heaven and Earth, this is the virtue of the accomplished man.[4] ("Syncretists" 40/15/1–8)

XXXVI. The Spirit of the Sea and the River Spirit

It was the time of Autumn floods. A hundred streams flowed into the Ho, which swelled in its tempestuous course. The banks were soaked so far asunder that one could not differentiate an ox from a horse.

Then the master of the river laughed out loud from joy, that the beauty of the Earth was gathered to him. With the stream he traveled to the East, until he reached the Northern Sea. As he looked eastward and saw no boundary to the water, his expressions changed. He looked out over the plain, sighed and spoke to the Lord of the Northern Sea, "A common saying states that whoever has received a hundred sections of the truth thinks that no one compares to him. Such a one was I.[1] But now I have looked at your limitlessness. It would pain me had I not reached your home. I would have become for eternity the laughter of all enlightened ones!"

Thereupon, the Lord of the Northern Sea answered, "One cannot speak of the sea to a fountain frog; he cannot see out over his hole. One cannot speak of ice to a summer fly; it only knows of its own season. One cannot speak of Tao to a pedagogue; he is immured in his teaching. But now, since you have come out from your narrowness and have seen the great sea, you know your unimportance and I can speak to you about the primordial foundation.[2]

"There is no water under Heaven that could compare to the sea. Water without measure flows therein, and yet it does not overflow. Water without measure is withdrawn from it, and yet it does not wane. Spring and Autumn bring forth no alternations; flood and drought are likewise unknown to it. And it is so vast that it covers all rivers and streams. Nevertheless, I would never dare to boast of this. For I have received my form from Heaven and Earth, my life-breath from Yin and Yang.[3] Before Heaven and Earth I am like a stone or a small tree on a great mountain. I know my unimportance—what remains for me of which I could boast?

"The land between the four seas is to Heaven and Earth like a small heap of stones is to a swamp. The Middle Kingdom is to the land between the four seas as a grain of rice is to a granary. Of the entire myriad of created beings, man is but one. Of all men who live in the nine spheres of the Earth who feed on its fruits and travel in boats and wagons, the single man is but one. Is he in the abundance of things not like the tip of a hair on a horse's hide?"[4]

"Should I thus," asked the Lord of the river, "regard Heaven and Earth as unconditionally great, the tip of a hair as unconditionally small?"

"Absolutely not," answered the Lord of the sea. "Dimension knows no boundaries; time knows no standstill; destiny knows no symmetry;[5] becoming knows no certainty. So the sage[6] gazes into space and does not consider the small unimportant, the good appreciable; for he knows that dimension knows no boundaries. He watches the lapse of time and does not grieve over the distant, does not rejoice over the near; for he knows that time knows no standstill. He looks at fullness and deficiency and does not delight in success, does not falter at failure; for he knows that destiny knows no symmetry. He watches the changing course of things and is not intoxicated with life, does not despair over death; for he knows that becoming has no certainty.[7]

"For that reason, the accomplished man[8] deems that he does not do evil to others, but neither mercy nor benevolence.[9] He seeks no profit, but he does not scorn those who do. He does not strive after property, but does not deem this as good. He asks for no assistance, but he does not deem this as independent and does not scorn those who let themselves advance. He acts differently from the masses, but he does not deem this as uncommon; and while others go with the majority, he does not scorn them as hypocrites. The honors and profits of the world are no incentive for him, its punishments and dishonors no inhibition. He knows that right and wrong could not be differentiated, great and small could not be bounded.

"This I have heard said: The man of Tao has no reputation; perfect virtue knows no success; the accomplished man does not know of self—this is the peak-point of self-determination."

"But," asked the Lord of the river, "how is it then that we separate the inner and outer antitheses of worth and worthlessness, of largeness and smallness?"

"Seen from Tao," answered the Lord of the sea, "there is no antithesis of worth and worthlessness. But the isolated one values himself as high and the other as petty, and the collectivity deprives the individual of the right of judgment in adjudicating himself.[10]

"From comparison,[11] if we say one thing is great or small only because it is great or small in comparison to another, then there is nothing in the world that is not great, nothing that is not small. To know that Heaven and Earth is a grain of rice, the tip of a hair is a mountain—this is called cognition of comparability.

"From the relation,[12] if we say a thing is genuine or it is not genuine only because it performs or does not perform in relation, then there is nothing in the world that is not genuine, nothing that is genuine. To know that east and west are exchangeable and yet inflexible, this is called the regulation of relations.

"From worth,[13] if we say a thing is good or bad only while it is good or bad in our eyes, thus there is nothing in the world that is not good, nothing that is not bad. To know that the emperor Yao and the tyrant Chieh each thought himself good, each thought the other bad—this is called the arrangement of standards of measure.[14]

"Therefore, those who will hold up the right without its antagonist, wrong, or who hold up good-doing without its opposite, evil-doing—they do not seize the primordial foundation of Heaven and Earth nor the nature of things.[15] That is as good as if one could suppose the existence of Heaven without the existence of Earth, or the existence of Yin without the existence of Yang, which is evidently an inconceivability. When they continue their talk in spite of the demonstration of the truth, they must be fools or rogues.

"Rulers have renounced their throne under various conditions, dynasties have been continued under various conditions. Those who missed the correct moment and stood in opposition to their era were known as usurpers. Those who met the correct moment and stood in harmony with their era were known as friends of the fatherland. Be content, Lord of the Ho: how could you know what is worthy and what is worthless, what is great and what is small?"

"If that is so," said the Lord of the river, "what should I do and what should I not do? How should I arrange my refusal and acceptance, my grasping and yielding?"

"Seen from Tao," answered the Lord of the Sea, "worth and worthlessness are as changeable as elevation and depression, depending on where one stands.[16] To consider something as persevering is called striving against Tao. Few and many are as exchangeable as gifts, depending on whether they are considered by the giver or the receiver. To consider them as persevering is called violating Tao. Be judicious as a ruler who rules impartially. Be composed as a protective spirit[17] who distributes impartially. Be broadly sincere like the space that has set no boundary. Embrace all things in your love, and none will be better sheltered than another. This means to be unconditioned, to be a united view, to be out of all separation."[18] ("School of Chuang Tzu" 42/17/1–3, 4–13, 14–18, 24–34, 37–44)

XXXVII. The Pleasure of the Fish

Chuang Tzu and Hui Tzu stood at the bridge that led over the Hao.

Chuang Tzu said, "See how the minnows spring about! That is the pleasure of the fish."

"You are not a fish," said Hui Tzu, "how can you know wherein lies the pleasure of the fish?"

"You are not I," answered Chuang Tzu, "how can you know that I do not know wherein lies the pleasure of the fish?"

"I am not you," confirmed Hui Tzu, "and do not know you. But I do know that you are no fish; so you cannot know fish."

Chuang Tzu answered, "Let's return to your question. You asked me, 'How can you know wherein lies the pleasure of the fish?' At base you knew that I knew, and thus asked. No matter. I know it out of my own pleasure over the water." ("School of Chuang Tzu" 45/17/87–91)

XXXVIII. When Chuang Tzu's Wife Died

When Chuang Tzu's wife died, Hui Tzu went to him to convey his condolences.

Chuang Tzu sat on the ground, stretched out his legs, sang, and beat time on a pot.

"When a woman has lived with a husband and reared children with him," cried Hui Tzu, "and then dies in her old age, it seems to me bad enough not to lament. But to beat a bowl and sing, this is a peculiar undertaking."

"Not so," said Chuang Tzu. "When she died, I submitted to it. But soon I remembered. She had already existed before she was born, without form, without substance. Then a transformation occurred in the primordial mixture, the spirit came into being, the being to form, the form to birth.[1] Now a further transformation has occurred, and she is dead. So one goes from Spring to Autumn, from Summer to Winter. At present, she sleeps restfully in the great home. If I were to weep and lament, I would no longer have a sense of all this. So I withdrew myself." ("School of Chuang Tzu" 46/18/15–19)

XXXIX. The Dead Man's Skull

One day, Chuang Tzu bumped into a dead man's skull that was bleached, though its form was still preserved. He grazed it with his riding whip and said, "Were you once an ambitious man whose unregulated aspirations have brought him into this state? A statesman who ruined his land with corruption and was executed with an axe?[1] A creature who bequeathed his generation a heritage of shame? A beggar who died in the pain of hunger and cold? Or have you reached this condition in the natural course of old age?"

After he had spoken to the end, he seized the skull and lay on it as a pillow under his head as he went to sleep. During the night, he dreamed that the skull appeared to him and said, "You set your words carefully, sir; but they are all based in the lifetime and in the confusion of the living. In death is nothing of all this. Do you wish to hear of death?"

"I wish it," answered Chuang Tzu.

The skull spoke, "In death is no overlord and no subject. The workings of the ages are unknown. Our settled existence is the existence of Heaven and Earth. The bliss of a prince among men is nothing of our bliss."

But Chuang Tzu did not believe him and said, "If I persuaded the lord of destiny that he grant your life to be born again, and renew your bones and flesh, and therewith you would return to your elders, to your wife and children, to your friends and confidants[2]—would you not want that?"

At that the skull opened its eyes wide and wrinkled its brow and said, "How should I reject my kingly good fortune and plunge into the misery of the lot of the humanity?" ("School of Chuang Tzu" 46/18/22–29)

XL. In Tao

Lieh Tzu said to Kuan Yin, "The accomplished man wanders through solid things without being hampered, steps through fire without being singed, treads on the air without trembling.[1] How does he attain this?"

Kuan Yin answered, "What matters is that he preserves the unconditional purity.[2] It is not cunning and not skill. Sit down, and I will explain it to you.

"What has form, sound, and color is known as thing. In one sense, all things are alike; none can reach the existence that is beyond them all; they are only what they seem. Only man has the means to become formless and constant. If one can reach this in perfection, how could things hinder him? He persists in his regulation and resides in the endless concealment. He embraces the beginning and the end of all that is existing. He brings his being to the oneness and from that nourishes his life-force, he gathers his virtue and penetrates through to creation. If in this way his Heavenly is without failure, his spirit is without breach, how could things tread into him?[3]

"A drunken man who falls from the wagon may get wounds, but he will not die. His bones and joints are like those of others, yet his injury is different; his spirit has not been touched.[4] He did not know that he climbed into the wagon; he does not know that he fell out of it. Death and life, angst and dismay do not penetrate into his breast, so he remains unhurt in his heart.

"If one can reach such from wine, how much more from Heaven! The sage is sheltered in Heaven and nothing can damage him."[5] ("School of Chuang Tzu" 48/19/7–16)

XLI. The Cicada-Catcher[1]

When Confucius walked on his way out of a wooded area toward the state of Ch'u, he saw a hunchback who was catching cicadas with a sticky rod as though he were picking them up with his hand. "You are skillful!" he cried. "Is there a way to do that?"

"There is a way," answered the hunchback. "I practiced for five or six months long, rocking two balls on my rod. When they no longer fell, I only missed but a few cicadas. When I could rock three balls, I only missed one out of ten cicadas. When I could rock five, I caught cicadas as though I was picking them up with my hand. I held my body like a tree stump, my arm like a withered branch. Of Heaven and Earth, so great they are, and of the many things therein, I know nothing but the wings of my cicadas. I do not turn myself, I do not bend myself to the side; I do not exchange the wings of my cicadas for all things. How should it not succeed for me?"

Confucius looked at his students and said, "Where the will adheres to *one thing,* the spirit collects its power.[2] This is the teaching of the hunchback." ("School of Chuang Tzu" 48/19/17–21).

XLII. The Ferryman

Yen Hui said to Confucius, "When I was crossing over the rapids of Shang-shen, the ferryman steered his boat as quickly as a spirit. I asked him whether one could learn such guidance of a boat. 'One can,' he answered. 'The comportment of those who know how to keep the vessel over water is of such a kind as though they were abandoning a sinking one. They row as though the boat were not there.' What I wanted to know he did not tell me. Is it permitted for me to ask about the meaning?"

"It means," answered Confucius, "that such a man forgets the water around him. He regards the rapids as if they were solid land. He considers a capsized boat as the stalling of a wagon. Capsizing or stalling, he who is so unmoved by it, what shore should he not be able to reach safely?

"A man who plays for clay shards will play well. If he bets a bronze clasp, he will be uneasy. If he bets gold, he will be bewildered.

His destiny is in each case the same, but he is agitated by the worth of this stakes. And whoever yields to the outer weight will be helpless inside." ("School of Chuang Tzu" 48/19/22–26)

XLIII. The Priest and the Pigs

The priest of the sacrifice, in his dark and rectangular garments, stepped into the pigsty and thus spoke to the pigs: "How could you resist going to your death? I will feed you three months long with fine corn. I will mortify myself ten days long and stay awake for three days. I will lay out for you the mats of white grass. I will lay your body on the carved sacrificial dish. Does that not satisfy you?"

Then he went for a moment upon the point of view of the pigs and said, "It would indeed seem better for them to feed on bran and stay in the sty . . ."[1]

"But," he set forth again from his own point of view, "to obtain honor, each will gladly die on the battlefield or in the basket of the executioner."

So he rejected the point of view of the pigs and adopted his own point of view. To what extent was he different from the pigs? ("School of Chuang Tzu" 49/19/35–38)

XLIV. The Gamecocks

Chi Hsing-tzu was training a gamecock for the prince.

After ten days, the prince asked whether the bird was ready. "Not yet," he answered, "he is still completely quarrelsome and wanton."

After another ten days, the prince asked again. "Not yet," answered Chi, "the voice and sight of other cocks still agitate him."

After another ten days, the prince asked again. "Not yet," answered Chi, "the anger in abdomen and eyes still shakes him."

But as yet another ten days elapsed and the prince asked again, he answered him, "Now he is fit. Other cocks may crow for him as much as they want, but he will not pay attention to it. If you look at him, you might say that he is made of wood. His virtue is complete. Foreign cocks will not dare to pit themselves against him; they will run away." ("School of Chuang Tzu" 50/19/46–49)

XLV. The Chimepost

Ch'ing, the master of woodworking, carved a chimepost. When he was done, the work seemed to everyone who saw it as though it were made by spirits.[1] The prince asked the master, "What is this secret in your art?"

"Your servant is only a craftsman," answered Ch'ing, "what secret could he possess? And yet there is something. When I went there to make the chimepost, I guarded against each diminishing of my life-force. I composed myself to bring my spirit to unconditioned rest.[2] After three days, I had forgotten all the rewards that I could acquire. After five days, I had forgotten all the glory that I could acquire. After seven days, I had forgotten my limbs and my form. The thought of your courtyard, for which I should work, also vanished. Thus, my skill was collected, no longer disturbed from outside. Now I went to the high woodlands. I looked at the shapes of the trees. When I beheld one that had the right shape, the chimepost appeared to me and I went to work. Had I not found this tree, I would have had to give up the work. My heavenly-born manner and the heavenly-born manner of the tree converged thereupon. What now was credited to spirits was only grounded therein."[3] ("School of Chuang Tzu" 50/19/54–59)

XLVI. The Beautiful Woman and the Ugly Woman

When Yang Tzu traveled to the state of Sung, he spent one night in an inn.

The innkeeper had two concubines, one beautiful and one ugly. He honored the ugly one; he scorned the beautiful one.[1]

Yang Tzu asked of the innkeeper why this was so. He answered, "The beautiful one knows of her beauty and we do not see her beauty. The ugly one knows of her ugliness and we do not see her ugliness."[2] ("School of Chuang Tzu" 54/20/68–70)

XLVII. Silence

When Confucius came upon the sage[1] Wen-po Hsüeh-tzu, he spoke
no word. Afterward, Tzu-lu asked him, "Master, you have desired
for a long time to see Wen-po Hsüeh-tzu. How is it that you, now
that you saw him, have no words to speak to him?" Confucius
answered, "With a man like this one, merely his view is needed,
and Tao appears. Thus, there is no room for talk." ("School of Chuang
Tzu" 55/21/12–14)

XLVIII. The Perpetual Dying

Yen Hui asked Confucius, "Master, when you go at a step, I go at
a step. When you go at a trot, I go at a trot. When you go at a
gallop, I go at a gallop. But when you chase past the bounds of the
dust, then I can only stand waiting and stare after you. How does
that happen?"

"Tell me what you mean," said Confucius.

"I mean," continued Yen Hui, "this: when you talk, I talk. When
you demonstrate, I demonstrate. When you preach Tao, I preach
Tao. But when I say that, 'When you chase past the bounds of the
dust, then I can only stand waiting and stare after you,' I mean
that you do not speak and everyone believes you, you are not zealous and everyone agrees with you, you do not entice and everyone
congregates around you. That is what I can not understand."

"Why do you wish to go into something unreasonable?" said
Confucius. "Nothing is worth such grief as the death of the mind.
The death of the body is of much pettier significance.

"The sun rises in the east and sets in the west. There is no thing
that is not guided by it; and all that have eyes and feet depend on
it to be able to do their work.[1] When it appears, life has appeared;
when it disappears, life disappears with it.

"And each man has his sun-mind on which he depends; when it
goes, he dies, and he revives when it returns.[2] But if I, a mind-
gifted body, stride toward the end without the perpetually life-
regenerating transformation,[3] if I resign myself to days and nights
of perpetual wearing out like a mere thing, if I am not aware of
perpetual dying, if I am only aware—in spite of the mind-gifted

body—of the one that cannot save me from the grave, then I consume life until it is thus in death, as though you and I had leaned one single time shoulder to shoulder, before we were forever separated! Is this not worth grief?

"But you fix your gaze at something in me that, when you look, has already passed away. And nevertheless you seek it as though it must yet be there, as one seeks a sold horse at the market. Look, what I admire in you is changeable. What you admire in me is changeable. Why do you worry? Even if my self dies at every moment, in the transformation the eternal preserves itself."[4] ("School of Chuang Tzu" 55/21/14–24)

XLIX. The Three Answers

As Cognition roamed northward over the black water and over the mountain of incomprehensible slope, he encountered Do-nothing-say-nothing and said to him, "I would like to ask you something. What does one think, what does one consider, to discern Tao? Where does one stand, what does one seize, to approach Tao? Whom does one follow, on what does one tread, to reach Tao?"

To these three questions, Do-nothing-say-nothing gave no answer. Why would he not answer? He could not.

When Cognition received no answer, he turned around and wandered southward, over the white water and over the mountain of illumination. There he met Delusion-whirlpool and submitted his questions to him.

"Ah!" cried Delusion-whirlpool. "I know. I will tell you . . ."

But as he was about to speak, he forgot what he had begun to say.

When Cognition received no answer, he went back to the palace. There he met the Yellow Emperor and submitted his questions to him.

The Yellow Emperor spoke, "There is nothing to think, nothing to consider, to discern Tao. There is nothing on which to stand, nothing to seize, to approach Tao. There is nothing to follow, nothing on which to tread, to reach Tao."

Then Cognition spoke to the Yellow Emperor, "Indeed, you and I know that, but these two do not know it. Who is in the right?"

The Yellow Emperor answered, "Do-nothing-say-nothing is truly in the right, and Delusion-whirlpool is near to the right. You and I are wholly in the wrong. For those who take hold of it do not speak of it, and those who speak of it do not take hold of it."[1]

Thereupon, Cognition spoke to the Yellow Emperor, "I asked Do-nothing-say-nothing. He did not answer me. Why did he not answer me? He could not. I asked Delusion-whirlpool. He was about to speak, but he did not speak. Why would he not? He was about to speak, but he forgot what he had begun to say. Now I asked you, and you have answered me. How is it then that you are totally in the wrong?"

The Yellow Emperor spoke, "Do-nothing-say-nothing was truly in the right, because he did not know. Delusion-whirlpool was near to the right, because he forgot. You and I are wholly in the wrong, because we know."

When Delusion-whirlpool heard of this, he thought that the Yellow Emperor had spoken like a knowledgeable man. ("School of Chuang Tzu" 57/22/1–7, 13–16)

L. To Have As One's Own

Emperor Shun asked Ch'eng, "Can I obtain Tao so that I have it as my own?"

Ch'eng answered, "Your body is not your own. How could you possess Tao as your own?"

"If my body," said Shun, "is not my own, whose is it?"

"Your body," answered Ch'eng, "is the form designated by Heaven and Earth. Your life is not your own. It is the harmony designated by Heaven and Earth. Your particularity is not your own. It is the malleability designated by Heaven and Earth. Your posterity is not your own. It is the renewal designated by Heaven and Earth.

"You walk, and do not know what drives you. You rest, and do not know what carries you. You eat, and do not know what enables you to taste. This is the strong, effective power of Heaven and Earth. How could you possess Tao for your own?" ("School of Chuang Tzu" 58/22/25–28)

LI. The Place of Tao

Tung-kuo Tzu asked Chuang Tzu, "What you call Tao, where is it to be found?"

Chuang Tzu answered, "There is nowhere where it is not."

"Give me but an example," said Tung-kuo Tzu.

"It is in this ant."

"So low!"

"It is in the weeds."

"Lower still!"

"It is in the clay shards."

"Lower still!"

"It is in the shit-pile," said Chuang Tzu.

Tung-kuo Tzu was silent.

"Your question, sir," continued Chuang Tzu, "does not have a hold on being. When Huo, the chief inspector of the markets, questioned the market manager about the fatness of the pigs, the test was made on the parts where one could take the least fatness for granted. But search for nothing that stands out in particular; for there is no thing that it denies. Of such a type is the perfect Tao. And of such a type is also the prototypic word. Wholeness, completeness, all-ness, these are the names that sound diverse and yet mean the same. Their purport is the one.

"Attempt with me to reach the palace of nowhere and there, amidst the oneness of all things, follow your discourse into endlessness. Attempt with me to practice non-doing, therein you can rest unmoved, pure, and blissful. Thus my mind becomes detached.[1] It does not wander, and yet is unconsciously at rest. It comes and goes, and yet is unconsciously stopping. Backward, forward, unconscious in all purposes—up and down in limitlessness, where likewise the greatest idea can find no end.

"That which makes things what they are is not restricted to things. The limits of things bind only their thing-ness. Tao is the limit of limitlessness, the limitlessness of the limited. We speak of fullness and emptiness, renewal and decay. Tao effects fullness and emptiness, but it is neither full nor empty. It effects renewal and decay, but it is neither renewed nor decayed. It effects root and crown, but it is neither root nor crown. It effects collection and dispersion, but it is neither collected nor dispersed." ("School of Chuang Tzu" 59/22/43–52)

LII. Tao the Unknown

Primordial Purity asked Boundless, "Do you know Tao?"

"I know not," said Boundless.

Primordial Purity asked Actionless, "Do you know Tao?"

"I do know Tao," said Actionless.

"Is there a motif," asked Primordial Purity, "to knowing Tao?"

"There is a motif," said Actionless.

"What is it?" asked Primordial Purity.

"I know," said Actionless, "that Tao honors and disgraces, binds and loosens. This is my motif to knowing Tao."

Primordial Purity repeated these words to Beginningless and asked, "Whose is in the right, the ignorance of Boundless or the knowledge of Actionless?"

Beginningless answered, "Not to know is profound. To know is superficial. Not to know is internal. To know is external."

Primordial Purity sighed and spoke, "Then ignorance is knowledge and knowledge ignorance! But tell me what kind of knowledge is the knowledge of not-knowing?"

Beginningless answered, "Tao cannot be heard. What can be heard is not Tao. It cannot be seen. What can be seen is not Tao. It cannot be spoken. What can be spoken is not Tao. What gives the form to the formed is itself formless; in this manner Tao is nameless."

Beginningless spoke further: "Whoever answers one who asks of Tao does not know Tao. Even if one hears of Tao, he in truth hears nothing of Tao. In Tao no questions are valid, of Tao no answers are valid. To ask the unaskable is frivolous. To answer the unanswerable is unessential. And whoever pairs the frivolous with the unessential, who has no outer perception of coherence, who has no inner perception of the primordial foundation—he will not ascend the summit of the sacred mountain, he will not vault into the great void." ("School of Chuang Tzu" 59/22/57–65)

LIII. Of Dogs and Horses

Hsü Wu-kuei the hermit was introduced by the minister Nü Shang to Prince Wu of Wei.

The prince greeted him in a sympathetic manner and said, "You are indeed suffering, sir. You must have experienced hard toilings in your mountain-life that you have decided to visit me."

Hsü Wu-kuei answered, "It is I, my prince, who has pitied you, not you me. If you give free rein to your passions, and pass on the machinery of hate and inclination, the inner conditions of your life will suffer. And if you discharge the passions and withdraw the machinery of hate and inclination, your senses, sight and hearing, will suffer. It is I, my prince, who has pitied you, not you me."

The prince was so astonished that he could not speak. After a while, Hsü Wu-kuei continued, "I will try, my prince, to explain how I judge hunting dogs. Those who are of inferior breed eat themselves full and are then as contented as a cat. Those of middle breed are as if they were staring at the sun. Those of the highest breed are as if they separated from their selves.[1]

But I know of dogs not as well as I know of horses. But I judge horses thusly: their extension must be that of a line, their inflection that of a curve, their turning that of a square, their revolution that of a circle. This valuates the horses of the state. But they are not like the horses of the kingdom. The horses of the kingdom are magnificent. They move as though full of eagerness to vault the distance as if they had lost their way, as if they had separated from themselves. So they fly over all their rivals, over the unstirred dust, removed from sight."

The prince found great pleasure in this speech and laughed.

When Hsü Wu-kuei came out, Nü Shang asked him, "What must you have been saying to the prince? When I speak to him, it is either on things of peace and based on the sacred books of songs, of history, of rites, and of music, or on things of war and based on the 'Golden Command Roster' and the 'Six Combat Plans.' I have performed innumerable errands with great success; yet the prince has never honored me with laughter. What could you have said to him that so delights him?"

Hsü Wu-kuei answered, "I have only informed him how I judge dogs and horses."

"Was that all?" asked Nü Shang.

"Have you," said Hsü Wu-kuei, "not heard of the outlaw from Yüeh? After the first day of banishment he was joyous when he met one whom he had known in his homeland. After a month he was joyous when he met one whom he had seen there. After a year he was joyous when he met one who in any way resembled his countrymen. So, to be separated from his community increases even more the longing to be reunited with them.

"A man who is joyous in the wild, where the hellebore hinders the path of the weasel, and who now is soon striding further, soon standing still—how very glad he will be when the stride of another man penetrates his ears. How much more so when he hears the voice of a relative, a brother. It is long, it seems to me, since the prince has heard the voice of a true man at his side!"[2] (Not attributed to a source, though perhaps recognizable as "School of Chuang Tzu" 64/24/1–13)

LIV. Criminals

Po Chü was a student of Lao Tzu. "Am I permitted," he said to him, "to go into the world?"

"No," answered Lao Tzu, "the world is everywhere the same as you see it here."

But as he pressed further once again, Lao Tzu asked him, "Where will you begin your wanderings?"

Po Chü said, "I will begin with the state of Ch'i. There I will uncover the corpses of the sentenced criminals. I will seize them and put them on their feet. I will take off my festival garments and dress them in them. I will cry to Heaven and lament their lot. I will cry, 'You men, you men, confusion was on Earth, and the first to have fallen into it were you.' I will speak, 'Were you in reality robbers? Were you in reality murderers? Honor and dishonor were introduced and evil followed. Wealth was accumulated and the quarrels began. Evil that was introduced, quarrels that were accumulated, distress man and take from him tranquility. Where is there an escape from this?

"The rulers of antiquity attributed all successes to the people, all failures to themselves. What was right they credited to the people, what was wrong to themselves. When damage occurred, they blamed themselves.

"Not so the rulers of this time. They hide a thing and blame those who cannot see it. They impose dangerous labors and punish those who do not dare to attempt them. They decree overly hard burdens and chastise those who are not capable of bearing them. They order overly long marches and execute those who do not withstand.

"And thus the people, sensing that their powers are not equal to those of all others, take their refuge in deception. Then where such great lies reign, how should the people thus not be fraudulent? When their strength does not suffice, they take their refuge in deception. When their knowledge does not suffice, they take their refuge in deceit. When their property does not suffice, they take their refuge in robbery. And who is it that bears the blame and responsibility for such robbery?" ("School of Chuang Tzu" 71/25/43–50)

The Commentary
"Afterword"

1

Across the theories of races and cultures, in our time the old knowledge has been neglected, that the Orient forms a natural oneness, expressed in its values and works; that across its divisions of peoples arises a commonality that separates it from the destiny and creativity of the West in unconditioned clarity. The genetic explanation for it, which is not to be expounded here, has its foundation quite naturally in the diverse conditions not merely in space but also in time, for indeed the spiritually determining epoch of the Orient belongs to a moment of mankind other than that of the West.

Here, the oneness of the Orient is only implicitly to be demonstrated in one manifestation, which to be sure is among the most essential of all, in the manifestation of the teaching.

In its primordial state, the Eastern spirit[1] is what all spirit is in the primordial state: magic. This is its being, that it confronts the unrestraint of nature that is rushing with thousandfold menace, with its restraint, the binding that is inherent in magical power. Regulated word, ordered motion, incantation and magic gesture compel the demonic element into rule and order. All primitive technique and all primitive organization are magic; implement and defense, speech and sport, custom and bond arise from magical intention and serve in their primordial time a magical sense out of which their own life only gradually sets itself loose and becomes independent.

This setting loose and becoming independent carries itself out much more slowly in the Orient than in the West. In the West, the magical has living duration only in the folk religiosity, in which the undifferentiated wholeness of life has preserved itself; in all other domains, the loosening is fast and complete. In the Orient, it is slow and incomplete; in the products of separation, the magical character adheres even longer. Thus, for example, the art of the Orient still remains in many ways, even after the attainment of artistic freedom and might, in the magical intention, while with that of the West, the attainment of this height confers its own right and its own purpose.

Among the three foundational powers in which the indicating spirit of the East (I am here bypassing the forming spirit) constructs itself, and of which the Occident possesses creatively only two—these being called science and law—it is the third, this being called the teaching, that is able to loosen itself most completely from the magical primordial ground.

It appears to me that for an understanding of the Orient, it is necessary to draw these foundational powers into every distinction from one another.

"Science" comprises all information about an existence,[2] earthly and heavenly, which are nowhere and never separated from one another, but rather combine themselves into the world of existence, which is the subject of science.

"Law" comprises all commands of an obligation,[3] human and godly, which are nowhere and never separated from one another, but rather combine themselves into the world of obligation, which is the subject of law.

Science and law belong continually together, so that existence proves itself in obligation, obligation establishes itself in existence. The growing schism between existence and obligation, science and law, which characterizes the spiritual history of the Occident, is foreign to the Orient.

With science and law goes the teaching as the third foundational power of the Eastern spirit.

The teaching comprises no subjects, it has only one subject, itself: the one that is necessary.[4] It stands beyond existence and obligation, information and command; it knows only to say one thing, the needful that is realized in the truthful life.[5] The needful is by no means an existence and accessible to information; it is not found either on Earth or in Heaven, but rather possessed and lived. The truthful life is by no means an obligation and subject to command; it is not taken over either from man or from God, but rather it can only be fulfilled out of itself and is utterly nothing other than fulfillment. Science stands on the duality of reality and cognition; law stands on the duality of demand and deed;[6] the teaching stands on the oneness of the one that is necessary.

One can nevertheless transform fundamentally the sense that the words *existence* and *obligation* have in science and law, and denote the needful as an existence that is accessible to no information, the truthful life as an obligation that is subject to no command, and the teaching then as a synthesis of existence and obligation. But when one does this, one may not thereby make this speech—which is an absurdity for science and law—vain and ruined and presentable, that one replaces information and command through an "inner" information, through an "inner" command with which the teaching has to contrive. These phrases of a time-honored, belief-enlightening rhetoric are nothing but confused deceit. The dialectical antithesis of inner and outer can serve only for the symbolic illustration of the experience, but not to pick the teaching in its manner out from the other foundational powers of the spirit. It is not the peculiarity of the teaching that it be concerned with the internal or receive from it measure and right; it would be meaningless to wish to diminish science and law to an "inner information" not at all separable from the outer, to an "inner command" not at all separable from the outer. Rather it is the peculiarity of the teaching that it goes not upon manifold and singular, but rather upon the one, and that it promotes neither a belief nor an action, both of which are rooted in multiplicity and singularity, that it generally follows nothing but rather proclaims itself.

This essential distinction of the teaching from science and law documents itself also in the historical. The teaching constructs itself independently of science and law, until it finds its pure fulfillment in one central human life. Only in the decline that begins immediately after this fulfillment does the teaching blend with the elements of science and of law. Out of such a mixture arises a religion, a product of the downfall, of the contamination and destruction, in which information, command, and the needful are welded into a contradictory and efficacious whole. So now, belief, like action, is demanded; the one has disappeared.

Teaching and religion, both are not partial forces, like science and law, but rather represent the wholeness of life. But in the teaching, all antitheses of the wholeness have lifted up into the one, as the seven colors into white light; in the religion, they are allied into community, as the seven colors into the rainbow. The magic that bordered science and law but could not touch the teaching seizes possession of the religion. Its binding power constructs the elements that are striving with one another into an opalescent magical whirlwind that rules the times.

Between the teaching and the religion, leading from the one to the other, stand parable and myth. Both make themselves close to the central human life, in which the teaching has found its purest fulfillment: the parable as the word of this man himself, the myth as the deposit of his life in the consciousness of the time. Accordingly, the parable appears still to stand wholly on the side of the teaching, the myth still to stand wholly on the side of the religion. Nevertheless, both carry the mediation in themselves. This is to be understood out of the being of the teaching, as it is considered in its liaison to man.

The teaching has only one subject: the needful. It is realized in the truthful life. To be seen from man, this realization signifies nothing other than the oneness. But this is not, as it may seem, an abstract determination, but rather the very most vivid. For the oneness that is intended is indeed not the summarizing oneness of a world or of a perception, not the steady oneness of one God or of the spirit or of existence or of any thought or felt or willed things; rather, it is the oneness of this human life and this human soul that fulfills itself in itself, your life and your soul's oneness, you the one seized by the teaching. The truthful life is the unified life.

But as there are two types of good and two types of wisdom—elemental and obtained—so too there are two types of oneness in man, in which the teaching as their consecration can realize and prove itself: the oneness of the simple persons and the oneness of the persons who have become one. In the time of its formation, the teaching speaks only to the persons who have become one.[7] But as soon as the central man appears, whose attained oneness has the purity and the straightforward force of the elemental, he must seek the simple persons, his impoverished brothers in spirit, that their profound oneness, which preserves all its sins and foolishness in the womb, sanctifies itself beyond sin and foolishness. And he speaks to them in the language that they can hear: in parable. And when he dies, his life has to them become a parable. But a life that has developed into parable is called myth.

The parable is the engagement of the absolute into the world of things. The myth is the engagement of things into the world of the absolute.

Even so long as the teaching speaks only to the persons who have become one, it cannot dispense with parable. For the naked oneness is silent. Only out of things, events, and relations can it obtain speech; there is no human speech beyond the things, the events, and the relations.[8] As soon as the teaching comes upon things, it comes upon parable. So long, however, as the teaching speaks only to the persons who have become one, the parable is only a glass through which one gazes at the light framed by a border of colors. But as soon as the teaching begins to talk through its central man to the simple person, the parable becomes a prism. Thus, the fulfillment leads across to the dissolution, and all the intoxication of rites and all madness of dogma rest already germinating in the parable of the master.

And on the other hand, even the life of the central man is caught not in a mirror, but rather in a prism: it is mythicized. Mythos does not mean to bring the constellations down upon the Earth and to let them walk upon it in human form, but rather in it the enrapturing human form will be raised to heaven, and moon and sun, Orion and the Pleiades serve only to adorn it. Mythos is also not a thing of yonder and former times, but rather a function of today and all times, of the state in which I write and all places of man. One eternal function of the soul: the engagement of that which has been experienced into the world process that is soon more instinctual, soon more thoughtful, but even by the dullest somehow perceived, into the magic of existence. The stronger the tension and intensity of the experience, the greater the experienced form, the experienced occurrence, so much more compelling the myth-building power. Where the highest form, the hero and saviour, the most sublime occurrence, his life that has been lived, and the mightiest tension, that of the affected simple person, coincide, arises the myth, which compels all of the future. Thus the way walks in to the dissolution, for in the myth of the saviour already rests germinating the creed of the small miracle and the abuse of the truth of salvation and redemption.

The dissolution carries itself out in religion, and it completes itself in the perpetuated violent deed that calls itself "religion" and yet holds religiosity in fetters. Ever again awakens in the souls of the religious the ardor after freedom; after the teaching; ever again reformation, restoration, renewal of the teaching is ventured; ever again it must go wrong, the fervent emotion must flow into, in lieu of the teaching, a mixture of science and law, the so-called purified religion. For the teaching cannot be restored, cannot be renewed. Eternally the one, it must still eternally begin anew. The history of the highest manifestation of eastern spirit carries itself out in this path.

2

But that the teaching eternally begins anew, this is in no way perchance to be understood as if it were one content which has taken diverse forms, as is thought by those who scrutinize and compare the ways of the teaching in order to ascertain the commonality. The antithesis of content and form appears here as a dialectical antithesis that does not clarify but rather obscures history, just as it does not clarify but rather obscures the contemplation of art. The Logos of John's gospel, the symbol of primordial existence drawn significantly from the linguistic world, is set upright like a landmark against the encroachment of this dialectic. "The word" is, "in the beginning," since it is the oneness that is dialectically analyzed. Precisely for this reason, it is the mediator, since it sets to the products of this analysis, perhaps to divinity and humanity, or otherwise considered as to "God the Father" and the "Holy Ghost," the oneness that binds them, the original, divided and embodied oneness that again reconciles the elements. "The word" is therefore the companion of each human word, which also is indeed not a content which has assumed a form, but rather a oneness which has been analyzed in content and form—an analysis that does not clarify but obscures the history of the human word and the history of each single human word, and whose claim, therefore, cannot reach beyond the realm of conceptual classification. The same holds with the teaching.

The teaching proclaims what it is: the oneness as the needful. But this is in no way a content that assumes diverse forms. When we analyze each way of the teaching in content and form, we receive as the "content" not the oneness, but rather the talk of the kingdom of Heaven and sonship to God, or the talk of deliverance from suffering and the holy path, or the talk of Tao and non-doing. This cannot be otherwise; for the oneness was even more than the content of Jesus or Buddha or Lao Tzu, even more than what they wanted to articulate, it was the sense and the foundation of these men. It was more than the content of their word, it was this word's life and the word itself in its oneness. From that is the foundational comparison with which we are here concerned, not that of content and form, but rather, as is yet to be expounded, that of teaching and parable.

It has been now sought yet again to make the oneness into a content, into a "common" content, while making the oneness of the truthful life into the oneness of God or of the spirit or of existence, which is common to the way of the teaching—somewhat after the analogy of modern monism, which decrees a "oneness of existence" constituted in some manner. But it is quite unessential to the teaching to trouble itself over the essence of God as one existing being.[9] With Buddha this is indeed wholly evident; but indeed even in the Upanishads this is not, after all, the significance of the teaching of Atman that a declaration is made about the oneness of existence, but rather that what one calls existence is nothing other than the oneness of the self and that consequently the unified man confronts the world as existence, as oneness, as his self. In the same way, the original Christianity[10] does not deal with the oneness of God, rather with the identity of the unified man with God; here too, the existing being is, so to speak, only for the sake of the needful. And the same goes for the Tao-teaching, where all that is said of the "path" of the world points to the path of the accomplished man, and maintains in it its confirmation and fulfillment.

Of course, it must become difficult for today's Westerner to realize this wholly, particularly for the philosophically schooled, for whom the needful is perhaps existence seen *sub specie aeterni*, the oneness perhaps the act of harmonizing in cognition. The modern Westerner subsumes what is not to be subsumed. The teaching troubles itself with existence as little as it troubles itself with obligation, but only with the reality of the truthful life, which is primary and unsubsumable. It is, therefore, not even to be gotten to out of the separation of subject and object, where one has no longer moved the oneness into the object, but instead into the subject; rather, for the man of the teaching, this separation is either altogether not there or it is for him only the pure formula for that multiform dialectical antithesis out of whose abolition the teaching is built.

3

The way of the teaching is accordingly not that of the training of a cognition, but rather that of the pure fulfillment in a central human life. This is to be perceived, with greater or lesser clarity, in the three manifestations of the teaching that are handed down to us in sufficient documentation.

These three manifestations are the Chinese Tao-teaching, the Indian teaching of release, and the Jewish/original-Christian teaching of the kingdom of God. The documentation of even these manifestations is insufficient to survey their way wholly. Thus we know of the growing Jewish/original-Christian teaching something of the living community that bore it—from the Rechabites (apparently misunderstood, intentionally or unintentionally, by the redactors of the canon)[11] in Jeremiah 35 to the Essenes, to whom ancient tradition, despite all the exaggerations, surely points correctly—but very few of the words of this so-called underground Judaism that we can only meagerly surmise or infer out of the late sources. On the other hand, handed down to us in the writings of the Tao-teaching are sayings of the "ancients," that guarantee to us the long preexistence of the teaching, and this is also born out through the observations of the opposing sides; but of the life forms in which it spread we have only wholly insufficient information. Not even the Indian writings, the incomparably largest of all, offer a complete view of the connections.

Nevertheless, the material is sufficient to show how the teaching takes shape independently of science and law, and how it fulfills itself in the central man, who overcomes science and law without a struggle, solely through the teaching and the life. Thus, Buddha overcomes the Vedic science with the abolition of the "view" that does not belong to the accomplished man on the "path," and the Brahmin law with the abolition of castes in the order. Thus, Lao Tzu overcomes the official wisdom through the teaching of "non-being," the official virtue through the teaching of "non-doing."

And we can also see from the manifestations of the teaching that the central man brings no new element to the teaching, but rather fulfills it: "I have not come to undo, but to fulfill."[12] So Lao Tzu also says of himself that he has only to fulfill the unrecognized of antiquity, the presentiment of the one that rests in the word of the people. He once quotes the saying, "The violent do not attain their natural death," and adds, "What the others teach, I also teach; I will make of it a father-ground of the teaching."[13] This corresponds to the words of the Sermon on the Mount: "But I say to you," as violence is for Lao Tzu already in itself the dead, the lifeless in the world, because it is Tao-less. To fulfill here means, as there, to elevate something handed down out of the conditioned into the unconditioned.

The central man brings to the teaching no new element, but rather fulfills it; that is to say, he elevates it at the same time out of the unrecognized into the recognized, and out of the conditioned into the unconditioned.

This unconditionality of the fulfilling person, which sets the world of the conditional against him, demonstrates itself in its highest reality; this, his strength of fulfillment, demonstrates itself in his life.[14] In incomparably higher measure than for the great ruler, for the great artist, and for the great philosopher, it is valid for him that all that is dispersed, volatile, and fragmentary coalesces in him to oneness; his life is this oneness. The ruler has his organization of people, the artist has his work, the philosopher has his ideology; the fulfilling person has nothing but his life. His words are pieces of this life, each executor and originator, each comforted by destiny and snapped up by destiny, the multitude of voices transforming through this human body into finality, the weak impulses of many dead bound in him into might, he the cleat of the teaching, fulfillment and abolition, salvation and decline. Around that are the logia, that no doubt can touch and that, standing through the generations, even without writing, preserve themselves unblended by virtue of the imprint of destiny and the elemental uniqueness of the fulfilling speech. For the fulfilling person, who is bound from everything and yet comes from nothing, is the most unique man. Although all those who search wanted him, and all meditation presaged him, he is, when he appears, recognized by few, and those few are doubtless not among those who presaged him and wanted him. So great is his uniqueness, so unoriginal, so plain, so utterly the last genuineness of humankind.

This is most conspicuous with Jesus, for whom the witness was, as it seems, accomplished through death, the unique absolute that man has to give up. Next to him stands Buddha. Lao Tzu's life offers itself the least. It is of consequence that it was precisely the life of his teaching, a concealed life. In the meager account of the historian, everything is said about that: of his life, "His teaching was the concealment of self; this was to become nameless, after which he strove"; of his death, "No one knows where he ended; Lao Tzu was a concealed sage."[15]

4

Like the life of Lao Tzu, so too his teaching is the most concealed, for it is the most without parable.

The naked oneness is silent. As soon as the oneness develops from foundation and goal of a separated humankind submerged in the wordless wonder into the teaching, as soon as the word stirs itself in this man—in the hour of silence, before day, where there is but no Thou other than the I, and in darkness the secluded speech measures across and back the abyss—the oneness is already touched by the parable. Man speaks his words as the Logos speaks man; it is no longer pure oneness, it is already the manifold, the parable therein. But as the manifoldness of men is still bound to the oneness so long as they are children, and the parable rests upon them only as the smile upon their lips, so the speech of the separated man in the hour of silence is touched only at first by parable like a smile. And as the multiplicity of men, if they should grow up and themselves bear children, absolves itself from the oneness and the parable thus flows into them like blood in their veins, so the speech of the fulfilling man, when he goes among men, is flowed through with parable as with blood.

But as between childhood and manhood stands the time of youth, the tragedy that imperceptibly reconciles itself until it has disappeared, so between solitude and sermon stands the time of transition, that certainly does not imperceptibly reconcile itself, but rather decides itself.[16] Buddha calls it the time of temptation. He speaks to the tempter, "I shall not, oh evil one, enter into nirvana, until this my blameless conduct will have thrived and come to blossom, spread afar to be found by many, richly unfolded, so that it is beautifully manifested by man."[17] At this time, the parable is no longer the smile, yet not the blood; it is still upon the spirit, already in the spirit—like a dream. As youth stands in the dream, so the transition stands in the dream. Therefore the word of the solitude is the cry, and the word of the sermon the narrative, but the word of the transition is the image.

There is, nevertheless, a life in which the transition leads not from the solitude to the sermon, but rather from the solitude of the question to the solitude of the fullness, from the solitude of the abyss to the solitude of the sea. This is the concealed life.

I believe that this man is tempted as are the others. And like the others, he does not enter into nirvana, but he does not even go among men; he goes into concealment. The concealment should bring forth to him his children. "He who knows his brightness veils himself in his darkness," so Lao Tzu styles it.[18]

What is the sermon to this man? "Heaven does not speak and yet knows to find the answer."[19] What is manhood to him? "He who loves his manhood, holds on to his womanhood, he is the river-bed of all the world."[20]

This man talks not to himself and not to man, but rather in concealment. Although he himself is not on the way to man, his word is yet necessarily on the way to the parable; he is not in transition, but his word has remained the word of transition: the image. His speech is not a complete speech of parables, like that of Buddha or Jesus, but rather a speech of images. It is like a young man who has not yet been absolved from the oneness into the parable[21] like a man, who is no longer bound to the oneness like a child. But this would be a young man as we presage him somewhat in Hölderlin's poems, one who does not have the aspiring beyond self of dream and of tragedy, but only the prophetic fullness of youth, turned into the unconditional and eternal, where dream has become divination and tragedy the mysterium.

Concealment is the history of Lao Tzu's speech. Even if the Sermon of Banaras, the Sermon on the Mount may be so mythicized, that a great truth lies at the foundation of the myth is unmistakable. In Lao Tzu's life is nothing that corresponds to this. One notices everywhere in his speech, in the book, that it utterly was not what we call speech, but rather only like the roaring of the sea out of its fullness when a light wind touches upon it. In the scanty account of the historian, this has also been communicated or represented. Lao Tzu goes into his final concealment; he leaves the land in which he dwelled. He reaches the border-pass. The commander of the border-pass speaks to him: "I see that you are going into concealment. Will you yet write a book for me before you go?" Thereupon, Lao Tzu wrote a book in two sections that is the book of Tao and the virtue, in five thousand and some words. Then, he goes. And immediately thereafter it concludes itself in the account that I earlier quoted: "No one knows where he ended." Information or symbol, no matter; this is the truth of Lao Tzu's speech. "Those who know it do not speak it; those who speak it do not know it," it is said in his book.[22] His speech is only like the roaring of the sea out of its fullness.

The teaching of Lao Tzu is imaginative, but without parable, provided that we think of the complete parable that develops from image to narration. So he delivered it to the time. Hundreds of years passed over when the teaching came to one who—surely, like all great poets, collecting in himself a great deal of folk parable— composed its parable. This man was called Chuang Tzu.

Consequently, the parable in the Tao-teaching is not, like that in the teaching of Jesus or Buddha, the immediate word of fulfillment awakening in the central man, but rather it is the poetry of one to whom the teaching has been delivered already in its fulfillment.

The manifestation of the Tao-teaching is split into the first word, which stands so near to the naked oneness like no other word in the human world, and into the second word, in which the oneness bears such rich and tender garment as in no other word of the teaching, but only in the great poems of the human world.

But only both together give us the perfect form of the teaching
in its purest fulfillment, as they proclaim Tao, "the path," foundation and sense of the unified life, as the universal foundation and
the universal sense.

5

Chuang Tzu lived in the second half of the fourth and in the first
half of the third century before Christ, thus about 250 years after
Lao Tzu.[23] But whereas that other great apostle who did not know
his master in the flesh, Paul, broke up his teaching of the oneness
of the truthful life and perverted it into an eternal antithesis of
spirit and nature—which one can never abolish, from which one
can only flee—Chuang Tzu was in reality an emissary of his teaching: its emissary to the things of the world.[24] For that he composed
its parable, this is indeed not to be understood as though he had
"explained" it on things or "applied" it upon things. Rather, the
parable carries the oneness of the teaching into all the world, so
that, as the universe previously cherished it within itself, now the
universe appears full of it, and no thing is so petty that it refuses
to fill it. Whoever in such a way does not spread the teaching
zealously, but rather manifests it in being, he also allows each now
to discover and animate the teaching in oneself.

Such an apostolate is silent and solitary, as the mastery that it
serves was silent and solitary. It no longer dwells like the former
in concealment, but it is bound with man through no obligation and
through no purpose. The historian imparts to us almost nothing of
Chuang Tzu's life other than this: that he was poor and the offices
that were offered to him were declined with the words, "I will never
accept an office. Thus I will remain free to follow myself." The same
emerges from the biographical information scattered through his
book, evidently originating from the hands of his students. And the
account of his death purports nothing else. He forbade them from
giving him a funeral: "Heaven and Earth for my coffin and tomb,
sun and moon for me the two round holy symbols, the stars my
jewels, the infinite things my cortege of mourners—is this together
not all? What could still be added to it?"[25]

It is not surprising that the world of the conditioned rose against him. His time, which stood under the dominion of the Confucian wisdom of the moral management of life according to obligation and purpose, called Chuang Tzu a useless man. In parables like that of the useless tree (16) he has given his answer to the time. Men do not know the use of the useless. What they call purposeless is Tao's purpose.

He trampled upon the public opinion which was the law of his time, against it not in regard to any content, but fundamentally. Whoever flatters his princes or his elders, he said, whoever agrees with them blindly and groundlessly praises them, is by the multitude called unfilial and faithless; but not whoever flatters the multitude itself, blindly agrees with it, groundlessly praises it, who directs his comportment and his expression thereupon to win its favor. But he knew the inanity of the multitude and articulated it; he knew that only he wins it who himself enjoins it, and said so: "One man steals a purse and is punished. Another steals a state and becomes a prince."[26] And he also knew that the teaching of the Tao cannot itself enjoin the multitude. For indeed the teaching brings nothing to man, but it says to each person that he has the oneness when he discovers it and animates it in himself. But so it is with man: "All strive to grasp what they do not yet know, no one strives to grasp what he knows."[27] The great is inaccessible to the multitude, because it is simple. Great music, says Chuang Tzu, the multitude does not accept, over street songs it rejoices; thus perfect words are not heard, while common words have dominion; two earthen bells deaden the metal bell's tone. "Thus the world has gone astray; I know the right path; but how can I lead it?"[28]

And so the apostolate exhausts itself in the parable, which is not zealous, but in itself remains visible and yet concealed. The world, says Chuang Tzu, stands against the path, and the path stands against the world; the world cannot acknowledge the path, and the path cannot acknowledge the world, "therefore the virtue of the sages is concealed, even if they might not reside in the mountains and in the forests; concealed, even when they conceal nothing."[29] Thus the apostleship of Chuang Tzu found its issue in that which the mastery of Lao Tzu had had its rein: in the concealment.

6

The word "Tao" signifies the way, the path; but since it also has the sense of "speech," it is sometimes rendered with "logos." For Lao Tzu and his disciples, where it is always developed metaphorically, it is tied to the first of these meanings. Yet its linguistic atmosphere is related, in fact, to that of the Heracleitian Logos, given that both transplant a dynamic principle of human life into the transcendent, but at base mean nothing other than that it is the human life itself that is the carrier and realization of all transcendence. I shall here explain this about Tao.

In the West, Tao has been understood, for the most part, as an attempt at world explanation; remarkably, the world explanation that is perceived therein continually conflates with the inclinations of the present time's philosophy; so Tao is valued first as nature, then as reason, and lately it is to be merely energy. Contrary to these explanations must be pointed out that Tao means in general no explanation of the world, but rather this: that the whole sense of existence rests in the oneness of the truthful life, will only be experienced in it, that it is precisely this oneness grasped as the absolute. If one wishes to disregard the oneness of the truthful life and consider what "lies at the foundation"[30] of it, then nothing remains left over but the imperceptible, of which nothing further is to be said but that it is imperceptible. The oneness is the only way to realize it and to experience it in such a reality. The imperceptible is naturally neither nature nor reason nor energy, but precisely the imperceptible for which no image suffices, because "in it are the images."[31] But that which is experienced is again neither nature nor reason nor energy, but rather the oneness of the path, the oneness of the truthful human way, that recovers the unified in the world and in each thing: the path as the oneness of the world, as the oneness of each thing.

But the imperceptibility of Tao cannot be so conceived as one speaks of the imperceptibility of some principles of religious or philosophical world explanations, in order to make a statement about it after all. Likewise, that which the name "Tao" states is not stated about the imperceptible: "The name that can be known is not the eternal name."[32] If one will consider Tao not as the needful whose reality is experienced in the unified life, but rather as an existence in itself, then one finds nothing for consideration: "Tao can have no existence."[33] It cannot be investigated, cannot be explained. Not only can no truth be stated about it, but it cannot be the subject of a statement at all. What is stated about it is neither true nor false: "How can Tao be obscured so that some "truth" or some "falsity" appears in it? ... Tao is obscured because we cannot take hold of it."[34] When it thus appears that Tao is in some time more than in some other, then this is no reality, but only like the falling and rising of tones in music, "it belongs to the playing."[35] We can discover it in no existence. When we seek it in Heaven and Earth, in space and in time, then it is not there, but Heaven and Earth, space and time, are founded in it alone. And when we seek it in the "mystery of the essence of God," then it is not there, but rather God is founded in it alone.[36] And nevertheless, "it can be found through the seeking:"[37] in the unified life. There it is not perceived and known, but rather possessed, lived, and done. "He who obtains it with silence and completes it with being, only he has it,"[38] it is said in the books of Lieh Tzu. And he does not have it as his own, but rather as the sense of the world: the oneness of the masculine and feminine elements that exist not for themselves but only for one another, the oneness of antitheses that exist not for themselves but only through one another, the oneness of things that exist not for themselves but only with one another. This oneness is the Tao in the world. When in a conversation narrated by Chuang Tzu, Lao Tzu says to Confucius, "That Heaven is high, that the Earth is broad, that sun and moon revolve, that things thrive, this is their Tao,"[39] this dictum is thus only intelligible through an old verse adduced to Lao Tzu in his book. It reads:

Heaven attained oneness and with it brilliance, Earth oneness and with it rest and repose.
The spirits oneness and with it understanding, the brooks oneness and with it full banks.
All being oneness and with it life, prince and king oneness in order to give the world the right measure.[40]

Thus the oneness of each thing decides in itself the manner and the being of this thing; this is the Tao of this thing, this thing's path and wholeness: "No thing can produce Tao and yet each thing has Tao in itself and eternally produces it anew."[41] This means that each thing manifests Tao through the way of its existence, through its life; for Tao is the oneness in the transformation, the oneness that proves itself, just as in the multiplicity of things, so in the multiplicity of the moments that follow upon one another in the life of each thing. Therefore, the perfect manifestation of Tao is not the man whose way elapses without transformations, but rather the man who unites the purest oneness with the most vigorous transformation. There are two types of life. The one is the mere vegetative living, the wearing out until extinction; the other is the eternal transformation and its oneness in the spirit. Whoever does not let himself be consumed in his life, but rather unceasingly renews himself and just in that way, in the transformation and through it, affirms his self—which indeed is not a fixed existence, but rather simply the way, Tao—he obtains the eternal transformation and self-affirmation. For here as always in the Tao-teaching, consciousness effects existence, spirit effects reality. And as in the connection of the life moments of a thing, so Tao proves itself in the connection of the life moments of the world, in the coming and going of all things, in the oneness of the eternal, universal transformation. Thus it says in the books of Lieh Tzu, "What has no primordial source and continually engenders is Tao. From life to life therefore, though ending, not decaying, this is eternity. . . . What has a primordial source and continually dies is also Tao. From death to death therefore, though never ending, yet itself decaying, this too is eternity."[42] Death is loosening, is transition to form, is a moment of sleep and of meditation between two worldly lives. All is becoming and transformation in the "great home"[43] of eternity. As separation and concentration, transformation and oneness follow upon one another in the existence of things, so life and death follow upon one another in existence of the world, together proving only Tao as the oneness in the transformation. This eternal Tao, which is the negation of all apparent existence, is also called "non-being." Birth is not a beginning, death is not an end, existence in time and space is without limit and suspension; birth and death are only entrance and exit through "the invisible gate of Heaven which is called non-being. This is the abode of the accomplished man."[44]

Here too the accomplished man, the unified man, is denoted as the one who goes through and experiences Tao directly. He looks at the oneness in the world. But this is not to be understood as if the world were a closed thing apart from him, whose oneness he penetrates. Rather, the oneness of the world is only a reflection of his oneness; for the world is nothing foreign, but rather one with the unified man. "Heaven and Earth and I came together into existence, and I and all things are one."[45] But since the oneness of the world exists only for the accomplished man, it is thus in reality his oneness that sets oneness into the world. This also emerges from the being of Tao as it appears in things. Tao is the path of things, their manner, their proper order, their oneness; but as such it exists in them only potentially; it first becomes operative in its contact with other things: "Were metal and stone without Tao, they would produce no sound. They have the power of sound, but it does not come out of them if they are not struck. So it is with all things."[46] Moreover, consciousness is never on the side of receiving but rather on the side of giving; "Tao is conveyed but not received."[47] And as the Tao of the thing becomes alive and manifest only though its contact with other things, so the Tao of the world becomes alive and manifest only through its unconscious contact with the conscious existence of the unified man. This is thus expressed by Chuang Tzu that the accomplished man reconciles and brings into harmony the two primordial elements of nature, yang and yin, that divide apart the primordial oneness of existence. And in a late Taoist tract, the "Book of Purity and Rest," which on this point appears to be based on an altogether limitedly held tradition, it says, "When man remains in purity and rest, Heaven and Earth return," that is, to oneness, to the undifferentiated existence, to Tao.[48] Also in this late, degenerated literature (the whole of later Taoism is nothing but increasing degeneration),[49] the unified man is also thus comprehended as the giving man. We may say that for the Tao-teaching, the unified man is the creating man; for all creating, seen from this teaching, intends nothing other than to evoke the Tao of the world, the Tao of things, to make living and manifest the dormant oneness.

An attempt to summarize it:

Tao in itself is the imperceptible, the unknowable. "The true Tao does not declare itself."[50] It is not to be put forward; it is not be thought, it has no image, no word, no measure. "Tao's standard of measure is itself."[51]

Tao appears in the becoming of the world as the original undifferentiation, as the primordial existence from which all elements originated, as "all beings' mother,"[52] as the "valley spirit" that bears all. "The valley-spirit is immortal; it is called the deep feminine. The deep feminine's gate which is called Heaven and Earth's root."[53]

Tao appears in the existence of the world as the constant undifferentiation, as the uniform change of the world, as its order. "It has its movement and its reality, but it has neither action nor form."[54] it is "eternally without doing and yet without non-doing."[55] It "perseveres and does not change."[56]

Tao appears in things as the personal undifferentiation, as the proper manner and vigor of things. There is no thing in which the whole Tao is not as this thing's self. But even here Tao is eternally without doing and yet without non-doing. The self of things has its life in the way in which things answer things.

Tao appears in man as the purposive undifferentiation, as the uniting that conquers all deviation from life's foundation, as the making whole that heals all separation and fragility, as the expiating that redeems from all disunity. "He who is in sin, Tao can expiate him."[57]

As the purposive undifferentiation, Tao has its own fulfillment as the goal. It wishes to materialize. In man Tao can become oneness so pure, as it cannot become in the world, in things.[58] The man in whom Tao becomes pure oneness is the accomplished man. In him Tao no longer appears, but rather is.

The accomplished man is shut into himself, all secure, unified out of Tao, unifying the world, a creating man, "God's companion,"[59] the companion of the universal, creative eternity. The accomplished man has eternity. Only the accomplished man has eternity. The spirit wanders through things until it flourishes to eternity in the accomplished man.

This word of Lao Tzu means this: "Climb the height of renunciation, embrace the primordial foundation of rest. The incalculable beings all rise up. Therein I know their return. When the beings have unfurled themselves, in the expansion each returns to its root. To have returned to the root means to rest. To rest means to have fulfilled destiny. To have fulfilled destiny means to be eternal."[60]

Tao materializes in the truthful life of the accomplished man. In his pure oneness it develops out of manifestation to direct reality. The imperceptible and the unified human life, the first and the last, touch themselves. In the accomplished man Tao returns from its world-wandering through manifestation to its self. It becomes fulfillment, becomes eternity.[61]

7

But what is the unified human life in its liaison[62] to things? How does the accomplished man live in the world? Which form does knowing assume in him, the coming of things to man? Which the doing, the coming of man to things?

The Tao-Teaching answers thereupon with a great denial of all that by man is called "knowing" and "doing."

What by man is called "knowing" is based on the tearing apart of the senses and the faculties of mind. What by man is called "doing" is based on the tearing apart of intentions and acts. Each sense takes this up differently, each faculty of mind arranges it differently, they all stagger through one another in endlessness: man calls this "knowing." Each intention pulls at the structure, each action interferes in the order, they all are entangled through one another in endlessness: man calls this "doing."

What by man is called "knowing" is no knowing. In order to demonstrate this, Chuang Tzu consolidated nearly all the grounds that the human mind has contrived to put itself into question.

There is no genuine perception because things unceasingly alter.

There is no perception in space, because to us not absolute but only relative extension is accessible. All great things exist only in comparison; "under Heaven is nothing that is greater than the tip of a blade of grass."[63] We cannot ourselves swing out of our measure; the cricket does not understand the flight of the giant bird.[64]

There is no perception in time, because to us even duration exists only in comparative value. "No being attains a higher age than a child that died in the cradle."[65] We cannot ourselves swing out of our measure; a morning mushroom does not know the varia-

tion of day and night, a butterfly chrysalis does not know the varia-
tion of spring and autumn.[66]

There is no certainty of life, for we have no criterion by which
we could decide which is the actual and determining life, the waking or the dream. Each condition holds itself as the actual one.

There is no certainty of worth, for we have no standard of measure by which we could decide what is beautiful and what is ugly,
what is good and what is bad. Each being calls itself good and its
contrary bad.

There is no truth in concepts, for all speech is inadequate.

For Chuang Tzu, all this means only one thing: that which by
man is called "knowing" is no knowing. In separateness there is
no knowing. Only the unseparated man knows, for only the one
in whom there is no separation is not separate from the world,
and only he who is not separate from the world can know it. Not
in the standing opposite, in the dialectic of subject and object,
only in the oneness with the all is there cognition. The oneness is
the cognition.

This cognition is put into question through nothing, for it comprises the whole: in the unconditionality of the all-embracing, it
overcomes the relation. It takes each pair of antitheses as a polarity, without wishing to delimit the antitheses, and it surrounds all
polarities in its oneness; it "reconciles the yes with the no in the
light."[67]

This cognition is without passion and without seeking. It is at
itself. "Not going out the door, one knows the world; not viewing
through a window, one see Heaven's way."[68] It is without delusional
knowledge. It has things, it does not know them. It carries itself
out not through the senses and faculties of mind, but rather through
the wholeness of being. It leaves the senses be, but only like playing children; for all that they bring to it is only a variegated,
playing, uncertain reflection of their own reality. It leaves the faculties of mind be, but only like dancers, who make their music into
an image, faithless and unsteady and richly formed after the manner of dancers. The "music of Heaven,"[69] the playing of the oneness
upon the multiplicity of our nature ("as the wind plays on the
openings of the trees"[70]) has here become the music of the soul.

This cognition is not knowledge,[71] but rather existence. Because
it possesses all things in its oneness, it never stands against them;

and when it considers them, it considers them out from themselves, each thing out from itself; but not from its manifestation,
rather from the being of this thing, from the oneness of this thing
that it possesses in its oneness. This cognition is each thing that
it considers; and so it elevates each thing that it considers out of
manifestation to existence.

This cognition comprises all things in its existence, that is, in its
love. It is all-embracing love that abolishes all antitheses.

This cognition is the deed. The deed is the eternal standard of
measure, the eternal criterion, the absolute, the speechless, the
unchangeable. The cognition of the accomplished man is not in his
thinking, but in his doing.

What by man is called "doing" is no doing.

It is not an activity of the whole being, but a groping of a single
intention into Tao's texture, the intervention of single action into
the manner and order of things. It is entangled in the purposes.

In so far as they approve of it, it is by man called "virtue." What
by man is called "virtue" is no virtue. It exhausts itself in
"humanheartedness" and "righteousness."

What by man is called "humanheartedness and righteousness"
has nothing in common with the love of the accomplished man.

It is perverted, because it appears as obligation, as object of a
command. But love cannot be commanded. Commanded love only
brings to pass evil and grief; it stands in contradiction with the
natural good of the human heart, it obscures its purity and dis-
tracts its immediacy. For this reason, those who so preach pass
their days lamenting over the malice of the world. They injure the
wholeness and truthfulness of things and awaken doubt and disunity. Purposive humanheartedness and purposive righteousness
are not founded in the nature of man; they are superfluous and
troublesome like surplus fingers or other outgrowths.[72] Therefore,
Lao Tzu says to Confucius, "As gadflies keep one awake the whole
night, so this task of humanheartedness and righteousness plagues
me. Strive accordingly to restore the world to its original simplicity."[73]

But in yet another sense "humanheartedness and righteousness"
have nothing in common with the love of the accomplished man.
They are based upon man standing facing other men and then treating them "lovingly" and "rightly." But the love of the accomplished
man, after which each man can aspire, is based upon the oneness

with all things. Therefore, Lao Tzu speaks to Confucius, "For the perfected men of antiquity humanheartedness was only a transit place and righteousness only a night inn along the way into the kingdom of the undifferentiated, where they fed themselves in the fields of equanimity and dwelled in the gardens of duty-lessness."[74]

As the true knowing of Lao Tzu, when it is considered from human speech, is called "non-knowing"[75] ("He who illumines in Tao is like full night"[76]), so the true doing, the doing of the accomplished man, is by him called "non-doing." "The accomplished man does non-doing."[77] "The rest of the sage is not what the world calls rest; it is the work of his inner deed."[78]

This doing, the "non-doing," is an activity of the whole being.[79] To intervene in the life of things means to damage them and oneself. But to rest means to effect, to purify one's own soul means to purify the world, to collect oneself in oneself means to be helpful, to surrender oneself to Tao means to renew creation. Whoever enjoins oneself has the small, obvious might; whoever does not enjoin oneself has the great, secret might. Whoever does not "do," effects. Whoever is in perfect harmony, is one whom the receiving love of the world surrounds. "He is unmoved as a corpse, while his dragon-power manifests itself roundabout, in profound silence while his thunder-voice resounds, and the might of Heaven answers each movement of his will, and all things mature and thrive under the compliant influence of non-doing."[80]

This doing, this "non-doing," is an activity out of collected oneness. In ever new parable, Chuang Tzu says that each does right who in his doing collects himself to the oneness. Whoever is collected upon the one, his will becomes pure ability, pure activity; for when no separation is in the willing person, between him and the willed—the existence—there is no more separation; the willed becomes existence. The nobility of the being lies in its capability to collect itself upon the one. For the sake of this oneness, it is said by Lao Tzu, "He who has the fullness of virtue in himself is like a new-born child."[81] The unified man is like a child who, from the harmony of his powers, cries the whole day and does not become hoarse, out of collected virtue keeps his fist shut the whole day, out of undetached attentiveness stares the whole day at one thing, moves himself, rests, adapts himself without knowing, and lives beyond all trouble in a heavenly light.

This doing, the "non-doing," stands in harmony with the being and destiny of all things, that is, with Tao. "The accomplished man, like Heaven and Earth, has no humanheartedness."[82] He does not stand across from the being, but rather comprises it. Therefore his love is wholly free and unlimited, does not depend on the demeanor of man, and knows no alternative; this is the unconditioned love. "The good—I treat them well; the not good—I also treat them well; virtue is good. The true—I treat them truly; the not true—I also treat them truly; virtue is true."[83] And since he has no "humanheartedness," the accomplished man does not intervene in the life of beings, he enjoins nothing upon them, but he "helps all beings to their freedom,"[84] he also leads them through his oneness to oneness, he makes free their being and their destiny, he redeems Tao in them.

Like the natural virtue, the virtue of each thing exists in its "non-being," in that it rests in its boundaries, in its primordial nature, so exists the highest virtue, the virtue of the accomplished man in his "non-doing," in his activity out of oneness that is undivided, without antitheses, enclosed. "He shuts his exits, closes his doors, he breaks his sharpness, stretches out his fullness, makes mild his brightness, becomes one with his dust. This is called 'deep one-becoming.' "[85]

8

Oneness alone is true power. Therefore the unified man is the true ruler.

The liaison of the ruler to the kingdom is the highest demonstration of Tao in the mutual adaptation of beings.

The kingdom, the community of beings, is not something artificial and arbitrary, but rather something native and autonomous. "The kingdom is a spiritual vessel and cannot be manufactured. He who manufactures it destroys it."[86]

Therefore, what by man is called government is no government, but rather a destruction. Whoever intervenes in the natural life of the kingdom, who wants to determine, master, and direct it from without, he annihilates it, he loses it. Whoever unfolds and protects the natural life of the kingdom, who does not impose command and coercion thereupon, but rather sinks himself therein, listens to its secret message, and brings it to the light and to the work, he rules it in truth. He does the non-doing; he does not intervene, but rather unfolds and protects what wills to become. In the kingdom's need and drive, Tao's will reveals itself to him. He shuts his will on it, he becomes Tao's instrument, and all things change of themselves. He knows no violence, and yet all beings follow the suggestions of his hand. He practices neither reward nor punishment, and yet what he wishes to make occur, occurs. "I am without doing," speaks the accomplished man, "and the people change of themselves; I love rest, and the people become upright of themselves; I am without bustle, and the people become rich of themselves; I am without desires, and the people become simple of themselves."[87]

To rule means to adapt oneself to the natural order of manifestations. But the only one who can is the one who has found the oneness and out of it seen the oneness of each thing in itself and the oneness of things with one another. Whoever becomes rid of the differentiation and joins the infinite, who returns things, like himself, to the primordial existence, dismisses together both himself and the world, brings them to purity, redeems them out of the slavery of violence and machinery, he rules the world.

The kingdom has degenerated; it has decayed into the violent deed of the authorities. It must be liberated from this. This is the aim of the true ruler.

What is the violent deed of the authorities? The coercion of false might. "The more prohibitions and restrictions the kingdom has, so much more the people are impoverished; the more weapons the people have, so much more the country is alarmed; the more artifice and cunning the people have, so much more things atrocious spring up; the more laws and statutes are published, so much more there are robbers and thieves."[88] The authorities are a parasite who deprive the people of their life force. "The people hunger, because their authorities consume too much tax. Therefore they hunger. The people are difficult to rule, because their authorities are too busy. Therefore the people are difficult to rule. The people hold death in little account, because they desire in vain after fullness of life. Therefore they hold death in little account."[89] The true ruler frees the people from the violent deed of the authorities, while he

lets "non-doing" rule instead of might. He exercises his transforming influence upon all being, and yet knows nothing of that, for he
influences them in accord with their own nature. He makes it such
that man and things rejoice of themselves. He takes all their sorrow upon himself. "To bear the country's misery and pain, that is
to be the kingdom's king."[90]

In the degenerated kingdom, it is such that it is guaranteed to
no one to be able to follow his affairs after his own insight, but
rather each stands under the subordination of the multitude. The
true ruler frees the individuals from this subordination; he unblends
the multitude and lets each manage freely that which is his and
the community that which is common. But he does all this in the
manner of non-doing, and the people do not notice that they have
a ruler; they say, "we have become so of ourselves."[91]

The true ruler stands as the accomplished man beyond
humanheartedness and righteousness. Indeed to be praised is the
wise prince, who is righteous and gives to each that which is his
own; yet to be esteemed higher is the most virtuous, who practices
love and stands in community with all; but able to fulfill upon
Earth the kingdom, the spiritual vessel, is only the spiritual prince
who produces completion: oneness with Heaven and Earth, freedom from all obligations that conflict with Tao, the redemption of
things to their primordial nature, to their virtue.

The true ruler is Tao's executor on Earth. Therefore it is said,
"Tao is great, Heaven is great, the Earth is great, also the king is
great."[92]

9

I have considered the Tao-teaching not in its "development," but
rather in its oneness. The teaching does not develop, it cannot
develop after it has found its fulfillment in the central man; rather,
it becomes a principle, like the teaching of Buddha, if the apostolic
man who (never immediately) takes it over out of the hands of the
fulfilling man is an organizer like Asoka; or it becomes dialectic,
like the teaching of Jesus, if this man is a violent doer like Paul;

or it becomes poetry, like the Tao-teaching, if he is a poet like Chuang Tzu. Chuang Tzu was a poet. He had the teaching as it was given to us in the words of Lao Tzu, not "improved,"[93] but he has elaborated it to poetry. And to philosophy; for he was a poet of ideology, like Plato.

Chuang Tzu also has several other congenialities with Greek philosophy. He has been compared with Heracleitus; and in fact, there are Heracleitian words not to be compared with anything else with the same justification as with the Tao-teaching, like those of the unknowable yet in all-effecting Logos, of the oneness that is at the same time nameless and named, of its demonstration as the eternal order in the world, of the eternal transformation out of universality to oneness and out of oneness to universality, of the harmony of antitheses, of the comparison between waking and dream in the existence of the individual, of that between life and death in the existence of the world. But at that Chuang Tzu may perhaps be compared with the entire form of Greek philosophy, that did to the perfect what by him was only sketched out: that transferred the Tao-teaching out of the sphere of the truthful life into the spheres of the explanation of the world, the comprehensibility, and the ideological composition, and thus freely created something wholly particular and wholly powerful in itself.

It is truly tempting to compare Chuang Tzu also with Western poets, whereto even individual motifs present themselves in a rather curious way. One proceeds somewhat from an outer to an ever more inner affinity; one begins therein by putting the narration of the dead man's skull (55) next to Hamlet's churchyard speech, then throwing together "Silence" (60) and the narration of Fioretti[94] of the meeting of the Brother Aegidius with Ludwig of France, and finally to recover in the discourse of the perpetual dying (60) the blissful yearning of "Die and Become"[95] in sharper, lonelier, more thoughtful counterpart. But all this can only be a passage to a reception in which one no longer attempts to incorporate Chuang Tzu, but rather accepts him in his whole essential being without comparison and coordination; him, that is, his work, the parable.

Postscript to the 1910 Edition:
"Remarks on the Books of Chuang Tzu and This Book"

Of the literature that is known under the name of Chuang Tzu and comprises thirty-three sections or books, only a selection is imparted in this book. The selection has been determined from the view expounded in the afterword.

In addition to the words of Chuang Tzu and several anecdotes about his life, a number of uncharacteristic interpolations from ardent students, "continuers" and "explainers," appear in the book, set apart through no express indications. Chinese and European philologists have taken honest pains to separate the authentic from the inauthentic. But I was obliged to follow not them, but rather my view. It is therefore likely that among the texts and parables imparted by me and the sentences quoted in the afterword, we shall see several that were not written down by Chuang Tzu himself. Nevertheless, the fidelity that I have exercised appears to me to be suitable.

Apart from an analytical presentation of the text of the same sort as Carus did with the *Tao Te Ching*,[1] the translation was based on the textual explanations of Giles (*Chuang Tzu, Mystic, Moralist and Social Reformer,* London 1889) and Legge (The *Texts of Taoism,* volumes 39 and 40 of the *Sacred Books of the East*), from which I was particularly indebted a great deal to that of Giles for several parts From the Chinese commentators I have cited what I could make available to myself.

Glossary: "Remarks on Several Personages in the Parables"

Ai: Marquis of the state of Lu from 494 to 468.

Huan: Ruler of the state of Ch'i from 684 to 643.

Hui: The prince of Liang or Wei (370–333), whose discourse with Meng Tzu (Mencius) appeared at the beginning of his work.

Hui Tzu: One of his time's most famous dialecticians; confidant and opponent of Chuang Tzu. His principal teaching, according to what is mentioned by Chuang Tzu, seems to have been the theory of qualities as differentiated existences (thus not merely standing in relation, as the former taught). At the end of the book, which does not originate with Chuang Tzu, amid many hollow sophisms, several thoroughly buoyant and charming discourses are also adduced to him. Chuang Tzu supposedly said at his grave that he now no longer had anyone with whom he could speak (chapter 24).

Hu Tzu, who appears in the parable "The Magician and the Redeemed Man"[1] as the teacher of Lieh Tzu, is named only in the variant of this parable in the books known under Lieh Tzu's name, as well as in two other places in this book. At the commencement of it, Lieh Tzu imparts to his students a teaching of Hu Tzu's on the unborn birth-giver, that Faber ("Der Naturalismus bei den alten Chinesen") rightly equates with the *natura naturans*. It should be mentioned that in Lieh Tzu's variant of the parable, "The Magician and the Accomplished Man," here the nine names of the abyss are cited.[2] The section in Faber's translation: "The eddy where large fish remain is one depth, the eddy in standing water is one depth, the eddies in flowing, in overflowing, in undulating, in effervescing, in back-flowing, in dammed, in dissolving water are depths. These are the nine depths." Faber delivers this proposition incorrectly because of an interpolation. But it is certainly to be assumed that the version from Chuang Tzu is the original; the expansion is to be attributed to the need for completion on the part of redactors or a copyist.

K'ung Tzu (Confucius) appears in Chuang Tzu sometimes as an opponent of the Tao-teaching, sometimes as a follower of it, sometimes as a dabbler in Tao, but not one devoted to it. Certainly as the explanation for this contradiction it is narrated (in chapter 27) that Confucius had changed his views in the sixtieth year of his life, and what he until then saw as right he by this time saw as wrong. This conversion is obviously comprehended as a consequence of the historical encounter with Lao Tzu (see Strauss, *Lao-Tse's Tao-te-king,* page liii), cited by Chuang Tzu in several sections (in chapters 12, 13, 14, and 21). The longest and most important of these accounts is translated by Strauss on pages 347–357. In other sections, Lao Tzu says to Confucius, "What I speak, you cannot hear" (chapter 12); "You have brought confusion to man's spirit" (chapter 13); "Wash your soul that it becomes snow-whitened, and dismiss your knowledge" (chapter 22). In a fourth section (chapter 21) after the interview with Lao Tzu, Confucius says to Yen Hui, "Had the master not removed the veil from my gaze, I would not have distinguished the great essence of Heaven and Earth." The encounter is changed by Chuang Tzu to Confucius' fifty-first year of life; Lao Tzu had at this time already counted over a hundred years.

Kuan Yin: The commander of the border-pass Yin or Yin-Hsi, at whose suggestion Lao Tzu is supposed to have written his work, the *Tao Te Ching* (see Strauss, page lvi). I could not ascertain upon what Giles based the statement that he was was once a student of Lao Tzu and was entrusted by him with the publication of the work (Giles, *Chuang Tzu,* p. 231). But in any case, he was indeed scarcely a contemporary of Lieh Tzu, with whom the parable "In Tao"[3] brings him together. Yet we find in the book known under Lieh Tzu's name a variant of this parable (which misses both of the final paragraphs). Another remark of Kuan Yin's belonging here, which appeared in Chuang Tzu (chapter 33) and similarly occurs in the books of Lieh Tzu (chapter 4) and in the book ascribed to Kuan Yin, reads, "Whoever does not adhere to himself opens himself to the shape of things" (see Faber, page 100).[4]

Kuang Ch'eng-tzu, who appears in the parable "Immortality"[5] as the teacher of Huang Ti, is, according to the interpretation of several Chinese commentators, Lao Tzu in an earlier incarnation. This interpretation suits the sense of the parable: the self of the person who has become one has continuance in the human world.

Lieh Tzu: A Tao-Teacher of the fifth or fourth century before Christ, whose existence is doubted by several Chinese and European critics (see Balfour, *Leaves from my Chinese Book*, page 83: "A philosopher who never lived"; Giles, page 4: "A personage of whom nothing is really known. He is considered by the best authorities to have been of Chuang Tzu's own creation"),[6] apparently unjustly. On the other hand, it does appear certain that the books known under his name do not stem from him; yet they are surely not, as Giles thinks, a forgery passed off as one by a person invented by Chuang Tzu, but rather a work of several generations in which isolated handed-down dicta of the master are mixed with those of the most disparate and scholastic elements, wherein one may find raw wondrous tales and sensualist excursus set wholly against the Tao-Teaching (see de Harlez, "Textes taoistes," p. 286).[7] Moreover, given that it has gone astray not without extensive excerpts from other writings, it follows that numerous parts (the index prepared by Faber is incomplete)[8] were gathered from Chuang Tzu, including the parables: "To Have as One's Own,"[9] "In Tao,"[10] "The Ferryman,"[11] "The Cricket Catcher,"[12] "The Magician and the Redeemed Man,"[13] "The Beautiful Woman and the Ugly Woman,"[14] The Gamecocks."[15] Recently, Wilhelm put forth the view (*Lia Dsi, Das wahre Buch vom quellenden Urgrund, Jena 1911*) that the text by Lieh Tzu is the more original.[16]

Nü Yü: The name of a woman, according to the interpretation of a Chinese commentator.

Tzu Ch'i of Nan-kuo ("The Organ-Playing of Heaven")[17] seems to me to be identical to both Nan-po Tzu-kuei ("Steps")[18] and Nan-kuo-tzu (Lieh Tzu, chapter 4),[19] who, when Lieh Tzu and his students visited him, stood there transfixed "like a ghost" as though body and soul had separated, and only gradually awoke out of his rapture.

Chieh Yü, also known as Lu T'ung: a Taoist, who feigned insanity in order to escape a public career.

Wang Ni and **Nieh Ch'üeh**: Two sages who supposedly lived on Mount Ku-she, mentioned in the parable, "The Inactive Man"[20] (a depiction of the life on this mountain is in Lieh Tzu, chapter 2).[21]

Yen Hui or **Yen Yüan**, ("With Men"),[22] who died after twenty-three years and of whom his master said that he had been close to completion, appears in Chuang Tzu as a character as vacillating as Confucius himself.

-PART II-

The Hermeneutic Chapters

The Historical Question
The Matter of Textual Reconstruction

The Intended Meaning of the Author

From a modern sinological perspective, the extent of Buber's contribution toward explicating the thought of the historic Chuang Chou as manifest in the text of *Chuang Tzu* would likely be the central issue of any investigation into *Reden und Gleichnisse*. When dealing with ancient philosophical texts, sinologists have been predominantly (though not exclusively) concerned with the reconstruction of authorial intent, to the degree that most contemporary translators and interpreters implicitly equate it with textual "meaning," as though such an identification were self-evident to any reader. The standard methodology combines philological and historical analysis in order to produce a critical distillation of the cultural and literary currents that originally informed the particular document. As discussed in the introduction, the most sophisticated representative of this approach to *Chuang Tzu* is A. C. Graham, who has tentatively dated the separate strands of the text and provided extensive contextual analyses of both the authentic and inauthentic entries. A typical premise of this approach is Graham's convincing hypothesis that much of the content of the "Inner Chapters" can be made intelligible only when examined in the context of the then prevalent debates on logic, language, and disputation (Graham, 1969–70:137–159). More recently, the ramifications of this position have been further explored by Chad Hansen (1992:233–306) and others.

But despite the fact that Buber's work on *Chuang Tzu* contains a lengthy commentary and the most extensive German translation of its time, very few scholars have ever given serious consideration to the possibility that his work does offer a significant contribution

103

toward resolving the historical question. Ironically, most of those
who have engaged Buber's text have lacked sinological expertise,
and their interests in it reflected a range of other agendas. The
earliest notices came in the form of book reviews, appearing in
German newspapers almost immediately after publication and
written by emerging literary figures. As Buber's sometime colleagues,
the authors tend to be enthusiastic and uncritical in their celebra-
tion of the new availability of Chinese material.[1] Buber's work was
somewhat influential among leaders of the German Youth Movement, though they approach it with an ahistorical eye for political
inspiration and aesthetic appreciation.[2] In the instances over the
years where Buber scholars have addressed this work, all have
virtually ignored the translation in favor of the commentary, examining the latter only inasmuch as it espouses a philosophical perspective similar to that of *Daniel* and marks a transitional phase
in Buber's movement toward the life of dialogue. The essay's original points of reference, the texts of *Chuang Tzu* and *Lao Tzu,* are
rendered all but inconsequential.[3]

Until quite recently the only noteworthy sinological treatment of
this work was an obscure essay by O'Hyun Park entitled "Chinese
Religions and the Religions of China," from the 1975 edition of
Perspectives in Religious Studies. Park makes a modern statement
on the unity of the *san chiao*—the "three teachings," i.e., Confucianism, Taoism, and Buddhism—and argues that "the so-called
three *religions* of China all aim at attaining the *religion* of China
which proclaims the harmony of Heaven, Earth and Man" (190).
He furthers this case through a seemingly unorthodox approach, by
summarizing and evaluating the applicability of Buber's statements
from "China and Us," "The Teaching of the Tao," and "The Place of
Hasidism in the History of Religion," essays dealing ostensively
(according to Park) with Confucianism, Taoism, and Zen Buddhism
respectively.[4] Though Park offers no direct justification or explanation for this bizarre methodology, he does sympathetically examine
several key themes from Buber's afterword, particularly those of
unity and non-action, and bestow on it a measure of guarded praise:
"Buber's interpretation of Taoist religious thought and his evaluation of it comes as close as any to grasping its inwardness and to
an appreciation of its non-dualistic character, but his thought is
not wholly free of the entanglements of opposites" (176).

Nevertheless, while he contends that Buber may offer some helpful insights toward understanding ongoing trends in Chinese religion—e.g., the nontheological character of the teaching, the ontological rather than ethical connotation of inaction—Park shows no apparent interest in historical or textual questions. He makes only passing references to Chuang Tzu, Lao Tzu, and specific bodies of primary literature, all without directly citing any Taoist sources. In effect, he treats the three teachings not as concrete historical phenomena but as perennial philosophies.[5] Without a doubt, this explains why Park was the lone sinological exception who judged Buber's Chinese studies as worthwhile subjects of inquiry; in putting forth his perennialist agenda, he was not particularly concerned with method, and he simply took for granted historical and linguistic competence on Buber's part.[6] However, given the longstanding primacy of historical-philological method in the critical study of Chinese texts, most scholars have reasonably assumed that Buber, working nearly a century ago and without direct access to the material, could not have arrived at any relevant conclusions. Buber's work on *Chuang Tzu* has received minimal sinological attention only partially because the abstruse and aetherial commentary appears to reflect a philosophical agenda belonging more to Buber than to Chuang Tzu; the more pressing reason is simply that the secondhand translation does not meet contemporary scholarly standards. Therefore, it is no surprise that most scholars whose principal research deals with *Chuang Tzu* have never read *Reden und Gleichnisse,* and many have never heard of it; even the most thorough studies of *Chuang Tzu* have rarely included any mention of Buber's work as more than a minor footnote.[7]

However, the first sign that Buber's work might finally begin to penetrate beyond the margins of sinological discourse is Irene Eber's introduction to the recent *Chinese Tales* volume. Eber, not unlike Park, affirms that Buber successfully cuts through to the core of Chinese experience in some essential ways. Specifically addressing Buber's translated portions of P'u Sung-ling's *Liao Chai Chih-i,* Eber writes:

What seems remarkable is that Buber in his encounter with Chinese literature and without the benefit of a critical apparatus to point the way, perceived in these stories their philosophical substratum as well as important aspects of the Chinese worldview. In Chinese thought the idea of unity is that of an all-embracing order which encompasses this world and the world beyond. The two spheres, the sociopolitical order and the order of spirits and gods, are not hermetically sealed off from one another. They interact in often strange and unexpected, though never chaotic, ways. (1991:xiii)

Despite this acknowledgement of Buber's sensitivity to matters Chinese, Eber's historical interest throughout her introduction largely ignores matters of textual reconstruction and instead concentrates on the twentieth-century confluence of Chinese and German thought. "Buber's contribution," she states in a personal correspondence, "lies in having made accessible aspects of philosophical Taoism by furnishing interpretations that transposed Taoist ideas into a German intellectual discourse."[8] Eber does explore "how Buber understood the concepts of philosophical Daoism and which concepts were of significance to him" (xiv), yet she begins from the questionable presupposition that she understands the subject better than Buber does, and she criticizes his conclusions from her own perspective as though that represents an established body of knowledge. In particular, she notes that Buber does not appear to sort out the philosophical differences separating Lao Tzu from Chuang Tzu on matters such as sagehood and transformation (xv–xvii). The important point here is that to a great extent, Eber still approaches Buber's work assuming its inadequacy; because of Buber's linguistic and historical limitations, she discounts from the outset the possibility that he may provide insights into *Chuang Tzu* that would be of any sinological interest: "From the perspective of Chinese philosophy, Buber's work on the Chuang Tzu text, whether in the translated portions or as commentary, is not sufficiently rigorous to be taken into account."[9] Clearly, such an assumption influences exactly what one will find and what one will accept.

This legacy of sinological unconcern for Buber's work, as well as Eber's rejection aforethought of Buber's contributions to relevant matters of textual study, certainly does not suggest that sinologists are guilty of any more chauvinism or insularity than those in other scholarly disciplines. The sinological academy has recognized many important contributions by scholars deviating from established parameters, and it is nonetheless perfectly reasonable for cultural and literary specialists in any area to be skeptical of the commentator who proceeds without philological and historical expertise.[10] Yet, when such skepticism is replaced by a priori rejection of an interpretation because of its supposed methodological inadequacy, then there is the very real probability that breakthroughs will go unnoticed for some time. So while Eber is in fact very generous to Buber, she is still predisposed to explain away or overlook information that may require more serious attention. For example, she does note correctly that "the majority of the selections in Buber's translation are from the outer chapters," but she also distorts the significance of this by concluding that "he was not especially concerned with problems of authenticity" (1992:xii). True, Buber in his postscript to the original edition acknowledges indifference to philological research on the subject and admits that "of the texts and parables imparted by me and the sentences quoted in the afterword, we shall see several that were not written down by Chuang Tzu himself" (96). However, Buber hints that he is interested in a thematic rather than historical authenticity, and Eber does not find it noteworthy that the vast majority of "inauthentic" passages cited would later be demonstrated by Graham to be philosophically kindred to those of the "Inner Chapters." Eber also glosses over the fact that many of Buber's selections—notably "The Butterfly" (21) and "The Pleasure of the Fish" (54)—while holding no special charm for early Western translators, had for generations been among the most piquing for Taoist commentators.[11] Finally, she seems inclined to overstate the involvement of Buber's erstwhile colleague, Wang Chingdao. She writes that Wang "introduced" Buber to both *Chuang Tzu* and *Liao Chai Chih-i* and implies that he may have had some significant role in the actual translation of the former.[12] In a subtle way, this serves either to deny Buber's legitimate accomplishments or to ascribe them to someone else.

It should here be stressed again that the recurrence of certain oversights within a given scholarly field hardly suggests anything malicious or conspiratorial on the part of the particular academic community, although there are some highly vocal critics who would stake out just that position.[13] It should also be noted that an argument against a priori rejection of Buber's Taoist volume in no way suffices for actually claiming any relevance of the text for the historical issue at hand. It does, however, demonstrate that the responsible scholar may wish to reconsider how he or she approaches such a document, and that it is by no means an easy task to become totally open to appreciating its content while remaining faithful to the demands of rigorous scholarship.

The Teaching and Its Parable

The remainder of this chapter returns to the question of reconstructing the thought of the historic Chuang Chou, following from the assumption that it is at least possible that Buber does offer some valid contributions. Interestingly, the one claim of Buber's most worthy of attention has its strongest ramifications in the areas of methodology and textual self-definition, where he addresses not specific interpretations of Chuang Tzu's philosophical tenets or the text's didactic qualities, but rather the broader significance of Chuang Tzu and his text in relation to the whole of Chinese spirituality. In his commentary, Buber asserts that *Chuang Tzu* is actually a poetic parable-presentation of the "teaching" (*die Lehre*), a unique "foundational power" which, though long since stripped of its creative presence in the West, continues to define the collective character of the East. For Buber, the writings of Lao Tzu and Chuang Tzu represent two different expressions of the same impulse; the former supposes no audience and simply projects images of the teaching during the moment of its fulfillment within the life of the author, while the latter disseminates the teaching in the form of poetic narrative to the needful community. In either case, the teaching transcends the descriptive and the normative, the subjective and the objective. A text that embodies the teaching neither illustrates nor advocates, but calls for an encounter, an engagement through direct experience, that allows the reader personally to discover it and make it manifest. Hence, the text is always in process, vital, living, and actually comes to life in and though the person. Buber's concept of the teaching may or may not be correct, but it does call into question basic methodological assumptions by reminding us that a philological approach to reconstruction of a text such as *Chuang Tzu* lays no a priori claim to validity over a method grounded in aesthetic attunement and mystic insight. And though Buber's theory is essentially a self-defending hypothesis that traverses a range of cosmic, psychological, and sociological issues, it is nevertheless possible and appropriate to explicate systematically the nuances of his position, to explore whether it finds any textual basis in *Chuang Tzu,* and to compare Buber's work with important subsequent scholarship.

A worthwhile starting place is Buber's intended connotations of the term *Lehre* itself, a subtle and compelling formulation that elaborates on a theme only partially developed in Victor von Strauss's early translation of the *Tao Te Ching.*[14] Buber repeatedly contrasts the teaching with science and law, the realms of existential knowledge and moral imperative respectively. In so doing, he stresses two closely related characteristics of the teaching: its resistance to reification, and its unified and unifying presence. For Buber, both science and law resolve into discrete bodies of categorical propositions, the former to "information" (*Kunde*) about "existence" (*Sein*), the latter to "command" (*Gebot*) derived from "obligation" (*Sollens*), both of which are scrutable and objectifiable. That is to say, the principles of science and law are intellectually abstractable from both the disciplines themselves and the objects to which they refer. Science describes the totality of phenomena, and these descriptions are processed as independent bits of data; law normalizes the totality of responsibility, and these norms are processed as independent statements of duty. On the other hand, the teaching cannot be reified; it cannot be reduced to propositions or conceived apart from its actualization in the human life. On the surface, this appears indistinguishable from the apologies of most mystical writers, who claim that their special knowledge or experience is characterized by what William James calls "ineffability" (1961:299–300).[15] However, Buber attributes this conceptual inaccessibility not to any transcendent experience or esoteric quality of the teaching, but to an "all-quenching oneness" (20), a unity so complete that no specific properties can be separated out of the whole and that the whole cannot be separated from life. At this juncture it is worth repeating a crucial passage from Buber's commentary:

The teaching comprises no subjects, it has only one subject, itself: the one that is necessary. It stands beyond existence and obligation, information and command; it knows only to say one thing, the needful that is realized in the truthful life. The needful is by no means an existence and accessible to information; it is not found either on Earth or in Heaven but rather possessed and lived. The truthful life is by no means an obligation and subject to command; it is not taken over either from man or from God, but rather it can only be fulfilled out of itself and is utterly nothing other than fulfillment. Science stands on the duality of reality and cognition; law stands on the duality of demand and deed; the teaching stands on the oneness of the one that is necessary. (70–71)

It is on this idea of oneness that Buber's discussion becomes extremely delicate. The unified teaching—which addresses the whole, and yet is inseparable from it—cannot be expressed in descriptive or normative statements, each of which would necessitate a certain dialectical tension, a distancing between subject and object. Any attempt at reification thus presents a dualism that ultimately misrepresents the unity of the teaching. One cannot describe the "needful," for that would suggest a chasm between its existence and the perception of it; it does not exist apart from its being lived. Similarly, one cannot advocate the "truthful life," for that would suggest a chasm between its imperative and the enactment of it; it makes no obligation apart from its being fulfilled. Buber is indeed aware that such a radical collapse of conventional distinctions may appear oxymoronic when subject to analytical evaluation,[16] yet he is tenaciously resistant to any explanations that may smuggle a dualism into his model. He denies that the teaching is in any way a synthesis of science and law, or that it embraces "inner" (rather than "outer") descriptions or norms. He maintains that the teaching is not a doctrine *about* oneness, not a principle that *underlies* the truthful life, not a content that finds expression in some form. Perhaps the most affirmative statement is that the teaching concerns itself "only with the reality of the truthful life, which is primary and unsubsumable" (76). As such, the teaching has no didactic intent to promote beliefs or actions; it simply proclaims itself in its oneness and is consequently experienced and embodied only in its totality. In this sense, though Buber would certainly be reluctant to identify the teaching as a "symbol," it does function in a modality that Susanne Langer, in her epistemological discussions of symbolic transformation, might have termed a "presentational symbol," which functions in a "simultaneous, integral presentation" and "widens our conception of rationality far beyond the traditional boundaries." (1942:97).

For Buber, this pervasive quality of oneness is more than a conceptual scheme; it is a defining characteristic of Eastern experience, and as Eber notes, it is a central theme of Buber's *Liao Chai* translations as well.[17] His commentary on *Chuang Tzu* begins with a claim that "the Orient forms a natural oneness" (69), an obscure statement that is only elaborated in any detail in his infrequently cited 1912 essay, "The Spirit of the Orient and Judaism."[18] Here, Buber hypothesizes that the "supraracial structure" of the diverse Asian peoples defines a "unified spiritual core," which is grounded in the possession of "totality" and is inaccessible through scientific or analytical method: "The great complex of Oriental nations can be shown to be one entity, an organism whose members, no matter how functionally different, have a similar structure and a similar vitality" (1967:56–57). Also in this essay, Buber hazards a "genetic explanation" for this phenomenon, as he suggests that the Oriental is a "motor-type man" for whom "the basic psychic act" is a "centrifugal" process, whereby "an impulse emanates from his soul and becomes motion." (58).[19] As such, there is no dichotomy of perception and action; the latter is not the deliberated result after a period of cogitation, it occurs as though it were identical to the former: "It does not grow in him, but strikes through him" (58). As a corollary to this, the plane of experience consists of fluid motions, undifferentiated from one another and inseparable from the subject doing the perceiving: "Though he perceives individual things, he does not perceive them as separate entities, each reposing and complete in itself, but only as an aggregate of nodal points for an infinite motion, which flows through him as well" (59).

Parenthetically, it should be noted that such an interpretation of oneness does not preserve the integrity and distinctness of the particular entities making up the whole, and it thus appears antithetical to Buber's mature dialogical thought. Nowhere is this more evident than in Buber's contrast of the teaching with what he

views as its reified and degenerated counterpart, "religion" as a
totally social and historical phenomenon, "a product of the downfall, of the contamination and destruction, in which information,
command, and the needful are welded into a contradictory and
efficacious whole" (71). Buber illustrates the oneness of the teaching through the metaphor of white light, the pure whole whose
parts are fused so seamlessly that one could not even justify regarding it as a synthesis. On the other hand, Buber compares the
supposed oneness of religion to the rainbow, a compelling but de-
ceptive whole created out of separations and juxtapositions, which
he describes pejoratively as "an opalescent magical whirlwind that
rules the times" (72).[20] Because his dialogue with Chinese thought
was consumed by this zest for an obliterating unity,[21] Buber would
later repudiate his early Taoist work (without specifically repudi-
ating Taoism), regarding it as "a stage that I had to pass through
before I could enter into an independent relationship with being,"
adding that this "mystical" phase included the "belief in a unifica-
tion of the self with the all-self" based on "a genuine 'ecstatic'
experience." One inclined toward this attitude will "regard every-
day life as an obscuring of the true life," and will "constantly flee
from it into the experience of unity, into the detached feeling of
unity of being, elevated above life," to the point that "the great
dialogue between I and Thou is silent" (1957:ix–x).[22]

However, despite these statements on the subject of oneness and
Buber's own later assessments of his position, his commentary does
demonstrate traces of what would most appropriately be considered "proto-dialogical" thought, as though he were discerning in
Chuang Tzu a more subtle concept of unity and at the same time
recognizing for himself some ambivalence about a pure monism.[23]
While Buber asserts that the cognition of oneness—a state identified more with being than with knowing—"overcomes the relation"
(89)[24] that exists in the world of polarities, he nevertheless notes
that when such a state engages individual things, "it considers
them out from themselves, each thing out from itself" (90). Here,
Buber does not go so far as to acknowledge ontological distinctions
among things; he still subordinates the diversity of existential
manifestation to the oneness embodied by each thing, yet his tone
indicates an appreciation of things as subjects in themselves rather
than as arbitrary repositories of unity. The tension between a pure,

undifferentiated oneness and an integrative proto-dialogical oneness is not always successfully resolved, and it occasionally gives
rise to apparent contradictions.

The Nature of the Parable

The first significant proto-dialogical formulation occurs when Buber
discusses the complex relationship between the teaching and its
parable, as he makes a claim as to how and why Chuang Tzu's text
came into being. Here, Buber presents a somewhat developmental
scheme, as he offers a quasi-historical account of the teaching in its
various existential manifestations.[25] In its elemental oneness, the
teaching is accessible only by the "man who has become one" (*der
Einsgewordenen*), alternately described by Buber as the "central
man" (*der zentrale Mensch*), the "accomplished man" (*der Vollendete*),
the "fulfilling man" (*der Erfüllende*), and the "unified man" (*der
geeinten Mensch*). The prime example is Lao Tzu, and his expression of the teaching, the *Tao Te Ching*, represents "the immediate
word of fulfillment awakening in the central man" (80). However,
this document occupies a unique position, because the totality of
the teaching—which is resistant to reification and differentiation—
theoretically should not find expression within the dualistic con-
fines of language; "the naked oneness is silent" (73), yet the existence
of Lao Tzu's words would present an important anomaly. Buber
reconciles this by ascribing to the *Tao Te Ching* a quality of
liminality, as he asserts that the text operates at the border of
silence and speech, qualifying as neither wordless solitude nor
spoken sermon, and thus occupies the instant of transition between
the oneness of the teaching and the multiplicity of manifestation.[26]
This transition is likened to the margin between childhood and
manhood, or, in a more aesthetic though abstruse analogy, to the
dream state between smile and blood. But unlike ordinary threshold stages, which invariably dissolve when the transition is complete, the moment embodied by the *Tao Te Ching* represents a state
of ongoing liminality, since Lao Tzu does not actually complete and
in no way anticipates the passage to speech and narrative. The
document born from this moment cannot legitimately be characterized as communication, for its speaker "talks not to himself and not

to man, but rather in concealment" (79). Further, the anticipated locutionary tools of discourse and narration are absent; in their stead, one finds images (*Bilden*): "One notices everywhere in his speech, in the book, that it utterly was not what we call speech, but rather only like the roaring of the sea out of its fullness when a light wind touches upon it" (80).

On the other hand, because of the specific historical circumstances of Chuang Tzu's reception of the teaching as well as his intentions for its transmission, Buber contends that Chuang Tzu's text is distinguished from that of Lao Tzu by what might be understood as a divergence in ontological status. Unlike Lao Tzu, Chuang Tzu is an example of "one to whom the teaching has been delivered already in its fulfillment" (80), and the oneness that he experiences, though in no way diminished, is therefore "attained" rather than "elemental." As such, he remains socially and emotionally bound to the community of which he has always been a part, and is compelled to communicate the oneness to "the simple persons, his impoverished brothers in spirit" (72). While the words of Lao Tzu, images existing only in silence and concealment, do not actually constitute speech, Chuang Tzu's purposive narratives to a needful community clearly entail it.

According to Buber, this can be accomplished only through the language of parable. This is the only way by which the oneness can be made accessible and intelligible for the unenlightened masses. Explained metaphysically, the formless absolute requires a concrete means of manifestation by which it can speak to and become meaningful in the existential world, while somehow not sacrificing its pure unity. Buber's crucial point is that for the teaching to be brought into speech, there must occur an engagement of the oneness with "things, events, and relations" (73),[27] and that such a meeting necessitates the expression of the teaching in what he terms "parable" (*Gleichnisse*). That is to say, the parable arises not directly from the oneness, but through the existential multiplicities in which the oneness inheres. This is particularly noteworthy because it touches on a concept of unity that is compatible with—and, in some way, requires—a world of individuated phenomena that are in genuine relation with one another. As parable, Chuang Tzu's text embodies both oneness and relation, unitary as white light passing through a smooth pane of glass, spectral as colors emanating from a prism (73).[28]

This is the reasoning that underlies Buber's claim that there are "two types of oneness in man" (72), an oxymoronic proposition that both pure monists and dialogical philosophers would no doubt find unsatisfactory. The *elemental* oneness is the obliterating unity that awakens in one such as Lao Tzu, "where there is but no Thou other than the I" (78), and finds expression in a liminal and nondidactic speech of images. On the other hand, the *attained* oneness is the proto-dialogical unity that is delivered whole to one such as Chuang Tzu, and is transmitted in parable to a world of things in relation where "no thing is so petty that it refuses to fill it" (81). Though it appears that with this distinction Buber has accidentally slipped into an unavoidable dualism, he still attempts to resolve this tension with yet another synthesis into a greater totality: "But only both together give us the perfect form of the teaching in its purest fulfillment, as they proclaim Tao, 'the path,' foundation and sense of the unified life, as the universal foundation and the universal sense" (81). Thus, the parable is not only an inevitable moment in the life of the teaching, but also necessary to its fulfillment in the world.

While Buber offers cryptic or tautological definitions of parable—"the engagement of the absolute into the world of things" (73), "the poetry of one to whom the teaching has been delivered already in its fulfillment" (80)—he eschews specific descriptions of how the form and meaning of parable are distinguished from those of other types of discourse. It must be recalled that as a valid expression of the teaching, the parable is still resistant to reification; thus, any literary analysis of its structure or philosophical position is ultimately misdirected. Buber instead concentrates "without comparison and coordination" (95) on the role and effect of the parable as tenor and vehicle for transformation, how it "carries the oneness of the teaching into all the world" (81) and "allows each now to discover and animate the teaching in oneself" (81). The tremendous irony here is that those who hear this parable are called to do nothing more than to realize existentially that which is already ontologically so: the oneness that is manifest in all being.[29] "For indeed the teaching brings nothing to

man, but it says to each person that he has the oneness when he
discovers it and animates it in himself" (82). Thus, the parable
offers a unique transformation; it enables those who understand
it to realize their actuality, their most profound state of being
human.

At this point, one may begin to sense that what Buber is char-
acterizing as *die Lehre* is not entirely unlike a romantic concept
of "lore,"[30] a living body of accumulated wisdom that has its roots
in the primordial past, is sustained through direct personal transmission by means of a uniquely structured symbolic language,
and is both reflected and realized in the realm of earthly experience. Indeed, the fascination with an autonomous cultural legacy
that transcends history and philosophy is very much what attracted Buber to a number of different traditions during the first
part of this century. A telling example is Buber's early work with
Hasidism, which drew criticism from a number of places because
of his intentional reversal of an established hermeneutic. The
traditional perspective placed historical primacy on the canons of
intellectual literature, the theoretical statements of doctrine, while
deeming the collected folk tales as merely illustrative and historically subsequent. Buber, on the other hand, regarded the lore as
the quintessential expression of the Hasidic spirit (that has inevitably fallen victim to textual corruption) and the doctrine as a
later intellectual attempt at systematic explanation.[31] Buber's
formulation of the teaching may also reflect his passing familiarity with classical Indian literature; the Hindu canonical categories of both *sruti* ("that which is heard") and *smrti* ("that which
is remembered") encompass revelations that do not have a historical moment of origin, but continually make up the collective
memory and psyche.[32] This hypothesis is born out insofar as Buber
notes that "handed down to us in the writings of the Tao-teaching
are sayings of the 'ancients,' that guarantee to us the long preexistence of the teaching," and that Lao Tzu's purpose is "only to
fulfill the unrecognized of antiquity" (77). Even in his later writings, Buber would describe the teaching very much as a kind of
folklore; in the time of Lao Tzu, Buber writes, "China received,
mostly through oral tradition, the decisive imprint of a teaching"
(1958a:361).

The Historical Question In Context

In summary thus far, Buber argues that an understanding of *Chuang Tzu* is contingent upon the recognition of its historical and spiritual place as a parable that poetically proclaims the teaching, a unique foundational power that significantly defines the creative impetus of Asian experience and identity. As the teaching addresses the totality and wholeness of the truthful life, it cannot be understood through conventional dialectics such as those of subject and object, normative and descriptive; rather, it embodies a pure oneness that renders such reification and abstraction impossible. As this unity awakens in the life of one such as Lao Tzu, the elemental oneness can be expressed only through the language of images, the liminal ground between the silence of singularity and the speech of multiplicity. When it is received whole and transmitted to the existential realm by one such as Chuang Tzu, the attained oneness is expressed through the language of parable, genuine speech that poetically expresses unity by way of the manifold and represents how oneness can be compatible with the world of things in relation to one another. The parable is essential to the completion of the teaching through its transformative power to enable those who hear it to make manifest the oneness, thus suggesting that multiplicity is essential to actual embodiment of unity. As such, the teaching and its parable are, in a very crucial sense, the primordial lore of what Buber calls the Orient.

It is now appropriate to begin evaluating Buber's credibility as an interpreter of *Chuang Tzu* and to assess critically his contribution toward answering the originally framed historical question. Of course, in determining the heuristic value of Buber's commentary as a source for the reconstruction of authorial intent or textual self-definition, there are inherent problems in appraising arguments concerned with subjects such as "foundational powers" and "parables." The principal purpose here is to explore the plausibility of Buber's most significant hypotheses, by probing for textual justification for his positions and relating his work to the historical and critical scholarship of others. Due to the nature of the material and the arguments, the specific issues to be examined often need to be discussed in tandem, though they can essentially be understood as falling into two related categories: Buber's historical perspective (on which his philosophical interpretations are built), and his conceptualization of the teaching and its parable.

Much of Buber's argument hinges on his basic historical assumption about the lineage of the teaching—that Lao Tzu and the text that bears his name both antedated the historical Chuang Tzu—a presupposition that carries some interesting ramifications in light of recent scholarly developments. Clearly, Buber's first Taoist studies indicate virtually no awareness that Chinese scholars had for almost two centuries been debating the dating of the *Tao Te Ching* and the possibility of multiple authorship; he simply follows the traditional view that places Lao Tzu as a sixth century B.C.E. elder contemporary of Confucius and sole author of the text, and he even includes apocryphal conversations between the two men in both text translation and commentary.[33] However, in the years subsequent to Buber's publication, many scholars began to arrive at progressively later dates for the text, some placing it as much as two centuries after Chuang Tzu. By the time of the final edition of *Reden und Gleichnisse*, virtually any date between the sixth and second centuries would find some support among both Chinese and Western scholars.[34] To this deluge of new speculation, Buber replies with nothing more than a footnote in Friedman's 1957 translation: "I cannot agree with the late dating of Lao-tzu that is recently gaining ground" (81 n. 23).

The prevailing scholarly consensus (if such a thing exists) on this controversy is articulated fully in the 1990 translation by Victor H. Mair,[35] where he argues that the *Tao Te Ching* is actually "a selection of proverbial wisdom from a larger body of sayings attributed to one or more old masters," which was "the result of a period of oral composition that lasted approximately three centuries (650–350 B.C.)," and that "seems to have coalesced beginning sometime during the fourth century B.C. and was probably written down during the second half of the third century B.C." Mair lists numerous indications of the text's origins in orality, including repetition, formulaic language, mnemonic devices, homonymic scribal errors, and intrusive editorial additions (1990:119–123). The early date for much of its content is corroborated by other scholars such as Chad Hansen (1992:202–203), who notes that the text's total lack of certain technical language (relating to logic and disputation) places the authors either prior to the fourth century or totally removed from the ongoing philosophical discourse, the latter being an unlikely possibility. The comparatively late date for the commitment of the text to writing is evidenced by other works from the period; in texts before the latter half of the third century, authors (including Chuang Tzu) cite Lao Tzu without explicit mention of a written document, and their citations vary considerably from each other and from what appears even in the Ma-wang-tui versions of the text, thus suggesting that a single form of the material had not yet existed (Mair 1990:125).

Of course, this historical information would seem to render some of Buber's claims questionable at best, notably that the *Tao Te Ching* records a single person's moment of awakening and functions as a wholly unified document, and consequently that Chuang Tzu was a disciple who received the text intact.[36] It is, in fact, Mair's contention that reading the text as if it were "constructed from start to finish by a single guiding intelligence" is the single most common flaw informing errant interpretations: "The results—while displaying valiant determination to make sense of the book as a whole and of its constituent parts—are often sheer gibberish" (1990:124). However, I would argue that the dubious historicity of Lao Tzu and the apparent incongruity of the text do not undermine Buber's most important interpretations. It should be recalled that his notion of oneness applies not to a doctrine expressed systematically in the text's propositions, but to the teaching and to the *life of the central man;* he ascribes unicity to the text not because of any sustained philosophical discourse, but because of the oneness that it embodies and expresses through the language of "images." Moreover, these images do not represent an intelligible essence underlying the unified truthful life, but evoke the undifferentiated experience of oneness within that life itself.[37]

Buber is, in fact, in fundamental agreement with Mair (and others) that one should not seek philosophical unity within the text. But, where Mair treats it as a philosophical document without unity, Buber treats it, in a manner of speaking, as a unified document without philosophy. It is especially interesting to note that similar perspectives have emerged in recent years. In one iconoclastic account, Michael LaFargue (1992) argues that what the reader may mistake as discordant, inconsistent philosophical constructs are actually hypostatized representations of a single "Laoist" state of mind and world orientation, expressive personal testimonies structured through a romantic internal language: "The 'point' of Laoist origin sayings is not instructional, but celebratory, celebrating the *existentially* 'foundational' character of Tao as concretely experienced in the self-cultivation of the ideal Laoist, experienced both as an internal personal center and a foundation for meaning in a transformed world" (208).[38]

More importantly, the historical-critical analysis—which may reveal the existing written form of the *Tao Te Ching* to be a comparatively late, philosophically variegated document—technically does not damage Buber's fundamental historical claim that Chuang Tzu received whole the teaching, which had come to fulfillment a few centuries earlier, after having been passed along orally for generations.[39] Again, the question of whether China possesses a foundational power called "the teaching" is all but impossible to verify one way or the other, but it is at this point appropriate to examine the text of *Chuang Tzu* to see if its authors demonstrate any consciousness of being heir to such a legacy. In Buber's text translation, the isolated noun *Lehre* appears only twice, and the contrast between the two instances is striking. In the first case, the term is used pejoratively, in juxtaposition with the higher knowledge of Tao:

> One cannot speak of the sea to a fountain frog; he cannot see out over his hole. One cannot speak of ice to a summer fly; it only knows of its own season. One cannot speak of Tao to a pedagogue; he is immured in his teaching. But now, since you have come out from your narrowness and have seen the great sea, you know your unimportance and I can speak to you about the primordial foundation. (51)

Here, the teaching is a set of explicit propositions, which, in the context of this episode, is portrayed as a refuge for the shallow and self-absorbed, as static dogma that inhibits one from learning of the "primordial foundation." This conventional teaching is certainly not the unified teaching expounded in Buber's commentary.

On the other hand, the second occurrence of the term concludes the brief vignette on "The Cicada-Catcher," the hunchback who effortlessly performs his task to perfection, with blithe indifference to other phenomena. An awed Confucius voices the final comment, "Where the will adheres to one thing, the spirit collects its power. This is the teaching of the hunchback" (57). In this particular case, the one possessing the teaching is characterized by his experience of subject-object continuity, singularity of intent, and total attentiveness to the mundane world; such a depiction of spiritual realization no doubt provides a glimpse of what Buber calls "the oneness of the truthful life." And as illustrated in the segment, the unified teaching is not a reifiable doctrine or specific set of instructions, but an evocative parable of the human life in achievement of its potencies. Other episodes in the text translation provide similar aesthetic metaphors; "The Wheelwright" labors with a "secret skill" that he "cannot teach (*lehren*)" even to his own son (48), while "The Mutilated Man" rivals Confucius for the regional teaching authority (*Lehregewalt*) and "teaches information that finds no expression in words" (28).[40] Through the multiple layers of translation, this latter predicate corresponds to the Chinese phrase, *pu yen chih chiao*, "a wordless teaching" or "an unspoken teaching," which appears repeatedly in both *Chuang Tzu* and the *Tao Te Ching*.[41] As might be expected, beneath many appearances in the German of *Lehre* or *lehren,* the original text employs *chiao* (as in *san chiao,* the "three teachings") as either a noun or verb.

As a noun, *chiao* is the most appropriate literary Chinese equivalent to "the teaching," and its varied usages in *Chuang Tzu* and other texts of the period parallel the tension between Buber's two applications of *Lehre*, the conventional teaching and unified teaching.[42] In most cases, particularly in Confucian classics such as *Mencius,* the term is analogous to the former, referring to a specific set of moral or literary lessons or instructions, sometimes even to education in general; and, as indicated by the concrete results, the connotations are certainly positive.[43] "Be attentive to the teaching in village schools, extending it by way of filial and brotherly rightness, and those with grey hair will not be on the roads carrying burdens on their backs or on their heads."[44] As Buber's single pejorative use of *Lehre* correctly demonstrates, it is precisely this understanding of the teaching that is sometimes criticized, even satirized, in portions of *Chuang Tzu.* In one episode, Confucius admonishes Yen Hui for his "teaching and blaming" which "belong to antiquity," claiming that they amount to "too much administering regulations and no discernment" ("Inner Chapters" 9/4/21–22).[45]

By contrast, even in Confucian texts, there is an occasional use of the term that is considerably more delicate. The most salient example is from the metaphysically tinged *Chung Yung* ("The Doctrine of the Mean"), which begins with the brief series of definitions: "That which Heaven charges is called the nature; the following of the nature is called the way; the cultivating of the way is called the teaching; as for the way, it cannot be deviated from for even an instant."[46] In a comprehensive study of the text, Tu Wei-ming notes that "the statements are presented not as freshly argued propositions but as notions which . . . are self-evidently true . . . that heaven-endowed human nature defines what the Way is, which in turn characterizes what teaching ought to be" (1976: 2–3). However, if one departs slightly from Tu's interpretation, by considering the characterization of teaching as descriptive rather than normative, then it makes the somewhat different existential statement that the teaching is the lived fulfillment and realization of that which is ontologically so—the way that is inseparable from human existence and, paradoxically, entails the human execution of Heaven's charge—that it addresses nothing more than "the needful that is realized in the truthful life."[47] And again, the reference point for the teaching is the way not as a conglomeration but as a whole, though the text certainly has in its background the full gamut of specific Confucian duties. Chuang Tzu, on the other hand, takes this a step further, by arguing that the realization of the teaching differs from conventional learning: "As for the (perfect man's) teaching, there is no learning; to receive its intention is not that."[48] The most striking appearance of *chiao* in *Chuang Tzu* occurs in the following passage:

The great man's teaching is like form to shadow, sound to echo. If there is a question, he answers it, drawing out all that is in his bosom, and becomes a match to all-under-Heaven. He finds a place in the echoless, travels in the directionless. Move beyond the annoyance of going and returning, and by this journey the borderless, with no margin between coming and going, each day renewing the beginning. In your extolling and discussing form and body, harmonize in the great sharing. In the great sharing, there is no self; and without self, how could one obtain and have? The one who perceives as having is the gentleman of former times; the man who perceives as not having is the friend of Heaven and Earth. ("School of Chuang Tau" 9/4/21–22)

In many ways, this passage captures the heart of what, according to Buber, one can and cannot say about the teaching.[49] Likened to both form and sound, the genuine essences at base of shadow and echo respectively, the teaching is here characterized as the "foundational power" that underlies and permeates concrete existence in Heaven and Earth. And just as shadow and echo follow immediately upon that which engenders them, the "truthful life" is neither experientially separable nor intellectually abstractable from the teaching. Where Buber states that "the fulfilling person has nothing but his life" (77), here the one who fulfills the teaching is portrayed as embodying the pure unity, of himself as a whole being ("drawing out all that is in his bosom"), of the world as an undifferentiated totality ("journey the borderless, with no margin between coming and going"), and of himself as an integrated part of the world ("a match to all-under-Heaven" who will "harmonize in the great sharing"). The specific details of the unified life are, nevertheless, evoked only in parable, as the great man is depicted simply as "the friend of Heaven and Earth." Finally, Buber regards the teaching as a primordial lore "in the beginning" that "eternally begins anew" (74); here, the great man is "each day renewing the beginning." Again, while the historical reality of the teaching is far from explicitly confirmed, there is evidence to suggest that the author or authors of *Chuang Tzu* have some concept of it as a more complex spiritual reality.

Some of Buber's other interpretations concerning the teaching and its relationship to the text of *Chuang Tzu*—e.g., the juxtaposition against both the descriptive and the normative, the distinction between elemental and attained oneness, and the transformative quality of the parable—are considerably more difficult to corroborate through isolated textual examples. What is so interesting, however, is that these positions do resonate well with approaches found in several important recent scholarly works; mainstream sinologists are now unintentionally echoing what Buber wrote nearly a century ago. With regard to the last of the three issues, the transforming power of the parable, it is presently a fairly common assumption that the text is not a straightforward discourse, but a much more subtle literary device. Using language that recalls bits of Buber's terminology, Harold H. Oshima writes, "The exact understanding of most of its ideas . . . lies buried . . . in the parable and imagery of the text, and must be salvaged from them." He adds that such a "set of interpenetrating images and pictures," in fact, "bears little resemblance to the systematic, logical elaboration of ideas to which we are accustomed" (1983:64). The maverick modern interpreter and outspoken critic of undiluted historical-philological method, Wu Kuang-ming, offers the following elaborate description of the text's inner dynamic:

> The *Chuang Tzu* is poetic in that its thoughts cluster in a web—one thought points to another which explains it, then the pair point to another, and the movement goes on—and back. Clusters of thought co-mirror, co-imply into layer after layer of meaning. A spiral of thought loops in loops, twisting back to itself only to start over again in a new direction, from a fresh perspective. "Loop" sounds linear. It is rather a co-deepening co-resonance; to enter its pulsing rhythm is to enjoy life. (Wu 1990:23)[50]

But more importantly, what establishes Wu and Buber as kindred spirits is that the former is representative of a recently emerging, perhaps even fashionable, trend to argue that any attempt at systematization—any analysis that seeks a supposed philosophical position underlying the document—is ultimately untrue to both the original intent of the author and the actual history of the text. Unlike Oshima, Wu claims that *Chuang Tzu* does not simply employ metaphors to represent some other ideas that could have been made discursively intelligible, but that it creatively applies them through a method of "evocative indirection" (1982:23) that induces a unique experiential state in those who receive it:

> In metaphorical indirection, the author does not state but, by silences or by irrelevancies, evokes in us the desire to create something significant ourselves. Sometimes the author states

things so obviously atrocious that they provoke our own discoveries in the light of what is said, and often in revolt of what is said. (51)

In a manner of speaking, Wu is arguing that a faithful interpretation would not explicate what the text *says*, but would demonstrate what it *inspires*, what spiritual response it comes to elicit. This fascinating position maintains that *true* historical reconstruction in the case of *Chuang Tzu* entails not an archaeological expedition through an archaic discourse, but an enterprise bent on exploring, in the words of Paul Ricoeur, "the horizon of a world toward which a work directs itself" (1981:178). Wu does not actually justify his hermeneutic beyond the internal consistency and raw aesthetic appeal of his "interpretations"—book-length meditations and narrative operas—which are delivered in a presentational style more analogous to Chuang Tzu's parable than to literary or philosophical analysis. Nevertheless, other scholars affirm the implication that textual interpretation and spiritual realization are here one and the same. Guy C. Burneko, for example, states that *"Chuang Tzu* welcomes us to a guerilla hermeneutic whose practice alters our consciousness" (1986:178). Robert E. Allinson, attempting to build on Wu's work, reminds that the text's parabolic nature is the crucial ingredient in its transformative powers, that "the disconnectedness of the text and the highly oblique literary form of the text have a systematic correlation with the technical means of accomplishing the goal of self-transformation" (1989:3). And, as Buber would suggest that such a transformation is to nothing other than the actualization of the truthful life that already exists in potentiality, Wu claims that this text which "imaginatively reconstructs . . . human actuality" (1990:24) serves "to goad the reader into self-scrutiny and awaken him into becoming himself in the world" (1982:24). Again, all of these positions are quite congenial to Buber's understanding of the text's self-definition.

On the subject of Buber's distinction between elemental and attained oneness, a dichotomy that evidently reflects his own ambivalence about a pure monism and what I have called a proto-dialogical position, there ironically exist parallel tensions at work in both *Chuang Tzu* itself and recent trends in scholarship. If credence is given to Kuo Hsiang's traditional interpretation of the text, one can then detect a pantheistic, monistic tendency, as well as a principle of particularity and distinction. On the one hand, Isabelle Robinet, in her elaborate studies on Kuo Hsiang and Chuang Tzu, explains that Tao is recognized as a universal, non-entified process of "self-engenderment" that is "omnipresent, engulfing all things and penetrating all things" (Robinet 1983:78). Livia (Knaul) Kohn adds that a perfect acquiescence to this mechanism, the identification of oneself and all things with the unifying principle, results in "the state of mystical union with the Tao" (1985:436). On the other hand, in a step that anticipates Buber's point that parable results when unity comes upon "things, events, and relations," Kuo Hsiang's reading allows for ontological distinctions between and among things, by virtue of a principle of differentiation that provides them with unique potentialities and demarcations. Thus, all things possess a complementary nature, in that they are, by definition, both manifestations of a pervasive unity and particular entities in their own right (Robinet 1983:80–84).[51] To transpose Buber's language onto this, it may be appropriate to argue that the elemental oneness is the overarching universal process, while the attained oneness is that which inheres in and integrates things that are made distinct by virtue of existential reality.[52] Interestingly, the scholarly community appears divided, sometimes bitterly, on exactly how much of a unity is actually meant by the concept of 'Tao' and how things are related to it and to one another.[53] One advocate of an absolutist reading is Donald J. Munro, who writes that Tao is "a permanent unitary entity that permeates the many changing phenomena" (1969:123). Arguing the contrary position, Chad Hansen, a former protege of Munro, writes, "Chuang-tzu is a relativist and not an absolutist, that is, he is best understood as speaking of many taos, and taos are to be understood as ways (i.e., prescriptive discourses)" (1983a:31). In an attempt to sum up the various interpretations, Robert E. Allinson argues rather abstrusely that scholars (himself included) have actually staked out five different epistemological positions on this issue (1989:111–116).[54]

As to Buber's juxtaposition of the teaching with both science and law, that it proclaims itself in a way neither descriptive nor normative, it is well worth noting that even sophisticated proponents of rigorous philological analysis have made similar observations about *Chuang Tzu*. In one intriguing essay, A. C. Graham argues that "the underlying logic of the Taoist position escapes the dichotomy of fact and value (1983:21), that Chuang Tzu's conflating of (or, perhaps, never even considering separation between) the poles of "is" and "ought" keeps him out of the Western logical abyss of attempting to argue from indicative to imperative or to combine objective and subjective. For Graham, Taoist spontaneity is neither a purely objective response to things as they are, nor a purely subjective response to engender things as they should be, but rather a holistic, centered response that reflects nothing other than a generalized "awareness":

It will now be clear from the Western point of view there is something very peculiar about the Taoist attitude. We are accustomed to think in terms of a dichotomy: either as a rational agent I detach myself from nature, study the objective facts about it, make my own choices, resist becoming the plaything of physical forces like an animal, or else I welcome the Romantic idea of spontaneity, as the free play of impulse, emotion, subjective imagination. The Taoist is somewhere where this dichotomy does not apply. He wants to remain inside nature, to behave as spontaneously as an animal, to be caused rather than to choose, and concepts resembling those of stimulus and response come easily to him without the science which for us provides their context; on the other hand, he has a contempt for emotion and subjectivity, a respect for things as they objectively are, as cool and lucid as a scientist's. (10–11)

To summarize, Buber approaches *Chuang Tzu* from a unique interpretive paradigm based on a specific understanding of the historical and spiritual circumstances of the text and its author. A distillation of modern scholarship and critical analysis of the text indicates that Buber's individual suppositions and premises are somewhat uneven in quality; many of them are strikingly perspicacious and resonant, while others are merely misapplications of historical data. But, the cumulative result is that the general spirit of Buber's argument on the teaching and its parable is certainly plausible, and that his linguistic and historical limitations do not prevent him from evincing a tremendous sensitivity to the subtleties of Chinese thought. Perhaps even more importantly, Buber's interpretive paradigm provides a hermeneutic framework that is, at the very least, interesting; the conclusions that follow from it shed new perspectives on Chuang Tzu and his text. Therefore, the next step at this stage is to move out of the purely historical question of textual self-definition and, with the details of Buber's approach firmly in place, to begin assessing the thematic issues addressed in both text translation and commentary, and to reexamine the original text in light of these new hypotheses. Buber's hermeneutic reading of *Chuang Tzu* approaches the text as a parabolic expression of the teaching eliciting a personal transformation; we can now explore exactly which portions of the parable attracted Buber's attention and how he responded to them.

The Hermeneutic Question
The Matter of Textual Interpretation

The Interpretive Framework

Certainly, at issue is not whether Buber understood or misunderstood the Chinese texts. Hermeneutics is an ongoing process pursued by philosophers, intellectuals, thinkers, and all those people whose acute engagement with their time and its ideas constitutes their life's work. To become plausible in ever new and changing contexts, such persons must infuse ideas—whatever their source—with meanings that are commensurate with a particular time and place. Ideas are not disembodied entities, existing in a vacuum. They function within a discourse; otherwise they are meaningless, of no consequence, or forgotten. (Eber 1991:xx)

Although Eber maintains that Buber's text translation and commentary lack the historical perspective necessary for them to find a place within the modern Chinese philosophical discourse, she does acknowledge that the sometimes questionable scholarship informing this work does not negate the potential influence and heuristic value of its conclusions. Indeed, Buber's interpretations take on a life of their own, and they serve to animate the words of Chuang Tzu—however culturally altered or interpolated in their transmission—within a new intellectual and spiritual context. This dynamic of tradition and transformation is one of the profound realities of human religious history, as the most significant break-throughs can often be traced back to creative "mistranslations" of primary texts or "misappropriations" of material across cultural boundaries, which are nevertheless put forth and understood as continuous with an unbroken lineage. One interesting example

129

relevant to the study of Asian religion is the case of Dogen Kigen Zenshi, the thirteenth century founder of the Soto branch of Zen, whose intentional misreading of a single philosophical statement from the *Maha-Parinibbana Sutta* captures in microcosm his adaptation of Chinese Ch'an Buddhism to the Japanese worldview. Playing on ambiguities of the Chinese character *you*—which can mean either "to be" or "to have"—Dogen read the phrase "all sentient beings possess Buddha-nature" as "all is sentient being, all existences are Buddha-nature," a formulation entirely compatible with the indigenous Shinto tradition's radical non-dualism.[1] From the Japanese perspective, this is not merely an interpolation but a natural development, the result of new questions and challenges realizing aspects of Buddhism latent in the original tradition.

By establishing *Chuang Tzu* as the parable of a primordial teaching, Buber finds the historical grounding he needs to justify examining the text ahistorically. That is to say, a crucial ramification of Buber's argument is that it allows him to bring to the document an interpretive agenda quite separate from the previously discussed historical question, and that it is therefore inappropriate to evaluate his work solely on the basis of a reconstructionist model of meaning. Instead, one must consider Buber's own hermeneutic position concretely in order to establish a specific model by which his work may be assessed, a process that begins with a determination of exactly what questions Buber is asking of the text and how he adapts the text to those questions. Some indications of Buber's interpretive presuppositions are implicit in his commentary and choice of translated material, but perhaps most illuminating are his other works of the same period, specifically the translations and interpretations of Hasidic material, which methodologically parallel his Chinese studies in a number of important ways.[2] What is particularly striking is not only how Buber's Hasidic texts continue to inspire fervent debates on matters of hermeneutic freedom and historical fidelity, but also how the various scholarly positions are analogous to those that are central to this present study. A detailed summary of this ongoing controversy will bring to light some of the more compelling parallels and their ramifications.

As mentioned briefly in the previous chapter, Buber's Hasidic studies have been widely criticized for methodology supposedly lacking in historical and philological grounding, the same reason

why his Chinese studies have been ignored.[3] The first significant
negative judgment came from Gershom Scholem, whose scholarly
mission has been to determine the historical development of various occurrences of Jewish mysticism and to situate them in their
proper historical relation to one another. As one primarily concerned with discerning social continuities and isolating correct lines
of doctrinal transmission, Scholem rebukes Buber for "present(ing)
Hasidism as a spiritual phenomenon and not as a historical one,"
objecting chiefly to Buber's propensity for interpolations and selective omissions ("he combines facts and quotations to suit his purpose") (1971:230–231).[4] Scholem claims that Buber's work therefore
represents a misinterpretation, a projection of his own agenda onto
a tradition that has its own objective history. "The spiritual message he has read into these writings is far too closely tied to assumptions that derive from his own philosophy of religious
anarchism and existentialism and have no roots in the texts themselves" (247). Louis Jacobs, a chronicler of Jewish mystical testimonies, is somewhat more charitable toward Buber's selectivity, but
he is equally firm that "what Buber is not entitled to do is to read
his ideas into the Hasidic tales since the tales are based on the
doctrine and were told to illustrate that doctrine" (1985:96).

Nowhere is the dogma of historicity more evident than in Steven
Katz's essay, "Martin Buber's Misuse of Hasidic Sources" (which
actually includes a chapter entitled "Buber's Exploitation of the
Legendary Materials"), where the author both echoes Scholem's
point that Buber gives undue primacy to the narratives and also
suggests that he misappropriates and decontextualizes them as
well (1985:74–86). Here, Katz betrays a narrow appreciation for
the hermeneutic process, as he so quickly dismisses Buber's own
defense of his work, his belief that he was "commissioned" to present
the material in a new way and to interpolate in response to that
calling:

> Buber suggests that duty is the cause of his retelling the
> Hasidic tales. But "duty" to whom and to what? To the Hasidim
> and their form of life or to Buber's own philosophy of dialogue?
> Insofar as Buber denies all external norms and categorically
> rejects the ordinary rules by which one assesses the nature of
> duty in favor of a subjective account of responsibility, we find

it difficult to understand what restraining effect the invocation of the notion of duty has here. If it allows Buber to disregard all questions of the dating of the sources, their authorship, and their authenticity, and also to omit parts of texts when it suits him and, on other occasions, to quite arbitrarily combine texts and materials that come from different sources, etc., without answering to any independent criteria or procedures of authentication, then the meaning and value of the term "duty" becomes uncertain. (75–76)

Katz evidently defines textual fidelity in terms of historical "objectivity" alone; he even proposes sixteen tentative "methodological strictures" by which one may judge the validity of a rendering of Hasidic material (76–78). And while he acknowledges that an interpretation operating outside of the reconstructionist paradigm may have a certain aesthetic or literary merit, he maintains that when viewed from a critical perspective, it must be deemed nothing more than radical subjectivism. Stated very simply, textual "meaning" is here construed as the exclusive domain of the historian.[5]

There are, of course, a small number of Judaica scholars who defend the historical fidelity of Buber's works; Arthur Green, for example, challenges the position that the theoretical texts have historical primacy over the narrative folklore (1979:368). Similarly, Maurice Friedman observes that there had historically been an uneasy contention between the two streams of Hasidism, and that Buber's area of interest had been unjustly relegated to secondary status (1988a:449–467). However, in a series of influential articles and a recent book, Steven D. Kepnes heroically attempts to liberate Buber altogether from the historical question, employing rigorous hermeneutic theory to demonstrate that Scholem and Buber labor under different, though equally valid models of meaning, each thinker tracing his methodological roots to a specific nineteenth-century German tradition. The former, Kepnes argues, is heir to (and occasional critic of) the legacy of the *Wissenschaft des Judentums,* advocates of which employed "ideational, philological, and historical" scholarship in order "to present a picture of the history of the Jewish culture throughout the ages so that Jews and non-Jews could see the riches of the Jewish people and understand the historical antecedents of the present Jewish situation" (1987:88).[6]

With this in mind, Scholem brings to Hasidism a specific set of questions, dealing principally with topics such as textual authenticity, the connection between Hasidism and past forms of Judaism, and the impact of the movement within a particular time frame (81).

On the other hand, Kepnes establishes Buber's considerable debt to the "romantic" *Verstehen* hermeneutic school of Friedrich Schleiermacher and Wilhelm Dilthey, which likened textual interpretation to "thought transfer," some kind of direct connection between the minds of reader and author. Complete understanding "entails not only grammatical and stylistic analyses but also a process of intuiting or 'divinizing' meaning," which thus "requires an act of genius that parallels the genius of the author" (83).[7] While such an enterprise still amounts to a type of historical "reconstruction," its focus, particularly in Dilthey's model, does not end with the discernment of a frozen philosophical position, but continues on to the re-creation and re-living of the life-experience of the author (Kepnes 1988:196). Buber's own introductions to his Hasidic publications clearly acknowledge kinship with this approach, while at the same time expanding upon it; in a passage cited more than once by Kepnes as evidence of Buber's "romantic" interpretive lineage, Buber writes:

> I have received it and told it anew. I have not transcribed it like some piece of literature. I have not elaborated it like some fabulous material. I have told it anew as one who was born later. I bear in me the blood and spirit of those who created it, and out of my blood and spirit it has become new. I stand in the chain of narrators, a link between links; I tell once again the old stories, and if they sound new, it is because the new already lay dormant in them when they were told for the first time. (1956a:i)

Where Scholem is concerned with discerning matters of historical continuity and textual authenticity, Buber is interested in experiencing and finding contemporary significance for the timeless messages latent in the Hasidic texts, the subtle spiritual essences that find modes of manifestation and transmission appropriate to the given temporal and spatial realities, but which are not to be equated with the actual manifestations. "Using Dilthey's principles, Buber took old tales into his imagination and attempted to re-imagine them, to discover new continuities, and to complete them in a new way" (Kepnes 1988:199). For Buber, the "meaning" within the texts of Hasidism is "the power that once gave it the capacity to take hold of and vitalize the life of diverse classes of people," and the role of interpreter is "to help our age renew its ruptured bond with the Absolute" (1963:218). Clearly, Buber's model of meaning is predicated on the self-defending hypothesis that mystical experience or insight can have some unique, essential quality that transcends historical context, thus suggesting that textual "meaning" in this case is more the domain of the fellow mystic than of the historian. And while the historian may question the reliability of talk about spiritual essences and divine communion, the issue still has yet to be resolved to the satisfaction of any scholarly consensus.[8]

The digression into the matter of Hasidic textual interpretation is particularly salient because Buber's association with Dilthey's hermeneutic school reached its apex in the years when he was preparing both *Reden und Gleichnisse* and *Chinesische Geister- und Liebesgeschichten*.[9] And not so coincidentally, his place in the sinological discourse is analogous to his place in the Hasidic discourse, that of romantic exegete whose works, despite finding a popular audience, would eventually be met with skepticism or unconcern from a discipline increasing in historical rigor and sophistication. But again, it must be emphasized that this is simply due to a disparity in models of meaning and goals of interpretation. Where A. C. Graham, applying his own "methodological strictures," seeks to reconstruct concretely the historic Chuang Tzu's philosophical outlook as it relates to a culturally specific debate (1981:31–33), Buber seeks to be receptive to the parable of the primordial teaching, to participate in its transformative influence, and to evoke and perhaps transmit anew the wholeness of the unified life, all of which is contingent upon direct insight into the life experience of the author, the central man. Buber thus takes on the unique interpretive mission of attempting to find contemporary speech to animate what he understands as an unreifiable totality, which even through parable can be neither described nor advocated, but simply presented and proclaimed.

Given the obvious limitations of historical and philological criticism in this particular case, there is still the problem of how best to establish some degree of objectivity, how to employ criteria by which one may judge the validity of interpretations emerging from Buber's alternative hermeneutic position. In his discussions of Buber's Hasidic texts, Kepnes notes the analogous problem and suggests that the solution may well be found within the modern transformations of the German *Verstehen* school, particularly those of Hans-Georg Gadamer's "philosophical hermeneutics" and Buber's own later "dialogical hermeneutics." Both approaches share the breakthrough of granting equal respect for the integrity of text and reader, and locating the gist of interpretation within the interactive "conversation" or "play" between the two, a process which both Buber and Gadamer predicate on a state of distanciation between subjects and liken to the authentic I-Thou relation.[10] This represents a major paradigm shift in the hermeneutic science, as it moves the locus of inquiry away from the dubiously postulated fixed body of "authorial intent" onto the flexible and organic "meeting of horizons, the horizon of the text and that of the interpreter" (Kepnes 1988:208). Building on the direction of this school, Paul Ricoeur notes that the faithful reading of a text produces not a recapitulation of ideas and experiences from the past, but an exploration of ideas and experiences yet to emerge in the life of the interpreter:

Ultimately, what I appropriate is a proposed world. The latter is not *behind* the text, as a hidden intention would be, but *in front of* it, as that which the work unfolds, discovers, reveals. Henceforth, to understand is *to understand oneself in front of the text*. It is not a question of imposing upon the text our finite capacity of understanding, but of exposing ourselves to the text and receiving from it an enlarged self, which would be the proposed existence corresponding in the most suitable way to the world proposed. (1981:143)

This model of meaning—foreshadowed by Buber's statement that Chuang Tzu's parable "allows each now to discover and animate the teaching in oneself" (81)—seems especially appropriate to the study at hand. However, it is crucial to note that within their hermeneutic writings, both Gadamer and Buber caution against simple subjectivism or impressionism; while they do place a new emphasis on the disposition of the interpreter, they do not subjugate the autonomy of the text to it. Both thinkers demand that the reader's conclusions or inspirations follow from a genuine dialogue with the text rather than a projection of one's presuppositions onto the text, which is precisely the same concern so often voiced by those who put forth a reconstructionist model of meaning. What is different in this approach is that conclusions are justified not by a depersonalized textual objectivity, but by the integrity of the process that informed them. Thus, the critical question that remains is whether Buber's poetic presentation of the contours of the unified life represents merely a personal philosophical stage coinciding with his reading of the text, or an actual transformation before the text, an enlargement of self involving new understandings legitimately catalyzed by the text. Ironically, a complete answer to this question requires something of a reconstruction, a piecing together of Buber's process of interpretation, which includes a determination of how and why he reaches his conclusions.

While it would be virtually impossible to assemble all of the complex social and psychological details relating to Buber's ongoing engagement with *Chuang Tzu,* Buber himself provides a glimpse of what is certainly the most significant intermediate step of his interpretive process: his text translation, the body of *Reden und Gleichnisse,* which has been universally ignored by sinologists and Buber scholars alike.[11] Buber offers these fifty-four passages (as well as the citations included in the commentary) not merely as a collection of his favorite vignettes and aphorisms, but as support for and illustration of the themes developed in his essay (15). In the language of literary theorist E. D. Hirsch, Jr., the translation is the closest approximation of what Buber discerns as the text's meaning ("what the author meant by his use of a particular sign sequence") based upon his distillation of various resources, while the commentary expresses what he regards as the text's significance ("a relationship between that meaning and a person, or a conception, or a situation, or indeed anything imaginable") following from his imaginative reflection on and extension of that meaning to contemporary life-experiences (Hirsch 1967:8). Similarly, phenomenologist Wolfgang Iser distinguishes between two poles of a literary work—the "artistic" ("the text created by the author") and the "esthetic" ("the realization accomplished by the reader")—thus suggesting the mutual dependence of work and interpretation that informs a fully actualized text (Iser 1974:125–146). The issue here is that in order to establish the heuristic value of Buber's appropriation of Taoism, it is necessary not only to work through his specific argument as presented, but also to evaluate thematically the relationship between translation and commentary, to explore whether Buber's conclusions are, in fact, justified by the material he implicitly presents in their support. In this way, it can be established to what extent Buber's essay represents an authentic dialogue with the text and, therefore, stands as a valid interpretation of *Chuang Tzu*. And by extension, this will demonstrate one important example of whether classical Taoism can truly stimulate and inspire the twentieth-century mystical imagination.

The Teaching of the Tao: Creation, Transformation, and Salvation

Buber may state that the "teaching" has no subject, but his repeated references throughout the commentary to the "Tao-teaching" indicate the topic with which he is most concerned,[12] and it is no surprise that all of the important themes developed in the essay revolve around his discussions of Tao. After perfunctorily dismissing the typical interpreter who "continually conflates (Tao) with the inclinations of the present time's philosophy" (83) Buber then applies the term in two different capacities, mirroring his own tension between pure monism and a proto-dialogical unity. He begins by portraying Tao as an undifferentiated totality, a uniform and eternal presence; but in a crucial elaboration, he then addresses it as something concretely manifested within the phenomenal world. Of course, Buber is reluctant to offer any single characterization as a comprehensive definition of Tao—"Not only can no truth be stated about it, but it cannot be the subject of a statement at all" (84)—though he does advance a number of direct and indirect references which cumulatively silhouette a striking picture:

1. "... 'the path,' foundation and sense of the unified life, as the universal foundation (*Allgrund*) and the universal sense (*Allsinn*)." (81)[13]

2. "... that it is the human life itself that is the carrier and realization of all transcendence." (83)

3. "... Tao means ... that the whole sense of existence rests in the oneness of the truthful life, will only be experienced in it, that it is precisely this oneness grasped as the absolute." (83)

4. "... the oneness in the transformation, the oneness that proves itself, just as in the multiplicity of things, so in the multiplicity of the moments that follow upon one another in the life of each thing." (85)

5. "... the negation of all apparent existence ... also called non-being." (85)

6. "... the being and destiny of all things. "(92)[14]

By extrapolation, three of these statements—the first, fifth, and sixth—combine to schematize Buber's understanding of Taoist ontology, which, given that Tao "cannot be investigated, cannot be explained" (84), he is clearly reluctant to express as a conventional philosophical position. Still, Buber does acknowledge Tao as the original and ongoing source, the very real principle by which the universe is rendered existent, ordered, meaningful, and, most importantly, unified. But at the same time, noting that Tao is continually invoked in the language of non-being, he is cautious not to portray it as an entity or in any way to hypostatize it.[15] For Buber, the recurrence of negation in Chuang Tzu's parable is not a nihilistic ontological statement, but a poetic device whereby Tao can be deemed as ineffable, belonging to an order somehow different from that of mundane existence, but without implying an ontological dualism between source and creation, between that which engenders and that which is engendered. In other words, while one may indeed posit a foundation and intelligibility to the universe, a destiny to all constituents of reality, such a postulate categorically excludes the affirmation of any creative and sustaining influences separate from those of self-generation and self-perpetuation inherent within the universe and the constituents of reality themselves.[16] This elemental tension between affirmation and negation of Tao is evoked most deftly in the following passage from the original text, which, though not actually appearing in Buber's text translation, is cited in the commentary in smaller isolated fragments:

As for Tao, there is actuality, there is reliability; there is no doing, there is no form. It can be transmitted but cannot be received, can be gotten but cannot be seen. It is itself the basis, itself the root. When there were not yet Heaven and Earth, it existed firmly since antiquity, making spiritual the ghosts, making spiritual the gods, engendering Heaven, engendering Earth. It is in precedent of the ultimate extreme, but is not deemed high; it is beneath the six extremes, but is not deemed deep. It was born before Heaven and Earth, but is not deemed longstanding; it is elder to antiquity, but is not deemed old. ("Inner Chapters" 16/6/29)[17]

Buber's text translation includes few passages concerned directly with matters of ontology—the commentary draws much of this data from the *Tao Te Ching* —but it contains no shortage of brief comments and allusions that together illustrate the abovementioned tension. In one instance, Tao is evoked as the "primordial one" *(uranfanglich Eine)* (42),[18] suggesting both its foundational, ancestral quality and its identification with unity. This is indicative of a recurring cosmogonic motif—"Tao appeared before the beginning was" (39)—as Tao is repeatedly associated (if not actually equated) with a gamut of images relating both to origins and to the undifferentiated whole: "primordial nature" *(Urbeschaffenheit)* (47), "primordial purity" *(Urreinheit)* (48), "primordial being" *(Urwesen)* (28), "primordial mixture" *(Urgemeng)* (55), "primordial wholeness of all things" *(uranfängliche Ganzheit aller Dinge)* (42), "primordial foundation of Heaven and Earth" *(Urgrunde von Himmel und Erde)* (53). Nevertheless, there is also a repeated indication that this creative principle is not substantial; Tao is portrayed as "the great void" (64)," "the kingdom of nothing," and "the wilderness of spacelessness" (37). This is stated most forcefully in the section entitled "Cosmogony" (one of two variants on creation mythology included in the text translation),[19] which commences with, "In the

primordial beginning (*Im Uranbeginn*) was the non-being of
nothing . . . the nameless," and even "the one stepped into existence, formlessly" (45). And of course, the negations and affirmations
are often in close contiguity or identified with one another: "Tao is
the limit of limitlessness, the limitlessness of the limited" (63).
Buber reads these images not as rigorous doctrine, but as snippets
of parable evoking the ineffable—"The essence of the perfect Tao is
profoundly hidden; its highness is lost in obscurity" (42)—and he is
therefore not always exacting in discriminating the different connotations of the jargon. His fundamental concern is not necessarily
the particular ontological position, but the ramifications that follow
from it. Still, he does not simply conflate apparent incongruities
such as "primordial purity" and "primordial mixture"; rather, he
views them as ambiguous, figurative depictions that point toward
"the imperceptible for which no image suffices" (83).

Buber's most significant observation on this matter is that as a
cosmogonic (or ontological) principle, Tao is present not merely "in
the primordial beginning," *in illo tempore*, but as a creative energy
immediately pervasive and totally embodied in all temporal or
spatial configurations. Although "Tao appears in the becoming of
the world as the original undifferentiation, as the primordial existence from which all elements originated" (87), it also appears in
"the existence of the world," in "things," and in "man" as the "constant undifferentiation," the "personal undifferentiation," and the
"purposive undifferentiation" respectively (87). In short, Buber understands the Taoist cosmogony as ongoing process, that creation
occurs "in all the coming and going of all things, in the oneness of
the eternal, universal transformation" (85).[20] In essence, this represents an extension of Buber's Taoist ontology, as he is specifying
that Tao is, in fact, the ontological basis for the transformations of
the existential world. It is this idea that informs and explains his
fourth definition of Tao, that it is "the oneness in the transformation, the oneness that proves itself, just as in the multiplicity of
things, so in the multiplicity of the moments that follow upon one
another in the life of each thing." Here, without invoking it directly,
Buber derives his own interpretation of the principle of equality
that is the subject of Chuang Tzu's second chapter.[21] Each transformation, each manifestation in time and space, is understood as a
legitimate presentation of Tao, consequently embodying its one-

ness. Thus, experiences that one may ordinarily differentiate with positive or negative judgments—e.g., health and illness, life and death—are actually equal components in a transformative process that knows no hierarchy: "Death is loosening, is transition to form, is a moment of sleep and of meditation between two worldly lives" (85).

This concept of oneness within transformation is perhaps the most memorable of the various themes illustrated by Buber's text translation. At times, the subject appears to be the impersonal processes of nature, "the changing course of things" (52) with its "perpetually life-regenerating transformation" (60). More often, the text turns specifically to the inexorable changes in human existence, the "resonances in the lot of humanity" (31). A particularly striking example is the vignette describing "The Four Friends" who are bound together by their common realization that "death and birth, life and lapse form one being," and that one should "make 'nothing' as the head, life as the spine, death as the tail of his existence." In this tale, one man falls ill and cautions his cohorts to recognize the numerous gruesome, almost comical changes in his appearance—"my chin is in the same hole as my naval"—as the variegated workings of the creator, who no doubt represents the hypostatized or anthropomorphized creative power of Tao. Importantly, this character advocates not an indifference to each passing transformation as though it were irrelevant to the whole, but a celebratory attentiveness to each step as an opportunity to enact the will of Heaven. "If (the creator) transforms my hips into cartwheels and my soul into a horse, I will travel in my own carriage" (34). While Buber ascribes no specific virtues to Tao or its processes, he nevertheless betrays some qualities of optimism, a quiet faith in the workings of a beneficent cosmos. This is reinforced in a number of sections that deal specifically with death, each of which dramatically advocates equanimity in the face of transformation. In one instance, a student of Lao Tzu declines to mourn for his master, because "for one who thus accepts the phenomena of birth and death, there is no complaint and sorrow" (22). In another episode, the skull of a dead man lectures Chuang Tzu on the "kingly good fortune" of death (56). Certainly the most memorable illustration is "When Chuang Tzu's Wife Died," where death is related explicitly to transformation and to Tao:

She had already existed before she was born, without form, without substance. Then a transformation occurred in the primordial mixture, the spirit came into being, the being to form, the form to birth. Now a further transformation has occurred, and she is dead. So one goes from Spring to Autumn, from Summer to Winter. At present, she sleeps restfully in the great home. (55)

An extremely important suggestion here is that every step in the transformative process is not an impersonal reconfiguring of matter and energy, but a *renewal and regeneration* of self. Some passages from the text translation even appear to affirm a permanent entity that remains unsullied throughout the processes: "Even if my self dies at every moment, in transformation the eternal preserves itself" (61). This motif is most evident in the chapter entitled "Immortality," where a mountain ascetic offers advice to the Yellow Emperor: "This self that all men believe to be transitory is inexhaustible. This self that men believe to be finite is limitless" (43). However, on further investigation, it becomes clear that Buber interprets this not as a static self that somehow endures transformation, but as a dynamic self that, as a constituent of an ongoing cosmogony, is continually recreated in the process of transformation. Two passages in particular—"Antitheses and Infinity" (19–21) and "The Butterfly" (21)—illustrate the simultaneous substantiality and fluidity of self through the metaphor of dream, the state in which one's perspective and sense of identity seem to shift from moment to moment.[22] In the latter, one of the text's most laconic and compelling narratives, Chuang Tzu awakens unsure of his own true self-identity after having dreamed that he was a butterfly.[23] Buber's transmission of the episode's conclusion contains much subtlety: "Between man and butterfly is a boundary. To cross over it is called transformation (*Wandlung*)." While *Wandlung* may appear to be a straightforward and innocuous rendering of the Chinese *wu-hua* ("transformations of things"), it is very likely that Buber—who in other instances employs the synonyms *Anderung* and *Umgestaltung*—has another connotation in mind. The entire passage is virtually a word-for-word translation from Giles, who rendered *wu-hua* as the very problematic "metempsychosis," a somewhat arcane designation for the transmigration of souls. This suggests that Buber may have intentionally, if only as an ironic jux-taposition, chosen *Wandlung* for its theological connotation of "tran-substantiation." Nevertheless, the example illustrates the perpetual renewal that is at the core of the life-process, as "all is becoming and transformation in the 'great home' of eternity" (85).

By positioning Tao as the ontological basis for transformation—i.e., for the ongoing cosmogony and regeneration of self—Buber establishes an absolutely crucial link between his discussions of Tao as undifferentiated and Tao as manifested.[24] Human fulfill-ment, Buber argues, occurs when one embraces Tao, not merely as a disembodied oneness, but as a oneness that generates and in-heres in transformation. The realization of Tao is thus that of a unity that is dynamic and affirming, rather than static and self-obliterating. Further, an important paradox here is that it is not sufficient for the human being to be a passive agent in the trans-formation; he or she must grasp squarely both the singularity and the manifestation, thus literally creating the self within the unfold-ing process. In essence, Buber identifies the realization of Tao with the realization of self:[25]

> Therefore, the perfect manifestation of Tao is not the man whose way elapses without transformations, but rather the man who unites the purest oneness with the most vigorous transformation. There are two types of life. The one is the mere vegetative living, the wearing out until extinction; the other is the eternal transformation and its oneness in the spirit. Whoever does not let himself be consumed in his life, but rather unceasingly renews himself and just in that way, in the transformation and through it, affirms his self—which indeed is not a fixed existence, but rather simply the way, Tao—he obtains the eternal transformation and self affirmation. (85)

The implication here is extremely significant, for Buber is relat-ing, perhaps even conflating, the ontological and soteriological di-mension of transformation. That is to say, transformation is not only the ongoing manifestation and recreation of being, it is also the analogue to "salvation" or "liberation," the ultimate goal of the human being, the state wherein the self continually becomes and

renews itself. This is certainly compatible with Tu Wei-ming's contention that throughout the history of Chinese thought and experience, "the emphasis is on learning to be human, a learning that
is characterized by a ceaseless process of inner illumination and
self-transformation" (Tu 1985:19). Moreover, Tu notes that this
transformation is not one of an ethical or formulaic anthro-
pocentrism, but one that is nothing less than a profound and dynamic sharing with the cosmic processes, though his account of it
clearly reflects Confucian priorities:

> The precondition for us to participate in the internal resonance
> of the vital forces in nature is our own inner transformation.
> Unless we can first harmonize our own feelings and thoughts,
> we are not prepared for nature, let alone for an "interflow
> with the spirit of Heaven and Earth." It is true that we are
> consanguineous with nature. But as humans, we must make
> ourselves worthy of such a relationship. (47)

Buber's discussion of transformation culminates with one last
profound and compelling paradox. "But since the oneness of the
world exists only for the accomplished man, it is thus in reality his
oneness that sets oneness into the world" (86). Although transformation in the world is, by definition, the ongoing creative working
of Tao, the repository of a dynamic oneness, it is in some way
contingent upon the realization of the sagely person, for "the Tao
of the world becomes alive and manifest only through its unconscious contact with the conscious existence of the unified man" (86).
In other words, to embrace Tao and its transformative impetus is
to affirm and regenerate the self, which is consequently *to affirm
and regenerate the cosmos*, to facilitate and/or complete
the transformation of things.[26] Stated a bit aphoristically, self-
transformation is in itself transformative; the "salvific" component
is, therefore, universal as well as personal. The "appointed person"
is called to be a "companion of the creator" (36), to participate in
creation, "the renewal designated by Heaven and Earth" (62).[27] It
is this interpretation that frames a number of important references
in the text translation, where those who seem to do little more
than affirm themselves demonstrate tremendous efficacy: "Speaking and doing happen freely from within, and the world is trans-

formed. One nod, one glance is sufficient, and all rush to follow it"
(47). Or more succinctly, "With a man like this one, merely his view
is needed, and Tao appears" (60). In other instances, there are
more direct allusions to cosmogony. For example, a dialogue between Confucius and Yen Hui slides from the subject of politics to
that of self-cultivation, but concludes with the apparently incon-
gruous statement, "This is the way to regenerate creation" (26). In
another passage, Confucius again describes the sage who "can bring
about the transformation of things, yet he preserves himself untouched in primordial being" (28). Finally, in the appropriately titled
"In Tao," Kuan Yin describes the sage who harnesses the primordial power: "He embraces the beginning and the end of all that is
existing. He brings his being to the oneness and from that nourishes his life-force, he gathers his virtue and penetrates through to
creation" (56).

It is in the light of this entire discussion on transformation that
one can understand the full import of Buber's second definition of
Tao, that it signifies "nothing other than that it is the human life
itself that is the carrier and realization of all transcendence." The
unified human life, as that which embraces creation and thus per-
sonifies creativity, is the ultimate locus of meaning. While Buber
does not belabor his use of "transcendence," he does seem to equate
it not with Tao specifically or with any other hypostatized entity to
which Tao refers, but simply with the oneness that has yet to be
discerned (and thus, created) within oneself and the world. This is
also the gist of Buber's third definition: "Tao means . . . that the
whole sense of existence rests in the oneness of the truthful life,
will only be experienced in it, that it is precisely this oneness
grasped as the absolute" (83). Ironically, the phenomenon of "tran-
scending" is the realization of that which is immanent, just as "all
creating . . . intends nothing other than to evoke the Tao of the
world, the Tao of things, to make living and manifest and dormant
oneness" (86).[28] Of course, this dialectic of transcendence and immanence inevitably returns Buber to the paradox that Tao is ubiq-
uitous as a unified totality, but inaccessible when sought through
any particularization: "We can discover it in no existence. When we
seek it in Heaven and Earth, in space and in time, then it is not
there, but Heaven and Earth, space and time are founded in it
alone. And when we seek it in the 'mystery of the essence of God,'

then it is not there, but rather God is founded in it alone" (84). One
need not look very far to find this tension illustrated in Buber's
text translation, as the two poles are sometimes juxtaposed in
consecutive vignettes. In "The Place of Tao," Chuang Tzu opines
that "there is nowhere where it is not," including even clay shards
and dung (63). Yet in "Tao the Unknown," the character appropriately named Beginningless states that "Tao cannot be heard. What
can be heard is not Tao. It cannot be seen. What can be seen is not
Tao" (64).

The Sage in the World: Non-Knowing and Non-Doing

But what is the unified human life in its liaison to things? How
does the accomplished man live in the world? Which form does
knowing assume in him, the coming of things to man? Which
the doing, the coming of man to things. (88)

With these questions, Buber notes that while each human being
is a caretaker of creation, one who is given the responsibility to
preserve both the oneness in the transformation and the great
transformation itself, this philosophical desideratum does not necessarily translate easily into a practical way of life, especially since
there is no self-evident resolution to the dialectic between the ac-
cessibility and inaccessibility of Tao. It may indeed be clear that
one must embrace all particulars as microcosmic configurations of
the oneness without creating a dualism between the particular and
the whole, but the steps toward establishing this orientation are
discussed largely at the level of suggestion and evocation. Certainly, it can be extrapolated that an ideal way of life is one that
is existentially integrative in order to preserve the integrity of the
whole (it is hardly a coincidence that "integrate" and "integrity"
share the same root),[29] and it is here helpful to recall how Buber
had previously contrasted the "teaching" with science and law, since
it is again his contention that existential knowledge and moral
imperative serve only to injure the oneness. It is the fatal flaw of
conventional knowing and doing that they are predicated on selectivity, differentiation, and, ultimately, disintegration. "What by man
is called 'knowing' is based on the tearing apart of the senses and

the faculties of mind. What by man is called 'doing' is based on the tearing apart of intentions and acts" (88). Just as the teaching simply presents itself to humanity, so too the sage simply presents himself to the world, by "overcom(ing) the official wisdom through the teaching of 'non-being,' the official virtue through the teaching of 'non-doing' " (77).

To some extent, Buber's position on the inadequacy of conventional knowledge can be captured in one straightforward statement, which again underscores the importance of transformation in his interpretative design: "There is no genuine perception because things unceasingly alter" (88). At first glance, this appears to be suggesting something of a primitive relativism, as Buber argues that the true contours of space and time are imperceptible because "not absolute but only relative extension is accessible" and "even duration exists only in comparative value" (88). And when he extends this motif to conclude that there are no available criteria for evaluating questions of truth or value—"Each being calls itself good and its contrary bad" (89)—he begins to tread dangerously close to the abyss of nihilism. However, Buber makes this claim not to deny the reality or attainability of truth, but rather to demonstrate the fallacy inherent in evaluations that presuppose and perpetuate distance between subject and object, between the knower and the world. Again, conventional knowing is problematic not simply because it is cognitive, but because it is dualistic. There is a suggestion of this point in the text translation, when Yen Hui tells Confucius that he has "forgotten everything," adding that "since I became free of my body and mind, I have become one with the all-pervasive" (37). This is illustrated more explicitly in Buber's rendition of the lengthy "Autumn Floods" dialogue, here titled "The Spirit of the Sea and the River Spirit." The story's protagonist argues that specific judgments of magnitude, genuineness, and correctness are conditional findings that arise when one compares, relates, and assesses value respectively, thus differentiating the object of perception from the subject and from other objects. When one recognizes the contingency and interchangeability of such judgments—e.g., "Heaven and earth is a grain of rice, the tip of a hair is a mountain"—then one has achieved "the cognition of comparability," "the regulation of relations," and "the arrangement of standards of measure" (53).

The conclusion here is not that there is no form of valid knowledge, but that true knowledge, which follows only from a unified
disposition, bears no resemblance to conventional dualistic knowledge. "Not in the standing opposite, in the dialectic of subject and
object, only in the oneness with the all is there cognition. The
oneness is the cognition" (89). As mentioned in the previous chapter, Buber often presents his understanding of unity in ways that
are anathema to his later dialogical principle, and it is on the
subject of knowledge that this monism is especially pronounced.
The unified knowing "overcomes the relation," as it "takes each
pair of antitheses as a polarity, without wishing to delimit the
antitheses, and it surrounds all polarities in its oneness" (89).[30]
This type of knowing is appropriately deemed "non-knowing," since
it is "without passion and without seeking" (89), relying not on the
mind's affective capacities for thought and sensation, but following
from a still and unified engagement in the world:

> (This cognition) is without delusional knowledge. It has things,
> it does not know them. It carries itself out not through the
> senses and faculties of mind, but rather through the wholeness
> of being. It leaves the senses be, but only like playing children;
> for all that they bring to it is only a variegated, playing,
> uncertain reflection of their own reality. It leave the faculties
> of mind be, but only like dancers, who make their music into
> an image, faithless and unsteady and richly formed after the
> manner of dancers. (89)[31]

The text translation illustrates "non-knowing" in two complementary ways, first by depicting the comical ineffectiveness (or
even destructiveness) of a conventional cognitive approach, and
then by depicting the efficacy of a nonpurposive cognitive orientation. In "The Strong Thief," the supposedly prudent precautions to
thwart a plunderer actually backfire and expedite the theft, as the
"Primitivist" author laments that "what the world knows as intelligence can be nothing other than subservient to the great
thieves . . . what the world knows as wisdom means nothing other
than protecting the great thieves" (40). This sentiment is echoed in
"Over-Indulgence and Non-Doing," where the same author again
argues, "Over-indulgence in knowledge leads to a prevalence of

artifice; over-indulgence of keen intellect leads to an expansion of passion for blaming" (40). In still another segment, "The Gardener" lambastes conventional knowing as divisive and self-aggrandizing, dismissing a Confucian student as "one of those who distend their knowledge in order to appear wise; who talk big in order to set themselves over the multitude; who sing lonely, melancholy tunes in order to spread their reputation" (46). On the other hand, in the brief search for "The Pearl," quasi-mythic characters named Knowledge and Clear-sight fail where Aimlessness succeeds (44–45), and in "The Three Answers," Knowledge learns that Do-nothing-say-nothing has the true understanding of Tao. Here, the Yellow Emperor explains: "There is nothing to think, nothing to consider, to discern Tao. There is nothing on which to stand, nothing to seize, to approach Tao. There is nothing to follow, nothing on which to tread, to reach Tao" (61). Finally, in the lengthy dialogue between "The Cloud Prince and the Primordial Mist," the latter figure casually describes his own enlightened comportment: "I wander without knowing what I seek. I roam about without knowing where I go. I stroll along for myself, arms folded, and watch how all things go their way. What should I know?" (43–44). He also offers the following advice to his companion, which again alludes to the universally salvific quality of one's own self-affirmation:

Spit out your mind-power. Forget things. Become one with the indivisible. Let loose your spirit. Make your soul free. Become empty. Become nothing. Let all beings return to their root. When they return to the root without knowledge, from there will come a simple purity that they will never lose; but knowledge would only bring deviation. Do not seek the names and relations of things; and all things will flourish of themselves. (44)

Paradoxically, it is by virtue of this "non-knowing," this knowing that stems from absolute unity, that one may break through the habituated conditions of separation and distance: "This cognition comprises all things in its existence, that is, in its love. It is all-embracing love that abolishes all antitheses" (90). This is a crucial step, because it completes the movement of the argument that began with ontology and soteriology, shifted briefly to a type of epistemology, and steps now toward what might be recognizable as ethics, or at least the inevitable question of the responsibilities involved in relationships between and among human beings.[32] Where the discourse had previously dealt with matters of perception and intellection, it is now concerned with human action in the world, as the unified knowledge produces a unifying love that necessitates some kind of outward activity. Or perhaps more appropriately, the action is the essential completion of the knowledge from which it is not truly separable: "This cognition is the deed. The deed is the eternal standard of measure, the eternal criterion, the absolute, the speechless, the unchangeable. The cognition of the accomplished man is not in his thinking, but in his doing" (90). As might be expected, Buber's understanding of ideal action is analogous to that of ideal knowledge, that it is a nonpurposive and nonaffective "non-doing" that "is an activity of the whole being" (91). As such, the expression of the highest virtue is to be distinguished from that of the conventional virtues of "humanheartedness" and "righteous-ness," which are both impractical and dualistic. They are imprac-tical in that they function as "objects of command," and "commanded love . . . stands in contradiction with the natural good of the human heart" (90). They are dualistic in that "they are based upon man standing facing other men and then treating them 'lovingly' and 'rightly'" (90). Once again, where Buber interprets non-knowing not as nihilism but as a knowing that arises from and creates unity, he interprets non-doing not as amorality but as a doing that also arises from and creates unity, the "oneness that is separated from no action" (25). In "The Magician and the Redeemed Man," Lieh Tzu's way of emulating the sage who appears before him "in a condition of undifferentiated all-unity" is to "put aside all the carving and painting and (return) to pure simplicity. There he stood like a clump of earth" (39).

The most important ramification is that this type of "non-action," which may on the surface resemble simple passivity, is actually infinitely efficacious, for "the accomplished man does not intervene in the life of beings . . . but . . . leads them through his oneness to oneness, he makes free their being and their destiny, he redeems Tao in them" (92). Stated more simply, "Whoever does not 'do,' effects" (91). This is the single theme that is most consistently associated with the traditions of Lao Tzu and Chuang Tzu, and it certainly appears more often in the text translation than does any other; it is hardly a coincidence that the very first passage is titled "The Inactive Man" (16). Typical references include the statement that "all things mature and thrive under the compliant influence of non-doing" (41) and the primordial mist nonchalantly telling the cloud prince to "persist in non-doing, and the world will be good of itself" (44).[33] This motif is often given an extra modicum of irony when the masses are inexplicably drawn to the idiosyncratic behavior of grotesques, misfits, and outcasts. In "The Mutilated Man," an amputee "stretches his might over Heaven and Earth and embraces all things," but also "moves to discern that all things are one." As a result, "the people voluntarily follow him, drag themselves to him, the one who moves no finger" (29). Similarly, in "The Leper," the character who "never preaches to the people" is compared to a water-balance where "the water remains peaceful within and does not overflow." The moral is that "when virtue supposes no outer form, things will not be capable of breaking off from it" (30–31). One particularly eloquent statement of non-doing comes in the passage about the "Pure Men," who "acted without calculation, did not seek to secure results, did not concern themselves with plans." Consequently, "the appointed man may destroy a kingdom and not lose the hearts of the people; without practicing humanheartedness, he makes happy the ten thousand generations" (32–33). In a word, Chuang Tzu's sages in Buber's selected passages are characterized by a quiet and composed equanimity; "if a man obtains Tao to live in, he needs no doing and is secure" (36). But, of course, this extends beyond the contentedness of the isolated individual: "Attempt with me to practice non-doing, therein you can rest unmoved, pure, and blissful" (63).

For that reason, the accomplished man deems that he does not do evil to others, nor mercy and benevolence. He seeks no profit, but he does not scorn those who do. He does not strive after property, but does not deem this as good. He asks for no assistance, but he does not deem this as independent and does not scorn those who let themselves advance. He acts differently from the masses, but he does not deem this as uncommon; and while others go with the majority, he does not scorn them as hypocrites. The honors and profits of the world are no incentive for him, its punishments and dishonors no inhibition. (52).

Buber's final topic, the significance of community and its government, follows from the ethical concerns inherent in the discussion of efficacious non-action. This is a subject that Buber does not develop in any great detail, and his granting of ontological status to society—"The kingdom, the community of beings, is not something artificial and arbitrary, but rather something native and autonomous" (92)—is not justified through any rigorous proof, though it may be ascertained by implication that human collectivity, "the mutual adaptation of beings" (92), is a natural product of the ongoing transformation of things. Nevertheless, Buber staunchly affirms the legitimacy of community, even if he offers almost no clue as to what its exact configurations would be, except that each member would "be able to follow his affairs after his own insight" (94). Buber's more pressing concern about community is the relationship between the ruler and the ruled, and, since "oneness alone is true power" (92), he places at the head of the ruling order the unified person, "one who has found the oneness and out of it seen the oneness of each thing in itself and the oneness of things with one another" (93). As anticipated by his earlier discussion, Buber argues that active, interventionist government, the dualistic setting of oneself against the natural course of society, is ultimately destructive. On the other hand, one who can "adapt oneself to the natural order of manifestations" is the one "who returns things, like himself, to the primordial existence" (93). Again, the key is the efficacy of inaction, the sense that action following from a paradigm of oneness excites in the world a spontaneous process of realization: "He exercises his transforming influence upon all being, and yet knows nothing of that, for he influences them in accord with their own nature" (94). In essence, the correct performance of non-doing is the most complete harnessing of Tao and its creative power:

Whoever unfolds and protects the natural life of the kingdom, who does not impose command and coercion thereupon, but rather sinks himself therein, listens to its secret message, and brings it to the light and to the work, he rules it in truth. He does the non-doing; he does not intervene, but rather unfolds and protects what wills to become. In the kingdom's need and drive, Tao's will reveals itself to him. He shuts his will on it, he becomes Tao's instrument, and all things change of themselves. He knows no violence, and yet all beings follow the suggestions of his hand. He practices neither reward nor punishment, and yet what he wishes to make occur, occurs. (92–93)

Although Buber discusses governmental and kingly non-doing with direct reference only to the *Tao Te Ching*, his text translation does in fact touch briefly on the issue,[34] such as when a nameless man urges a leader to "loosen the strength of your spirit to simplicity, the strength of your life to non-doing, surrender to the order of things, withdraw the selfness—and the kingdom will be ruled" (38). In another case, the Primitivist states: "Therefore, there is for the superior man, who will be appointed ruler in inescapable wisdom, nothing other than non-doing. Through non-doing he will be capable of resting in the natural conditions of existence" (41). Even though these examples are few and far between, it is evident that the transformative power of the sage extends throughout the networks of family, community, and world; each person who has become one is implicitly a leader. And while Buber's translated passages from *Chuang Tzu* do not explicitly address the necessity for a thriving and integrated community, they do cumulatively suggest that Chuang Tzu holds it as a tacit presupposition. Despite all of the quasi-mythic and nonhuman characters portrayed in the episodes, they also teem with figures occupying numerous social functions (cooks, gardeners, doctors, artisans, priests, musicians) and bound in traditional relations (teachers and disciples, ministers and subjects, friends, and spouses). It seems especially salient that Chuang Tzu's own close relationships with a wife and a network of confidants are never questioned.

The Hermeneutic Question in Context

It has been my intention in this chapter to build on the interpretive framework established in the previous chapter by determining the

suppositions and goals of Buber's hermeneutic agenda, establishing criteria by which one can evaluate the legitimacy of his conclusions, and exploring his translation and commentary in light of
those criteria. It appears that Buber approaches *Chuang Tzu* with
an interactive model of meaning that is heavily influenced by the
"romantic" *Verstehen* school of textual interpretation but also anticipates his own later dialogical hermeneutics, where meaning is
to be found in the transformation of self inspired by the good-faith
encounter between reader and text. As such, it is appropriate to
read Buber's work as a reception of Chuang Tzu's transformative
parable, and to evaluate the extent to which it represents a genuine encounter rather than a simple projection of ideas onto someone else's work. To this end, I have examined the relationship
between translation and commentary, in order to explore whether
Buber's conclusions find support in the body of the text as he
understood it, whether the two components of Buber's product hold
together as one plausible and consistent transmission of *Chuang
Tzu* and its teaching.

In summary, Buber argues that Tao is a singular and ineffable
cosmic principle that is accessible in the form of an obliterating
oneness that nevertheless provides an ontological basis for the transformation of things, which is an ongoing process of renewal and
recreation, an ongoing repetition of successive cosmogonic moments.
When one participates in the transformation and grasps the oneness, he or she undergoes a continuous affirmation and regeneration of self that is not only the highest form of personal realization,
but also paradoxically a catalyst to continuing and expediting the
transformation, thus serving a role that is responsible to the entire
cosmos and, in a manner of speaking, salvific. The actualized human life, the truthful life, is therefore the locus of meaning, the
access point at which one may discover and create the element of
transcendence. This fulfillment takes the form of knowledge and
action that are rooted in the oneness, thus appearing as subtle and
efficacious expressions of non-knowing and non-action, both of which
sustain and transform the greater community. At every step in this
argument, as illustrated by copious examples, Buber does find a
textual basis, though many of these bases are enhanced by imaginative renderings, interpolations, and decontextualizations. Nevertheless, this was all part of Buber's established method at the time,

which he attributed to an appreciation of phenomena that were spiritual as well as historical. *Reden und Gleichnisse* is itself contextual; it chronicles the germination of a Taoistically inspired transformation on Buber's part which would be completed in subsequent years. The completion of this process, of Buber's ongoing reception of the text, is the topic of the following chapter.

The Further Hermeneutic Question
The Matter of Textual Reception

The Interpretive Framework

The last of the three hermeneutic chapters addresses the possibility of relating Buber's dialogical principle directly to Chuang Tzu's mystical philosophy, a topic which on the surface seems only tenuously linked to the preceding analyses of Buber's contributions toward textual reconstruction and interpretation, which had focused more specifically on his text translation and commentary. Nevertheless, it will be demonstrated that there is a sound hermeneutic basis for such a line of inquiry, and that this approach does reflect an appropriate extension of the conclusions drawn from the previous chapters. More importantly, a focused investigation will in fact reveal a plausible analogue to the I-Thou relation in the original Chinese text, a resonance which not only provides the single most significant indicator that a comparative study of Chuang Tzu and Buber is ultimately worthwhile, but also carries important implications for the modern study of mysticism, which is currently dominated by a particularistic methodological paradigm.

As noted repeatedly in the previous two chapters, Buber's interpretive essay (especially when read apart from the text translation) presents a sometimes uneasy synthesis of a pure monism and a proto-dialogically suffused monism, where the former perhaps presents itself to the reader as the more pronounced of the two and certainly leaves a pantheistic imprint that is nowhere to be found in Buber's mature dialogical thought. Indeed, this vestige of Buber's pantheism is the one consistent thread that weaves together disparate parts of the commentary, from the largely methodological

groundwork on the oneness of the teaching, through the metaphysical treatment of the unity of Tao, to the epistemological and
ethical arguments on the non-knowing and non-doing of the unified
man.[1] The cumulative result of this presentation of oneness is a
misleading implication that Chuang Tzu displays a self-annihilating
and world-renouncing zest for the ecstatic experience of unity. Indeed, the text translation does verify that Buber found in *Chuang
Tzu* a significantly "escapist" motif, where the sage is portrayed as
one who "pays no attention to worldly things" (19), who leaves
behind the mundane reality of the existential world and chooses
instead to "swing on the light wings of emptiness beyond the six
directions" (37). In a number of passages, the return to the creative
source of being is depicted not as a renewal of self within the here-
and-now (as illustrated at length in the previous chapter), but as
a breakthrough to a qualitatively distinct realm, such as "that
height of great light, where the wellspring of the driving primordial power is, and . . . the gate of profound mystery, where the
wellspring of the restraining primordial power is" (42). And in a
few important cases, there is the serious implication that the experience of Tao entails a dissolution of self into the greater whole, an
idea that is most antithetical to Buber's later philosophy: "But I
finally came to enrapture; for enrapture means turned-out-from-
sense, turned-out-from sense means Tao, and Tao means the great
absorption" (50).

Buber's emphasis on this theme of unity and absorption is fur-
thered by his choice and adaptation of translated material, as he
disproportionately represents the core of examples that illustrate
various sages apparently reveling in some kind of mystical experience.[2] In these episodes, one can discern three closely related characteristics ascribed to the enlightened beings—otherworldliness,
immortality or imperviousness to harm, and superhuman powers—
all of which are likely metaphorical expressions of ecstatic experience. The "otherworldly" depictions are those which simultaneously
affirm some aetherial realm of existence and devalue that which is
immediate. "Who can climb to Heaven, roam through the clouds,
abandon space, forget existence, forever and ever without end?"
(35). At times, flight from the conventional world is explicitly identified with the experience of unity, as when reaching "the palace of
nowhere" places one "amidst the oneness of all things" (63), or

when the state of being "removed from all bounds" is to be "one with the all-pervasive" (37). Moreover, those who achieve ultimate freedom from and indifference to worldly realities are often represented as liberated from ordinary human vulnerabilities to pain or injury, since the usual causes of harm are relegated to the status of the merely mundane. "Thus they could scale heights and feel no anxiety; plunge into water and feel no wetness, step through fire and feel no heat" (32). In another episode, "The accomplished man wanders through solid things without being hampered, steps through fire without being singed, treads on the air without trembling" (56). This motif of imperviousness is occasionally even extended to one of immortality; the experience of absorption renders one preeminently alive and real, in stark contrast to the conditionality and evanescence of the secular world:

> In the present existence, all beings spring out of the Earth and return to the Earth. But I will accompany you through the gates of eternity into the kingdom of the infinite. My light is the light of the sun and moon. My life is the life of Heaven and Earth. I do not care who comes to me, who goes from me—all may die out, I will endure. (43)
>
> The accomplished man is a spiritual being. If the ocean evaporated, he would feel no heat. If the great rivers froze, he would feel no cold. If the thunder tore up the mountain and the storm catapulted up the great depth, he would not tremble. He would climb the clouds of Heaven, drive himself forth to the sun and moon, and stride to the boundaries of the four seas, where death and life have no more authority over man— let alone what is evil to him. (19)[3]

It may not be coincidental that Buber sometimes characterizes the person who achieves this state of oneness as a "spiritual being" (*geistiges Wesen*),[4] as there is a faint suggestion in the commentary either that the human spirit is the agent of such experience or that some less carefully defined universal realm of spirit provides the ontological basis for it. In a passage cited previously, Buber states, "There are two types of life. The one is the mere vegetative living, the wearing out until extinction; the other is the eternal transformation and its oneness in the spirit" (85). While this latter phrase could be construed as little more than a figure of speech—Buber's casual invocations of "the Eastern spirit" (69) or "foundational powers of the spirit" (71) do not appear to imply any rigorous metaphysics—there are other indications that spirit is somehow a crucial principle in the attainment of unity. In one depiction of the sage who is "unified out of Tao, unifying the world, a creating man," Buber concludes: "The spirit wanders through things until it flourishes to eternity in the accomplished man" (87). In the text translation, spirit is frequently seen as theoretically free from (and perhaps opposed to) the bonds of the existential world, thus furthering both the theme of otherworldliness and the hypothesis that spirit is the indivisible aspect that allows for unity:

> Life and death . . . preservation and decay, success and failure, poverty and wealth, virtue and vice, good and bad reputation, hunger and thirst, warmth and cold—they are all resonances in the lot of humanity. Day time, night time, they follow one another and no one can say where each begins. Thus, they must not be permitted to disturb the harmony of the living, and must not be permitted to enter the realm of spirit. To let flow the harmony of the living, bringing all souls to joy; to do this day after day without omission, that there be Springtime between one and the world of things; for all times and possibilities to be parallel—these are the signs of one whose talents are complete. (31)

And not surprisingly, it is incumbent upon those who have not yet experienced unity to cultivate or realize this elusive quality of spirit; persons with attachments to ego, body, things, or social structures are admonished to "let loose (their) spirit" (44) or "loosen the strength of (their) spirit to simplicity" (38). Finally, for the sage who has achieved such perfection—who "embraces the beginning and the end of all that is existing" and "brings his being to the oneness and from that nourishes his life-force"—it is stated that "his spirit is without breach" (56). At the risk of lapsing into a somewhat murky jargon, it seems evident that Buber understands the oneness of the central man as a state of "spiritual" wholeness.

Buber's implicit theory of spirit is particularly significant not simply because of the shaky metaphysics it suggests, but because it both anticipates and contrasts with his later use of the term in *I and Thou* and other subsequent texts, thus providing an interesting pivot on which to explore the tension between the monistic strain of the commentary and the dualistic tendency of the later dialogical writings. In *I and Thou,* although Buber would still insist that "the spirit is one," he would also elaborate that it "is not in the I but between I and Thou" (1958:39), thus placing it within an unambiguously dualistic context. Stated more concisely, "Only in virtue of his power to enter into relation is he able to live in the spirit" (39). Here, spirit is still understood as an organic whole, but it is a oneness based not on absorption or immersion but on ongoing response and connection. In fact, Buber's critique of mysticisms of unity (and, by implication, of his own earlier propensities) grows largely from his position that such processes diminish the potential of spirit by mislocating it within and confining it to the individuated self; the ecstatic experience becomes a temptation for one simply to "enjoy to the full this blessed concentration of his being, and without entering on the supreme duty fall back into dissipation of being" (89):

All doctrine of absorption is based on the colossal illusion of the human spirit that is bent back on itself, that spirit exists in man. Actually spirit exists with man as the starting point— between man and that which is not man. In renouncing this its meaning, its meaning as relation, the spirit that is bent back on itself is compelled to drag into man that which is not man, it is compelled to make the world and God into functions of the soul. This is the spirit's illusion about the soul. (93)[5]

At this juncture, there is certainly no cause to deny that the general thrust of Buber's commentary (bolstered by selected portions of the text translation) is his drive for a genuine and enduring realization of undifferentiated oneness, "the uniting that conquers all deviation from life's foundation . . . the making whole that heals all separation and fragility . . . the expiating that redeems from all disunity" (87).

However, even Maurice Friedman, who first cornered Buber on the "mystical" flavor of the commentary, acknowledges that the essay "focuses not upon mystical experience or upon a world-rejecting relationship to God but upon a central teaching and a central man," and that it reveals "a clear anticipation of Buber's mature religious existentialism" (1970:65–66). Unfortunately, this integrative "proto-dialogical" aspect of Buber's Taoist volume has seldom been fleshed out in any significant detail, again probably because so few Buber scholars have considered the commentary and text-translation portions of *Reden und Gleichnisse* in tandem. The idea of a unity predicated upon relationality, it should be recalled, has been an important subtext in the two previous chapters, particularly in the protracted discussion of the parable as an expression of the "attained" oneness coming upon "things, events, and relations," as well as that of the unitary Tao underlying the ongoing process of transformation. It is when Buber builds upon this latter point— Tao as diversely and concretely manifested in transformation— that the most significant proto-dialogical formulations occur. In an extraordinary statement, Buber writes, "Tao is the path of things, their manner, their proper order, their oneness; but as such it exists in them only potentially; it first becomes operative in its contact with other things" (86).[6] Here, Buber makes a striking parallel that is all too easily overlooked; just as the transformative power of the teaching is, for all intents and purposes, accessible only through the concrete language of parable, so too the creativity and efficacy of Tao is contingent upon differentiated and interactive constituents of reality. In other words, as transmission of the teaching is not complete without parable, so too actualization of Tao entails concretization and relation, for "the Tao of the thing becomes alive and manifest only though its contact with other things" (86).[7] Furthermore, the principle of microcosm, the potential for identification of the immediate with the absolute, is also a prominent feature here; where Buber states that "there is no thing in which the whole Tao is not as this thing's self" (87), he would later write, "by means of every particular Thou the primary word addresses the eternal Thou" (1958:75). Still, it should be noted that it is never anything less than a *oneness* that is maintained in such a state of relation; it is clearly appropriate to characterize this as a "proto-dialogical *unity*," where the voice of relation is in dialectical tension with the voice of monism.

The oneness of the masculine and feminine elements that exist not for themselves but only for one another, the oneness of antitheses that exist not for themselves but only through one another, the oneness of things that exist not for themselves but only with one another. This oneness is the Tao in the world. (84)

It is, in fact, quite understandable that among Buber scholars, the theme of unity has largely overshadowed the dialogical implications of passages such as the ones cited above. For Friedman and others, there has been little incentive to hunt for any more dialogical fragments, given that "the teaching of the unity of the central man and the world is still 'mystical' in a sense that Buber's mature thought is not" (Friedman 1970:66), thus reinforcing the view that Buber's initial engagement with *Chuang Tzu* marks a transitional philosophical stage (albeit a crucial one) that only anticipates his later dialogical principle.

It is, however, my contention that the fundamental ingredients of the I-Thou relation—the primacy of the existential sphere, the integrity of particular entities necessarily bound through interaction and relation, and the potential presence of the absolute within each coming together—are in fact already present within Buber's encounter with *Chuang Tzu*, although they have admittedly not yet coalesced or found articulate expression. Much of this is actually more evident in the body of the text translation, where Buber's choice of material and use of interpolation are quite telling. Where many passages indeed illustrate an otherworldly or absorptive mysticism, a considerable number of other episodes (or fragments of the same episodes) portray enlightened beings as finding transcendence directly within their appreciation of mundane activities or personal encounters.[8] In "The Magician and the Redeemed Man," Lieh Tzu finally achieves a measure of knowledge and clarity after several failed attempts, though all that is specifically revealed of the process is that he "helped his wife cook the family meal and fed his pigs as is if they were human beings" (39). Similarly, "The Gardener" rejects the "cunning implements" of speed and progress, choosing instead to dig an irrigation ditch slowly but meticulously (46). This latter snippet reveals Chuang Tzu's especially low regard for utility, a motif that recurs throughout the text translation, as when Chün Mang seeks no use for the ocean other than "going there to take pleasure in it" (46). This unquestionably foreshadows Buber's indictment of reducing people and things to objects of experience, "for the development of the ability to experience and use comes about mostly through the decrease of man's power to enter into relation" (1958:38–39). It is here important to note that Buber includes two related passages, "The Useless Tree" (16–17) and "The Holy Tree" (27–28), both of which illustrate the point that the worth of something deemed inutile can be recognized only when it is approached as a whole and as a subject in its own right, and that the entity's freedom from calculation and manipulation provides a model for the proper attitude of an enlightened person.[9] Moreover, there can be little doubt that these passages provided the inspiration for the unforgettable segment that appears toward the beginning of *I and Thou*, cited here in its entirety:[10]

I consider a tree.

I can look on it as a picture: stiff column in a shock of light, or splash of green shot with the delicate blue and silver of the background.

I can perceive it as movement: flowing veins on clinging, pressing pith, suck of the roots, breathing of the leaves, ceaseless commerce with earth and air—and the obscure growth itself.

I can classify it in a species and study it as a type in its structure and mode of life.

I can subdue its actual presence and form so sternly that I recognise it only as an expression of law—of the laws in accordance with which a constant opposition of forces is continually adjusted, or of those in accordance with which the component substances mingle and separate.

I can dissipate it and perpetuate it in number, in pure numerical relation.

In all this the tree remains my object, occupies space and time, and has its nature and constitution.

It can, however, also come about, if I have both will and grace, that in considering the tree I become bound up in relation to it. The tree is now no longer It. I have been seized by the power of exclusiveness.

To effect this it is not necessary for me to give up any of the ways in which I consider the tree. There is nothing from which I would have to turn my eyes away in order to see, and no knowledge that I would have to forget. Rather is everything, picture and movement, species and type, law and number, indivisibly united in this event.

Everything belonging to the tree is in this: its form and structure, its colours and chemical composition, its intercourse with the elements and with the stars, all are present in a single whole.

The tree is no impression, no play of my imagination, no value depending on my mood; but it is bodied over against me and has to do with me, as I with it—only in a different way.

Let no attempt be made to sap the strength from the meaning of the relation: relation is mutual.

The tree will have consciousness, then, similar to our own? Of that I have no experience. But do you wish, through seeming to succeed in it with yourself, once again to disintegrate that which cannot be disintegrated? I encounter no soul or dryad of the tree, but the tree itself. (7–8)

In the text translation, this motif develops into a new kind of universalism, as any entity or task, no matter how apparently insignificant or unappealing, can be seen as intrinsically meaningful. Thus, one character is exhorted to "embrace all things in (his) love, and none will be better sheltered than another" (54). This is illustrated most clearly in a passage where the integrity of supposedly insignificant entities (ants, weeds, clay shards, and dung) is affirmed, not because they are mere vehicles (for reaching Tao) which can be annihilated in favor of a greater unity, but because "there is no thing that (Tao) denies" and "there is nowhere where it is not" (63). Thus, there is the potential for a spontaneous realization of connectedness between self and other, where the two remain wholly distinct and self-conscious yet bound together in a moment of mutuality and reciprocity. This is why Chuang Tzu, through some cryptically explained act of perception ("out of my

own pleasure over the water"), can intuit the joys felt by fish swim-
ming under a bridge (54),[11] or why the priest of the sacrifice can
pause to consider the point of view of the pigs (58). At times, these
moments of connection occur in fleeting person-to-person encounters, as when Confucius speaks of having "leaned one single time
shoulder to shoulder" with Yen Hui (61), or when he maintains
silence in the face of a sage, since "with a man like this one, merely
his view is needed, and Tao appears" (60). But without a doubt, the
one encounter that gives the most sophisticated indication of dialogical thought occurs in a heavily interpolated passage, a developmental account of one ascending the steps toward an enlightened
state. This is particularly provocative given how Buber would later
dismiss his Taoist involvement as "a stage that I had to pass through
before I could enter into an independent relationship with being"
(1957:ix):

> After three days, the separation of things ceased for him.
> . . . After seven more days, the external ceased for him. And
> after another nine days, he stepped out of his own existence.
> After that, his mind became radiant like daybreak and he
> beheld being, his I, countenance to countenance. When he had
> seen this, he became without past and present. Finally, he
> entered the realm where death and life are no more, where
> one can kill without causing to die, and engender without
> causing to live. The one who is in Tao thus accompanies, thus
> finds, thus destroys, thus builds all things. Its name is
> Shattered-Unbruised, and its path is completion. (33–34)[12]

The climax is a revelation of sorts, depicted not as an absorptive
identification of the self with the absolute, but as a personal interactive encounter, where self-awareness is catalyzed through the
direct apprehension of and meeting with the eternal or essential.
Here, only by beholding being (*Wesen*) can one behold oneself, just
as Buber would later write that "through the Thou a man becomes
I" (1958:28), and "the person becomes conscious of himself as sharing in being, as co-existing, and thus as being" (63). It is also in
this description that there is a faint glimpse of one of Buber's most
important conclusions to *I and Thou*, where he looks beyond a
random succession of I-Thou moments and toward meeting with

the Eternal Thou: "The most powerful and the deepest reality exists where everything enters into the effective action, without re-
serve the whole man and God the all-embracing—the united I and
the boundless Thou." (89).

The sheer quantity of these proto-dialogical instances, com-
pounded by the subtlety and refinement of passages such as the
one just cited, renders all the more unsatisfactory the standard
hypothesis that the Taoist volume represents merely a transitional
stage in Buber's development and that *Chuang Tzu* is one of a
number of "influences" informing the dialogical philosophy. It is
here necessary to recall and extend the unique hermeneutic position that Buber establishes when he explicitly identifies the original text as a transformative parable of a primordial teaching and
implicitly defines textual interpretation as the transformation and
actualization of the reader occurring in his or her good-faith encounter with the text. With this in mind, it is my unorthodox (but
firm) contention that the tremendous thematic and linguistic continuity between the proto-dialogical position embedded in the Taoist volume and the mature dialogical philosophy articulated in *I
and Thou* strongly suggests that the latter represents, at least in
part, an extension of Buber's process of textual interpretation. That
is to say, based on Buber's own working hermeneutic, it is quite
reasonable to conclude that *I and Thou* continues, and perhaps
completes, the transformation of self that Buber had begun in his
initial engagement with *Chuang Tzu*. Or, in more familiar Buberian
language, *Reden und Gleichnisse des Tschuang-tse* is the chrysalis
to the butterfly taking shape in *I and Thou*.[13]

While the idea of considering one text as an indirect interpretation of another may seem to require some leap of the imagination,
there are some precedents found in modern hermeneutic theory
that lend support to such a possibility. In particular, Hans Robert
Jauss attempts to formulate an "aesthetic of reception," where he
indicts the "obvious backwardness of literary hermeneutics" and
laments that "no theory of understanding has been developed for
texts of an aesthetic character, and that the question of 'application' has been relegated to book reviewers' criticism as an unscholarly one" (1982:140). The "application" to which Jauss refers is the
third stage of a hermeneutic process first appearing in the theories
of Hans-Georg Gadamer, the totality of which "is to be conceived as

a unity of the three moments of understanding (*intelligere*), interpretation (*interpretare*), and application (*applicare*)." This sequence inspires Jauss's own triad of "aesthetically perceptual reading," "retrospectively interpretive reading," and "historical reading," which takes into account such matters as the shifting horizons of expectation and experience, the reality of repeated reflections on and struggles with a text after the original reading, and the "processlike effect" that the "poetic text" engenders (139–140). And while Jauss does not specifically address the kind of protracted interpretation that is being suggested here, he does argue that the final stage of reception "can satisfy the . . . legitimate interest of using literary communication with the past to measure and to broaden the horizon of one's own experience vis-à-vis the experience of the other" (147). Moreover, Jauss offers some choice words on a topic directly related to the present inquiry:

> Thus, for the interpretation of texts from other cultures, the aesthetic character of poetic texts from the western literary tradition can only offer heuristic advantages. Literary interpretation must compensate with the three achievements of the hermeneutic process for the fact that aesthetic perception itself is subject to historical exchange. It thereby gains the opportunity of broadening historicist knowledge through aesthetic understanding, and perhaps of constituting, through its unconstrained kind of application, a corrective to other applications that are subject to situational pressures and the compulsions of decision-making. (148)

Again, it is my contention that one important and as yet overlooked component in arriving at a complete appreciation of *I and Thou* is the realization that it can be understood as *a work of interpretation*, as the second interpretive layer of Buber's ongoing engagement with *Chuang Tzu*, the first being his commentary portion of *Reden und Gleichnisse*.[14] Naturally, this should be a matter of major interest for Buber scholars, although of more immediate relevance to this study are the sinological implications. If *I and Thou* can indeed be read as an interpretation of *Chuang Tzu*, then it becomes appropriate to evaluate whether it is a plausible interpretation, whether the dialogical principle is a legitimate lens through which one can read the Chinese text. Thus, correlating Buber's I-Thou relation to Chuang Tzu's mystical philosophy completes the task begun in the previous two chapters, that of assessing Buber's contribution toward the longstanding sinological problem of interpreting *Chuang Tzu*.

The Reader in Transformation:
Intraworldly Mysticism and the I-Thou Relation

Of course, the claim that *I and Thou* represents the crystallization of an ongoing reception of *Chuang Tzu* could simply be dismissed as postmodernist sophistry, were it not demonstrable that the dialogical principle does, in fact, bring much to an understanding of *Chuang Tzu*. Certainly, it has been evidenced that there are many ways in which the two texts are at least congenial or resonant with one another, but it is now necessary to employ sound sinological method in order to appraise the value of Buber's protracted reception, to determine the extent to which the I-Thou relation is actually latent in the pages of the original Chinese. This is clearly the most exciting facet of this study, for it is here where light will be shed on whether one may indeed understand Chuang Tzu as, in a manner of speaking, a dialogical philosopher. Obviously, it must be acknowledged at the outset that Chuang Tzu and Buber think and write within totally different cultural and linguistic contexts; Chuang Tzu neither speaks of the dialectic between the basic word pairs nor feels the need to accommodate such concepts as "wholly other" and "grace." The difficulty in executing this task properly lies in bridging the historical gulf without resorting to a perennialism that resorts to forced comparisons and assumes it own conclusions. What I propose, therefore, is to explore a dialogical reading of the Chinese text, just as others have considered psychological readings of Zen philosophy or Confucian readings of Kant. That is to say, what follows is an effort to render *Chuang Tzu* more intelligible, to add to its already rich history of textual interpretations, by applying dialogical philosophy to a careful reading of portions of the text and offering direct juxtapositions with relevant passages from *I and Thou*.

Specifically, this new interpretive framework proves most fruitful in supplying an important conceptual link between Chuang

Tzu's complex philosophical discourse on theoretical relation and his playful mystical vignettes illustrating personal relationship, which otherwise appear to be tenuously related. In the previous chapter's discussion of Taoist ontology, it was briefly noted how Buber's dialectical interpretation of oneness within transformation dovetailed comfortably with Chuang Tzu's principle of equality, a topic here to be fleshed out more fully. Once again, the point of departure is the metaphysical concept of Tao, which is generative and dynamic, simultaneously featureless and inexhaustible, and thus consistently invoked in the language of non-being.

> As for Tao, there is actuality, there is reliability; there is no doing, there is no form. It can be transmitted but cannot be received, can be gotten but cannot be seen. It is itself the basis, itself the root. When there were not yet Heaven and Earth, it existed firmly since antiquity, making spiritual the ghosts, making spiritual the gods, engendering Heaven, engendering Earth. It is in precedent of the ultimate extreme, but is not deemed high; it is beneath the six extremes, but is not deemed deep. It was born before Heaven and Earth, but is not deemed longstanding; it is elder to antiquity, but is not deemed old. ("Inner Chapters" 16/6/29)

Employing language reminiscent of Mircea Eliade's "archaic ontology," one can perhaps understand Tao as the ineffable yet omnipresent source of being, power, and creativity *par excellence,* as that which is preeminently real, efficacious, and productive:[15] "As for things already dead or alive, square or round, none knows their source, yet from antiquity the ten thousand things have remained firmly in existence ("School of Chuang Tzu" 58/22/18–19). Moreover, Tao straddles the overly convenient demarcation between transcendence and immanence, as it is independent of temporal and spatial categorization, yet is immediately pervasive and thoroughly embodied in all levels of existence: "Confused and hidden, as though having vanished, yet existing; lush, without form yet spiritual ("School of Chuang Tzu" 58/22/20–21). And of course, Tao is recognized as the progenitor of "the hundred transformations" and, consequently, of existential diversity:

The luminous is born from the obscure. The ordered is born from the formless. Quintessence and spirit are born from Tao. Form is originally born from quintessence, and through form the ten thousand things mutually give birth. Therefore, those with nine openings are womb-born, those with eight openings are egg-born. . . . Heaven cannot but be high, earth cannot but be broad, the sun and moon cannot but go their courses, the ten thousand things cannot but prosper. Is this not Tao? ("School of Chuang Tzu" 58/22/30–31, 32–33)

Certainly, this once again calls to mind the dialectical tension between the unity of Tao and the multiplicity of its manifestations, a topic already considered at great length. "To see things from their difference, there is liver and gall, Ch'u and Yüeh; to see them from their sameness, the ten thousand things are all one" ("Inner Chapters" 12/5/6). Although there may be a temptation to dismiss this as an unsophisticated relativism, it is crucial to note the ramifications of denoting human and cosmic multiplicity as the legitimate and essential manifestation of Tao. Each constituent of reality does exist in its own totality, but not in isolation, for "things certainly are mutually entwined, each kind summoning up another" ("School of Chuang Tzu" 54/20/64). And while these individual entities possess qualitative variations and distinctions from one another, they all recapitulate an impartial template that is resistant to any conceptual valuation:[16] "Heaven and earth exist together with me; the ten thousand things and I amount to one" ("Inner Chapters" 5/2/52–53). As a result, questions of priority, precedence, and valuation are irrelevant and, ultimately, ill-conceived: "For this reason, if one picks out a stalk or a pillar, a leper or Hsi-shih, the strange, the uncanny, Tao penetrates and deems as one" ("Inner Chapters 4/2/35). In other words, the elemental particularity of being is not hierarchical; the unique yet always transforming entities stand together in a state of metaphysical equality. This is an extremely delicate point, as Chuang Tzu encourages the aesthetic appreciation of the world in all its diversity, for as long as one can simultaneously withhold valuation from the parts and perceive the whole as an interwoven mosaic or symphony. On this subject, Kuo Hsiang, as translated by Fung Yu-lan, writes:

The flutes and pipes may differ in length; their notes may belong to different scales. Hence their resulting sounds may differ in innumerable ways, some being short, some long, some high, some low. But despite these myriad differences, their endowment conforms in every case to a single standard, so that there is no question of superiority or inferiority between them. (Fung 1952:227)

To repeat, the ontological condition established is one that affirms particularity and mutuality while rejecting (or rather, allowing no place for) hierarchy: "The ten thousand things are as they are, and by this they come together mutually" ("Inner Chapters" 6/ 2/78). This view is tremendously resonant with dialogical philosophy, as it not only maintains the reality and primacy of the existential world, but also authenticates a metaphysic of integrity and reciprocity. In *I and Thou*, Buber would similarly grant a kind of ontological status to the incipient dialogical potential—"in the beginning is relation" (1958:18)—the perfect, undifferentiated, primordial actuality that can be continually realized "in the sanctity of the primary word" (9). For Buber, relation is "the cradle of the Real Life" (9), a metaphor which recalls Chuang Tzu's image of the "treasury of Heaven," which when "poured into does not fill, poured from does not empty" ("Inner Chapters" 5/2/61). This latter image is also noteworthy because it appears in the midst of Chuang Tzu's most technical and controversial logical repartee, where it is likened to "a wordless discrimination, the unspoken Tao." ("Inner Chapters" 5/2/61).[17] In a universe governed by the principle of equality, any affected or cogitated demarcations and discriminations—ethical, epistemological, aesthetic—are not appropriate representations of reality; truly integrated participants in reality can be known in their totality, but cannot be objectified or circumscribed by fixed categories. Thus, "Tao has never had borders . . . it is by deeming something as so that there are boundaries" ("Inner Chapters" 5/2/ 55). For Chuang Tzu, the alternate presence or absence of "borders" or "boundaries" follows from two different ways of orienting oneself in the world. As if to comment on this, Buber begins *I and Thou* with, "To man, the world is twofold, in accordance with his twofold attitude" (1958:3), and he quickly brings this directly to bear on the topic of boundaries:

When Thou is spoken, the speaker has no thing for his object. For where there is a thing there is another thing. Every It is bounded by others; It exists only through being bounded by others. But where Thou is spoken, there is no thing. Thou has no bounds.

When Thou is spoken, the speaker has no *thing*; he has indeed nothing. But he takes his stand in relation. (4)

Although this point has already been made repeatedly, it is here prudent to stress once again that this existential condition without borders is understood not as a self-annihilating unity, but as an organic and unified integration. As such, the fully integrated participant in this state of being engages other participants directly, as genuine beings in and of themselves, rather than through the constraining filters produced by conventional subject-object cognition. Thus, Chuang Tzu writes, "the sagely person embraces them, the common persons make discriminations among them in order to show them to one another" ("Inner Chapters" 5/2/58). The implication is that each person possesses the capacity, by virtue of his or her "completed heart-mind,"[18] to know and respond to others on a level that is independent of symbolization. Much to the disdain of modern epistemologists and anthropologists who deny the possibility of "pure experience,"[19] Buber echoes Chuang Tzu in attesting to both the potentiality and meaningfulness of such an encounter. The I-Thou relation is, according to Buber, "unmediated" or "direct" (*unmittelbar*): "No system of ideas, no foreknowledge, and no fancy intervene between I and Thou. The memory itself is transformed, as it plunges out of its isolation into the unity of the whole."[20] Of the person who meets the world with such integrity, Chuang Tzu writes: "One who is ultimately secure in the universe brings forth Heavenly light."[21] And of the person who is met in such a manner, Buber writes: "But with no neighbor, and whole in himself, he is Thou and fills the heavens. This does not mean that nothing exists except himself. But all else lives in *his* light" (1958:8).

The crux of the matter is that despite "the essentials of nature and destiny," it is an unfortunate propensity of the human mind to lapse from wholeness and integrity and fall prey to an escalating spiral of valuation and differentiation.[22] Chuang Tzu does not elaborately speculate as to the first cause of this eventuality, but he does trace the devolution back to "the persons of antiquity," the first of whom "considered that there had not yet begun to be things." This regression moves through those who "considered that there were things but that there had not yet begun to be borders" and onto those who "considered that were borders but that there had not begun to be affirmation and negation." Chuang Tzu concludes this sequence with the superimposition of hierarchy, the moment that most indicates the loss of original integrity: "As for the ornamentation of affirmation and negation, it is the abatement of Tao" ("Inner Chapters" 5/2/40–42). In a similar fashion, Buber also locates the beginning of the decline in the dim reaches of "earliest history" (1958:23), and he too attributes it to the emerging awareness of things and borders:

> But this is the exalted melancholy of our fate, that every Thou in our world must become an It. It does not matter how exclusively present the Thou was in the direct relation. As soon as the relation has been worked out or has been permeated with a means, the Thou becomes an object among objects— perhaps the chief, but still one of them, fixed in its size and its limits. . . .
>
> Every Thou in the world is by its nature fated to become a thing, or continually to re-enter into the conditions of things. In objective speech it would be said that every thing in the world, either before or after becoming a thing, is able to appear to an I as its Thou. But objective speech snatches only at a fringe of real life. (17)

The primary implication of this is that the fundamental religious quest, the project of restoring meaning to a world where Tao is camouflaged by the veil of experience, is to unravel the habituated tendencies to objectify, utilize, and otherwise render existentially unequal an ontologically integrated order. That is to say, each person is faced with the responsibility to "sit and forget" the entire gamut of cognitive judgments ("Inner Chapters" 19/6/92), to strive instead to fulfill the human share of the creative work of Tao, which is nothing other than "to embrace the ten thousand things and, by this, deem as one" ("Inner Chapters" 2/1/31). Still, such a process by no means results in detachment from or homogenizing of the world; rather, it moves one toward an orientation where there is the capacity to recognize and engage the world as it is, where one who is poised on the "axis of the way" can "respond without end" ("Inner Chapters" 4/2/30–31). Ironically, the task of "equalizing" things in the world is simply that of returning to an unsullied way of perceiving; the newly equalized elements of the world are transformed into nothing more than their actualities. "I encounter," writes Buber at the finale of the pivotal passage cited earlier, "no soul or dryad of a tree, but the tree itself" (1958:8). In other words, the enlightened mind functions less as a transformer than as a transmitter, as a mirror that allows one to take his or her stand in direct relation to another:[23] "If even water in its stillness illumines, how much more so does the stillness of the quintessential and spiritual, the heart-mind of the sage, the mirror of heaven and earth, the reflector of the ten thousand things" ("Syncretists" 33/13/4). The mirror metaphor has been an especially popular topic for a number of modern scholars, and many suggest that it is a central image for Taoist mysticism.[24] However, it is crucial to note that in the Taoist tradition, the image of the mirror does not connote the mood of passivity that it normally would in a Western philosophical context. The Taoist mind is likened to a mirror when it is exquisitely attuned and receptive, a condition probably attained only through some type of conscious and possibly rigorous meditative practice:

Bring to completion what you have received from Heaven, but without eyeing gain, simply being tenuous. The utmost man uses the heart-mind like a mirror, neither taking hold of nor welcoming, responding but not storing up. Therefore he is able to bear the weight of things but without doing injury. ("Inner Chapters" 21/7/31–33)

Obviously, the task of mirroring reality, of reflecting the world as it is, demands the kind of subtle awareness where difficult tensions—unity of Tao and diversity of manifestation, particularity and reciprocity of being—are spontaneously resolved. But Chuang Tzu is also aware that the world to be reflected contains social and intellectual structures that have been and will continue to be generated by the inevitable human propensity for differentiation, and this too must be mirrored; the final tension to be resolved is the one between existential construction and ontological reality. And so in one clever vignette, the monkey-keeper indulges his charges' apparently irrational desires for four nuts in the morning and three in the evening (instead of vice versa), while not compromising the integrity of his intentions: "That is why the sagely person harmonizes them by way of affirmation and negation, and comes to rest in Heaven's balance. This is called carrying out both" ("Inner Chapters" 5/2/37–40).[25] Indeed, this is the final step that renders Chuang Tzu's philosophy truly "earthy" or "worldly"—in sharp contrast with the "otherworldliness" discussed earlier—as even a new orientation toward reality does not result in a total transcendence of the perspectives that are supposedly left behind, for that would amount to a kind of abandonment. Buber, too, is sanguine about the need to bring together the two perceptual and expressive worlds that are not in as strong an opposition as one might anticipate: "And in all the seriousness of truth, hear this: without It man cannot live. But he who lives with It alone is not a man" (1958:34). Maurice Friedman repeatedly argues that one of the most often misunderstood aspects of Buber's philosophy is this "basic dialectic approach, which sees a fruitful interaction of form and structure with life rather than an antagonism between them" (1989:198).

The text of *Chuang Tzu* contains numerous illustrations of the appropriately integrative and responsive attitude, usually in the form of sarcastic admonitions to abandon the urges for objectification and utilization, all of which render the world far more complex and confused than it need be: "You see an egg and seek a crowing rooster, you see a crossbow and seek a roasted owl" ("Inner Chapters" 6/2/76–77). Similarly, when Hui Tzu is stumped by a gourd that is too large to make into either a ladle or a bowl, Chuang Tzu simply exhorts him to "make of it a big tub and go floating in rivers and lakes" ("Inner Chapters" 3/1/41–42). Evidently, the presupposition of categorical demarcations guarantees that each thing will invariably be relegated to an inadequate category, as the entity in its wholeness is reduced to a part or a perspective on it. Thus, a "sacred tortoise" would certainly prefer "to be alive and dragging its tail in the mud" than to be dead and have its bones preserved for three thousand years in the ancestral temple ("School of Chuang Tzu" 45/17/81–84), just as a sea bird would rather eat small fish and enjoy the freedom of flight than be confined within a lavish human banquet ("School of Chuang Tzu" 47/18/33–35). And of course, the elimination of value judgments allows one to encounter things with complete impartiality, as a dying Chuang Tzu is totally indifferent as to which parasites will soon be given the opportunity to devour his corpse ("School of Chuang Tzu" 90/32/47–52).[26] This motif is extended into encounters with other human beings as well: "The sage when meeting with (human relationships) does not depart, when passing by them does not hold on" ("School of Chuang Tzu" 59/22/38). Nevertheless, none of these examples depicts a state of indifference of self to other, for it is in fact the condition of connectedness that enables such a mirroring of and participation in Heaven and earth. Thus, a distraught Confucius laments, "Crows and magpies hatch, fish blow out foam, the thin-waisted transform, there is a younger brother and the elder brother cries; for too long I have not been a fellow with the transformations" ("School of Chuang Tzu" 40/14/81). Perhaps stated most simply: "I send off what goes and welcome what comes; that which comes is not to be restrained, that which goes is not to be stopped" ("School of Chuang Tzu" 52/20/27).

Several scholars have devised worthwhile conceptual schemes for articulating this unique but seemingly simple way of living in the world,[27] though the one provided by Lee Yearley, who strives to place Chuang Tzu's philosophy in the context of different typologies of mystical insight or experience, is particularly creative and compelling. Yearley contrasts Chuang Tzu's approach with two more familiar forms of mysticism—"the mysticism of unity that arises in South Asia" and "the mysticism of union that arises in the West" (1983:13)[28]—and he introduces the new category of "intraworldly mysticism," which describes an aesthetically attuned and wholly earthbound state of being. What is so striking about the typology is that it posits a form of mysticism where "no absolute reality is sought" beyond the inherent meaning of that which presents itself existentially; indeed, a mystic of this variety seeks nothing more (or less) than "a way through the world" (131). For such an adept, life is recognized ontologically as "a series of new beginnings" and experientially as "change . . . unencumbered by the normal oppositions of good and bad that our language gives us," where, consequently, "each new moment is grasped as it comes and surrendered

as it goes" (135). Furthermore, personal encounters maintain a
distinct integrity of both the beholder and the beheld, as one neither revels in the subjective enjoyment of something external nor
collapses the self into indulgence in the object. Both participants
are, in a sense, made more fully alive and real in the face-to-face
meeting:

> Most important, the crucial notion is not that the mind dispels
> emotion by its possession of a general perspective. Rather the
> crucial notion is that the mind holds to and lets go of events
> as they arise, pass before you, and disappear. You hold to each
> moment, you are attached to it, but the attachment to any
> particular occurrence does not persevere. The attitude Chuang-
> tzu commends is a complex mixture of attachment and
> detachment. A total involvement with each moment and
> enjoyment of it combine with a detachment from the moment
> once it passes and a lack of desire that it return. (135)

And while there are certainly some ways in which Yearley's
characterization seems less congenial to the I-Thou principle,[29] it
does bring to mind one dialogical concept that truly captures much
of Chuang Tzu's mood and intent: the issue of "presence" or "the
present" (Gegenwart), which Buber describes as "not fugitive and
transient, but continually present and enduring" (1958:13). Like
Buber, Chuang Tzu bears witness to the need to live in the
"present"—even his writings themselves "are pervaded by the
sensation . . . of a man jotting the living thought at the moment of
its inception" (Graham 1981:48)—but this is only accomplished when
one is, in fact, "present" and can touch directly the "presence" of
another. Given the actual nature of reality, the present cannot exist
for a person in pure solitude; the mirror is by definition the facili-
tator of dialogue: "The present, and by that is meant not the point
which indicates from time to time in our thought merely the conclusion of "finished" time, the mere appearance of a termination
which is fixed and held, but the real, filled present, exists only in
so far as actual presentness, meeting, and relation exist" (Buber
1958:12).

It is precisely this dynamic quality of "presentness" that has
inspired numerous Buber aficionados to extend his philosophy to

a surprising range of disciplines and experiences, to stretch the
limits of the three spheres—"life with nature," "life with men,"
and "life with spiritual beings" (6)—in which one finds potential
for the I-Thou relation. For example, at the 1991 International
Interdisciplinary Conference on Martin Buber's Impact on the
Human Sciences, some of the more intriguing papers demonstrated
the relevance of the dialogical principle for matters as diverse as
feminist theory, psychotherapy, athletic competition, Shake-
spearean drama, and "self-help" programs.[30] In one especially
intriguing presentation, Virginia Shabatay characterized mutuality as a condition created by and allowing for true honesty between persons, a topic addressed directly by Chuang Tzu: "As for
those who travel (with Tao), the four limbs will be strong, the
intellect will be sharp and penetrating, the ears and eyes will be
astute and clear, his employment of the mind-heart will be without effort, his responses to things will be honest" ("School of
Chuang Tzu" 58/22/31–32). And in another case: "Report the constant facts of the matter, do not report exaggerated words, and it
may as well be perfect" ("Inner Chapters" 10/4/47). Most of the
dialogical applications delivered at the conference seemed to build
on Buber's observation that "only he who knows relation and who
knows about the presence of the Thou is capable of decision"
(1958:51), and his implicit corollary that virtually any environ-
ment is a suitable arena for dialogical expression as long as one
is driven only by "his repeated decision to approach his destiny"
(60). That is to say, the I-Thou world, as though shedding its
camouflage, can burst into the I-It world anywhere and anytime;
and this mutuality of presence, as the self becomes fully realized
in relation, is manifested in diverse forms of genuine creative
expression:

This is the eternal source of art: a man is faced by a form
which desires to be made through him into a work. This form
is no offspring of his soul, but is an appearance which steps
up to it and demands of it the effective power. The man is
concerned with an act of his being. If he carries it through, if
he speaks the primary word out of his being to the form which
appears, then the effective power streams out and the work
arises. (9–10)

This model of creative power following from one's whole being can be applied imaginatively to the text of *Chuang Tzu*, as it adds a fascinating nuance to the repeated illustrations of exemplars (often seen as simpletons or grotesques) who execute the most mundane tasks effortlessly, almost magically. What on the surface appear to be hyperbolic illustrations of the sense of personal freedom that supposedly characterizes Taoist enlightenment are actually vivid depictions—"strange lyric and dramatic episodes" (Buber 1958:34)— of actualized beings who create presence in the midst of areas normally dominated by objectification, who engage all constituents of reality as subjects in themselves. And so, one character mistaken by Confucius for a ghost swims on the crest of a treacherous waterfall, explaining how he can "enter together with the inflow, emerge together with the outflow, follow the way of the water without imposing a private will on it" ("School of Chuang Tzu" 50/19/52–53). Likewise, the hunchbacked catcher of crickets never misses a single insect, for "despite the vastness of heaven and earth, the multiplicity of the ten thousand things, there is only the cognition of the cicada's wings" ("School of Chuang Tzu" 48/19/20). The most memorable account is of the ox-carver who never has to sharpen his blade, as he simply discerns the configurations of matter and energy so clearly that he can slide the edge of the knife through the spaces between the joints:

> That which I devote myself to is simply Tao, which extends beyond skill. At the time when I first began to carve oxen, I could see nothing but oxen. Three years later, I was still not yet seeing the ox as a whole. And now, I meet it by way of spirit, and do not look with my eyes. The senses and cognition know to stop, and the spirit carries out as it deigns to. I trust in Heaven's pattern, strike in the large seams, cleave through the large openings, and follow by what is inherently so. Thus, I never touch the smallest ligament or tendon, much less a main joint. ("Inner Chapters" 7/3/4–5)

In many ways, this particular segment is a paradigmatic model of what might be called "dialogical praxis." Here, the butcher is intent on meeting the ox as a whole being, but not to the extent that he or the remainder of the world is annihilated; and when he accomplishes his task, he does so not through ordinary experiential data, but through spirit, the very quality that Buber sees as binding I and Thou in relation. Finally, the entire process is guided by an underlying confidence in the workings of the cosmos, an understanding that one can realize one's destiny in such practice.[31] A number of other vignettes—some of which appear at least in part in Buber's text translation—give similar illustrations of this profound expertise within conventional situations. For example, Chuang Tzu introduces the reader to the engraver whose bellstand virtually carves itself as he "observes Heaven endowing the form and substance (of the wood)" ("School of Chuang Tzu" 50/19/54–59), along with the wheelwright who employs his chisel with just the right tension and speed as he "takes it in the hands, but responds with the heart-mind" ("School of Chuang Tzu" 36/13/68–74). There is also the elderly fisherman who blends seamlessly into the landscape ("School of Chuang Tzu" 56/21/47–48), the ferryman whose boat glides easily across the water ("School of Chuang Tzu" 48/19/22–26), the forger who continues to craft perfect buckles when in his eighties ("School of Chuang Tzu" 60/22/68–69), the archer who never misses the smallest target ("School of Chuang Tzu" 64/23/71–72), and another archer who would have a second arrow drawn as soon as the first one was fired ("School of Chuang Tzu" 56/21/55–56). Perhaps the one passage that best captures the diversity of spontaneous expressions is the one that portrays a snake, a millipede, a mythical one-legged beast, and the wind, all of which achieve their own perfect varieties of motion without any specific interpretive awareness of the "Heavenly mechanism" which drives them ("School of Chuang Tzu" 44/17/53–60).

It is crucial to note that all of the characters mentioned above shunt aside any suggestions of demonic possession or self-dissolution, professing instead simply to know Tao, just as "in every sphere in its own way, through each process of becoming that is present to us we look out toward the fringe of the eternal Thou" (Buber 1958:6). Most importantly, they describe a new orientation toward their tasks, one characterized by presence of the whole being, immediacy of other, and attentiveness without attachment, which together form an analogue to the condition described by Buber where "unconditional exclusiveness and unconditional inclusiveness are one" (78). In each case, the subject retains his or her self-identity, which becomes further actualized in the course of practice, but which does not cause other entities to be reduced to objects of experience or perception. The locus of meaning is therefore found in the organic moments of interaction, which are characterized by the relational spirit that can suffuse any human engagement in the world. Persons and things have their innate integrity and substantiality realized by virtue of this participation; in a manner of speaking, the quality of transcendence is made manifest in the immanent encounter, and the immanent encounter itself becomes imbued with the quality of transcendence: "He who enters on the absolute relation is concerned with nothing isolated any more, neither things nor beings, neither earth nor heaven; but everything is gathered up in the relation. For to step into pure relation is not to disregard everything but to see everything in the Thou, not to renounce the world but to establish it on its true basis" (78–79). In Livia (Knaul) Kohn's words, "The absolute is the now; it is right here to be participated in absolutely" (1992:55). As if to comment on the specific examples of dialogical praxis and to bring the discussion full circle, Buber writes:

> This is the activity of the man who has become a whole being, an activity that has been termed doing nothing: nothing separate or partial stirs in the man any more, thus he makes no intervention in the world; it is the whole man, enclosed and at rest in his wholeness, that is effective—he has become an effective whole. To have won stability in this state is to be able to go out to the supreme meeting. (1958:77)

Building on the Taoist distinction between non-doing and purposive doing, Buber distinguishes between true will and "arbitrary self-will" (*Willkür*), and thus between true freedom and "establishing of a purpose and devising a means. (61) Buber's notion of true freedom is not the negative doctrine of "freedom from the world" that Burton Watson (1968:3) ascribes to Chuang Tzu, but the affirmative freedom to carve oxen, enjoy the pleasure of the fish, contemplate the tree, and even ride the clouds, a freedom that is manifest in every integrated performance: "But the free man has no purpose here and means there, which he fetches for his purpose: he has only the one thing, his repeated decision to approach his destiny (Buber 1958:60). Thus, to know Tao, to undo affected discriminations and to mirror reality, is to return to one's own humanity. In Chuang Tzu's language, it is to complete one's heart-mind; in Buber's language, it is to realize one's true will. And it is through the fulfillment of this process that one attains a state of unconditional freedom:

> The free man is he who wills without arbitrary self-will. He believes in reality, that is, he believes in the real solidarity of the real twofold entity I and Thou. He believes in destiny, and believes that it stands in need of him. It does not keep him in leading-strings, it awaits him, he must go to it, yet does not know where it is to be found. But he knows that he must go out with his whole being. The matter will not turn out according to his decision; but what is to come will come only when he decides on what he is able to will. He must sacrifice his puny, unfree will, that is controlled by things and instincts, to his grand will, which quits defined for destined being. Then he intervenes no more, but at the same time he does not let things merely happen. He listens to what is emerging from himself, to the course of being in the world; not in order to be supported by it, but in order to bring it to reality as it desires, in its need of him, to be brought—with human spirit and deed, human life and death. (59–60)

The Question of Reception in Context

It has been my intention in this chapter to complete the task of evaluating Buber's contributions toward an understanding of *Chuang Tzu* by extending the interpretive framework established in the previous two chapters and thereby establishing the hermeneutic justification for relating Buber's dialogical principle to the text. It has been demonstrated that there are three distinct factors which, when taken cumulatively, warrant a consideration of *I and Thou* as a continuation of the interpretive process begun by Buber with *Reden und Gleichnisse*. First, there is the tremendous continuity between the proto-dialogical position developed in the Taoist volume—especially evidenced in the choice of translated material and a handful of crucial interpolations—and the mature dialogical position represented in *I and Thou*. This is not a case where one work merely anticipates or influences the other; rather, the elemental components of the I-Thou relation—existential primacy, individual integrity, necessity for relation, immanent transcendence—are actually manifest in the Taoist volume. Second, Buber's own hermeneutic, which plausibly establishes *Chuang Tzu* as the parable of a primordial teaching, identifies interpretation with the ongoing transformation of self before the text, a process which may continue with subsequent readings and reflections. Third, hermeneutic theories such as Hans Robert Jauss's "aesthetic of reception" provide a further rigorous basis for regarding interpretation of poetic texts as a dynamic, protracted, and interactive process. Once again, it is these three points which together lay the theoretical groundwork for regarding *I and Thou* as, at least in part, a work of interpretation, and it therefore becomes appropriate to assess its heuristic value for sinological inquiry into the text of *Chuang Tzu*.

Toward this end, I have explored a careful dialogical reading of *Chuang Tzu,* in order to determine the extent to which this theoretically justified approach can be legitimately and concretely realized. Here, I have argued that Chuang Tzu's complex metaphysical discussions and playful mystical vignettes can indeed be brought together through the lens of dialogical philosophy. Chuang Tzu's ontology establishes Tao as the ineffable and inexhaustible cosmic principle which is the progenitor of existential multiplicity and equality, thus generating a universe where all constituents of reality are distinct and interactive, yet hierarchically undifferentiated. The religious quest is the task of restoring equality to a world rendered existentially unequal by the intellectual habits of objectification, utilization, and reduction of things to components of experience. The solution lies in the spontaneous engagement with the world and the mirroring of reality as it is, thus producing a state that integrates both the beholder and the beheld through the organic process of encounter. This new orientation to the world is intelligently characterized by Lee Yearley as "intraworldly mysticism," where one embraces things in themselves and thereby brings to full realization the inherent meaningfulness of both self and other. In Buber's terms, such a mystic may also be understood as embodying "presence" or dwelling in "the present," which gives rise to spontaneous action generated from the "whole being," action taking a wide variety of creative forms. It is precisely this type of presence that is illustrated in Chuang Tzu's portrayals of perfected beings effortlessly executing their ordinary tasks, where each performance stems from the true will and embodies absolute freedom. Of course, these tasks are permeated by the knowledge and presence of Tao, just as each I-Thou relation for Buber is a glimpse of the eternal Thou.

Conclusion
Cross-Cultural Interpretations
and Hermeneutic Implications

Multiple Levels of Meaning

To recapitulate briefly, this project evaluates the contributions of Martin Buber's much overlooked *Reden und Gleichnisse des Tschuang-tse* toward the ongoing sinological enterprise of interpreting the text of *Chuang Tzu*. The book includes both a series of annotated translations and rigorous analyses of the document's form and content with respect to three hermeneutic models: historical reconstruction, interactive interpretation, and aesthetic reception. In isolation, each hermeneutic chapter produces its own set of insights and challenges, yet what seems most significant is how readily the Chinese text lends itself to the various models of meaning, as well as how the models themselves fit together as components of one sustained argument. It is, in fact, the purely reconstructionist model which supplies the context for the discussion of the teaching and its parable, the discussion which itself generates and substantiates the new interpretive model focusing on the interaction between reader and text. Similarly, this dynamic view of interpretation is itself extended to produce a unique reception hermeneutic, one that makes meaningful an encounter between Buber's dialogical philosophy and Chuang Tzu's mysticism, by establishing the I-Thou relation as a legitimate lens through which to interpret the text. Thus, the combination of hermeneutic models employed in this study is imaginative, but not arbitrary. And the major themes elucidated in the three chapters—i.e., the text as parable, unity and transformation, the nature of presence— though brought to light through separate hermeneutic paradigms,

187

can be best understood as related moments within a singular yet organic and fluid interpretive process.

Certainly, it is quite apparent that these multiple layers of interpretation—the conclusions produced both directly and indirectly by Buber's Taoist volume—are of considerable significance for one narrowly focused discourse, the critical study of a specific Chinese text. However, because of the peculiar nature of the encounter between Buber and *Chuang Tzu*, and because of the delicate hermeneutic issues involved, these conclusions also carry important ramifications for several broader areas of study. First, the credible rehabilitation of *Reden und Gleichnisse* leads one to inquire of *Chuang Tzu* specialists (and, by extension, Chinese textual scholars in general) exactly why its significance had not yet been acknowledged, or at least to speculate how such an oversight might be avoided in the future. Second, the newly established connections between Buber and *Chuang Tzu* may give cause to Buber scholars to reconsider the scope of Taoist influence in the dialogical writings and to note other resonances between Taoist and Jewish forms of mysticism. Finally, the direct juxtaposition of dialogical philosophy with Chuang Tzu's mysticism may suggest that the respective concerns of sinologists and Buber scholars—Buber's contributions toward explicating *Chuang Tzu* and the role of *Chuang Tzu* in Buber's philosophical development—are more closely related than one might anticipate, and that this relationship carries important implications for the methodological debate currently raging within the academic study of mysticism. Some of the implications for each of the three disciplines—sinology, Buber studies, mysticism—are illustrated briefly below.

The Sinological Issue:
Textual Study and Hermeneutic Self-Consciousness

Although one can only speculate, albeit intelligently, as to the reasons for the legacy of sinological indifference to Buber's Taoist volume, one can assert with reasonable confidence that the interpretations represented by the text translation and commentary would continue to be deemed marginal or inadmissible were it not for the kinds of hermeneutic experiments undertaken in this study.

This could suggest that the real factor keeping *Reden und Gleichnisse* in the shadows is not Buber's historical or linguistic limitation, but his overall interpretive framework, a particular perspective and agenda which simply do not speak substantively to the core of *Chuang Tzu* scholars. That is to say, the great divide separating Buber from genuine sinologists—a chasm that can be closed only through applications of alternative models of meaning—may actually be a matter more of hermeneutics than of competence.

This hypothesis gains credence when one examines even briefly the fairly self-contained networks that have formed among modern scholarly readers of *Chuang Tzu*. With some exceptions, a surprising lack of interface among the established discourses testifies to a kind of "hermeneutic determinism." In one corner, a compendium of scholars concerned primarily with matters of history and language—Harold Roth, Chad Hansen, A. C. Graham, et al.—seems to be engaged in one continuing debate, as the individual participants frequently address questions to one another and respond to one another's arguments. In a second corner, a more exegetical school—pioneered by Wu Kuang-ming and continued by Robert Allinson—assumes textual authority and employs the commentary tradition to demonstrate the text's application as a living and culturally transplantable spiritual document. In still a third corner, a rapidly proliferating group—identified chiefly with the late Isabelle Robinet and Livia (Knaul) Kohn—addresses the history of later influence and interpretation, emphasizing chiefly the transformations of mystical philosophy and practice. Lastly, a more anthropological network—Michael Saso, John Lagerwey, et al.—considers the text only insofar as it bears directly on living religious traditions, with particular respect to ritual and meditation.

The serious differences among these approaches are evident not only in their respective loci of inquiry, but also in the methodological presuppositions informing their inquiries, especially in the varying degrees of "sacrality" granted to the text. In particular, the dominant historical-critical school devotes itself exclusively to precanonical history; the singular purpose is to unearth the human voices behind the Chinese characters by unraveling the convoluted tangle of textual clues. When viewed through such a treasure-hunt approach, the text is, in the words of Wilfred Cantwell Smith, relegated to its "pre-scriptural phase" and treated "as if it were not scripture" (Smith 1989). Regarding such an accusation, A. C. Graham appears wholly unconcerned, as he sharply rejects the tendencies of other translators and interpreters to treat *Chuang Tzu* "as though it were what is nowadays understood by a 'book'" (1981:30), since "ancient Chinese thinkers did not write books, they jotted down sayings, verses, stories, thoughts and by the third century B.C. composed essays on bamboo strips, which were tied together in sheets and rolled up in scrolls" (27). Even the "Inner Chapters" sequence, according to Graham, "is not sacred, since there is no reason to suppose that Chuang-tzu ever did put his jottings in a definitive order" (32). Thus, in his list of methodological guidelines, Graham argues that it is the intellectually responsible translator who omits portions thought to be spurious or unimportant and rearranges the text by topic or supposed author (31–33). In essence—and, very ironically—this reconstruction of authorial intent entails a deconstruction of the text itself.

But while Graham is technically correct that *Chuang Tzu* is not "a book," he nevertheless does not come to grips with the fact that it has been for perhaps two millennia, and continues to be, regarded as such. So, the concerns of the other schools—spiritual transformation, history of interpretation, religious practice—are simply not addressed. On the other hand, the historical-critical approach clearly rankles those for whom the inviolability of the text is a prerequisite for any valid interpretation. Wu Kuang-ming, for instance, cites Graham's work principally to express opprobrium, and this sometimes takes on an uncharacteristically vitriolic tone. In one case, Wu claims that "the rambling unintelligibility of A. C. Graham's 'restored' text . . . amply testifies to the limits of textual criticism" (1990:20), while in another he makes reference to "Graham's sadly stale description of Taoism" (11). For those concerned with Taoism as a living religious tradition, there is even some skepticism about placing such primacy on the literary word. Michael Saso writes: "If the written source and the dictionary seem opposed to field work and the living tradition, it is because our research has not been deep enough, not because the modern Taoist meditator is in error" (1983:155). Moreover, all of these modern approaches to the text are implicitly faulted by the late historian Michel Strickmann, who argues that the Western fascination with philosophical documents like *Chuang Tzu* is disproportionate to its actual role in Taoist practice and its relation to other volumes in the Taoist Canon.[1] Again, while it tends to be on matters of actual interpretation that debates are generated within a specific discourse, it appears to be on matters of hermeneutic method that divisions are created between and among discourses.

True, it may be argued that distinct hermeneutic orientations justifiably produce separate discourses, that the philosophical concerns of Graham and Hansen are so divergent from those of Wu and Allinson (both of which are so detached from the respective social and historical concerns of Saso and Strickmann) that any attempt to integrate them could only follow from pure whimsy. However, I would maintain that such a position would not be defensible until a reasonable attempt were made to bring the hermeneutic positions themselves, not the interpretive fruits therefrom, into fruitful dialogue with one another. In most studies relating to *Chuang Tzu*, a good deal of attention is devoted to explaining and justifying the methodologies appropriate for a given interpretive end (e.g., reconstruction, exegesis, etc.), while relatively little effort is spent legitimating the end itself. In short, there is a critical lack of what I would call "hermeneutic self-consciousness." For example, Graham presents an exquisite set of methodological strictures necessary for historical reconstruction, without ever explaining—probably because it seems self-evident to him—why he identifies the locus of textual meaning with authorial intent. Similarly, Wu offers minimal justification for his concern with the role of the text in spiritual transformation, while Saso and Strickmann simply proceed from the presumed primacy of the "living tradition" and social history respectively. This question of which model or models of meaning should be applied to an interpretive enterprise is hardly a trivial one.

One can speculate that a new hermeneutic self-consciousness among scholars of *Chuang Tzu* (and, perhaps, among other Chinese textual scholars) might allow the unique nature and history of the document at hand to contribute explicitly to the determination of appropriate interpretive frameworks. It might also bring to light necessary connections among the various hermeneutic models, thus moving a fragmented academy one step closer toward a comprehensive discourse. Buber's encounter with *Chuang Tzu* is of

special interest because it at least purports to predicate the interpretations on a discussion of textual self-definition. And in turn,
this study's critical reflection on that encounter illustrates a case
in point where one model of meaning can generate another. It is,
in fact, only one application of hermeneutic self-consciousness that
establishes the relationship between Buber's dialogical philosophy
and Chuang Tzu's intraworldly mysticism, for an inestimable range
of possibilities now exists. As if to put forth a Taoistic hermeneutic
in her review of several books on *Chuang Tzu*, Miriam Levering
writes:

> Looking at these works, one is tempted to suggest that a
> successful Way of reading the *Chuang-tzu* must blend three
> elements: (1) the historian's canons of evidence and concern
> for understanding things in their own historical and cultural
> contexts; (2) the philosopher's search for analytic clarity; and
> (3) various kinds of disciplined imagination (e.g., existential,
> literary, cross-culturally comparative). Any of these taken alone
> can produce fascinating and informative readings, but rarely
> undistorted or "complete" ones. A definitive Way of reading
> the *Chuang-Tzu* would of necessity combine these three in
> perfect balance and harmony. The new studies under review
> display these virtues, but in unequal proportions. Taken
> together they give clues to the well-rounded reading this text
> demands. (1989:229)

The Buberian Studies Issue: The I-Thou Relation as Taoist Mysticism

As discussed in the first hermeneutic chapter, the occasional interest shown by Buber scholars in *Reden und Gleichnisse* has been
chiefly to identify the transitional nature of the philosophical position expressed in the afterword and to establish the lasting Taoist
influences on Buber's later writings. The handful of relevant studies, which reflect no more than a rudimentary understanding of
Taoist philosophy and omit any significant mention of the text translation, are useful but ultimately incomplete, as they evidently follow from a pair of suppositions which are certainly untenable in

light of this study. First, they approach the commentary as though it puts forth an independent philosophical position wholly abstractable from the textual encounter that facilitated it; the fact that it is a reflection on material culled from a completely separate intellectual context is treated almost incidentally. Second, they assume that *Chuang Tzu* and Taoism represent fixed entities, readily intelligible historically and philosophically, and that a study of Buber's commentary and later works would demonstrate how he responded to and was influenced by these "entities." Simply stated, in these passing treatments of Buber's Taoist volume, the authors do not address the complex issues of cross-cultural encounter and hermeneutic method, perhaps due to their relative unfamiliarity with the Chinese materials or their presumption that the dimensions of Taoist influence are easily localizable. Even more to the point, they attempt to discern how Buber was influenced, without significant concern for what actually influenced him and why it did so. At this juncture, it is no longer plausible to try to gauge the importance of Taoism in Buber's development without a considerable understanding of Taoism itself, of the intricate sinological discourse Buber inadvertently entered, and of the interactive interpretive method he employed, all of which together will facilitate a very different perspective on matters of influence and integration.

The most germane issue here is the hypothesis presented in the third hermeneutic chapter, that Chuang Tzu was, in a manner of speaking, the original dialogical philosopher some twenty-four hundred years ago, and that *I and Thou* can be regarded in part as a work of interpretation, representing a protracted transformation of self before the text of *Chuang Tzu*. It is almost trivial to note that this position would necessitate revisions in the current understanding of Buber's later writings, to reflect the insight that the I-Thou relation is, in effect, a culturally transplanted accretion to Taoist mysticism, an organic growth of Chuang Tzu's philosophy in a new historical and spiritual context. In fact, it is no longer feasible to conceptualize this solely as a matter of "influence," of what Chuang Tzu contributed to Buber's philosophical development, for now it is partly a matter of "transformation," of how Buber transformed Taoist philosophy through the organic vehicle of textual interpretation. As such, the implications for Buber studies may be at least as dramatic as those for sinology, since matters as elemental as the actual experience of relation and the path to its realization are now possibly subject to reconsideration. Clearly, this opens up a daunting scholarly enterprise which is more correctly the domain of Buber scholars, though one can safely speculate about subjects of likely interest. One key possibility may be the repeated allusions in Chuang Tzu's dialogues to some kind of meditative training, a topic that is especially relevant given how Buber, staying true to his Jewish mystical roots, offers so little concrete direction concerning how one can break free of the I-It orientation and begin to speak the I-Thou basic word. For example, one recurring and particularly compelling theme in *Chuang Tzu* is that of "fasting," the process of figuratively starving one's faculties in order to limit conventional subject-object perception. It is this kind of fasting that is attested to, for example, by the engraver who makes himself increasingly free of judgment and arbitrary discrimination until he becomes wholly present in his work ("School of Chuang Tzu" 50/19/56–58). The ideal condition is one where the physical and psychological energies of the practitioner are so attenuated that he or she brings nothing less than the whole being to each encounter:

> Unify your will. This is not listening with the ears, but listening with the heart-mind. This is not even listening with the heart-mind, but listening with the ch'i. Listening stops with the ears, the heart-mind stop with what tallies, but when the ch'i is made tenuous it is in wait of things. Only Tao gathers together the tenuous; as for this attenuation, it is the fasting of the heart-mind. ("Inner Chapters" 9/4/26–28)

Here, one is admonished to cease perceiving and contemplating things, to make diffuse (and thus unified) those partial and objectifying sensory tendencies, which are differentiated out from the totality of the person and which differentiate things in the world into fragments of experience. At least on the surface, this seems to suggest much of the character that Buber ascribes to the dialogical encounter: "I do not experience the man to whom I say Thou. But I take my stand in relation to him, in the sanctity of the primary word" (1958:9). However, the undulation from I-It to I-Thou is not only the quieting of experience, it is also the activating of an incipient relational capacity—"the a priori of relation" (27)—that is extraordinarily elusive to those not at refined levels of awareness and is evoked only in highly metaphorical language. Thus, it may be relevant that part of Chuang Tzu's fasting of the heart-mind involves an active and affirmative component, the subtle cultivation of something other than the senses as ordinarily understood. For example, the student who is exhorted to "fast and practice austerities to clear and purge your heart-mind" is equally urged to "cleanse and purify your quintessence and spirit" ("School of Chuang Tzu" 58/22/29). Of course, such references to "quintessence," "spirit," and "ch'i" are not necessarily any more helpful for the uninitiated than are Buber's own references to taking one's stand in relation. But if these elements do indeed hold some practical key to entering into a dialogical orientation, then it becomes all the more potentially fruitful for Buber scholars, as well as aspirants for relation, to become conversant in the wider Taoist discourse.

Another notion put forth in *Chuang Tzu* that may suggest a related meditative technique is that of "sitting and forgetting," the process of progressively diminishing evaluative discrimination. "When there are no more categories of perception," Livia (Knaul) Kohn writes, "life and death subjectively cease to exist" (1991:14). Again, how this translates into concrete practice is not made at all explicit, though later interpreters would develop their own techniques and traditions (see Kohn 1987). Nevertheless, this does call to mind Lee Yearley's account of "intraworldly mysticism," as the specific method that he infers involves a variant of forgetting, where "intense involvement for a short time joins with forgetfulness" (1983:136):

> The ideal state sought by the radical Chuang-tzu is an intraworldly mysticism where you focus intently on the perception that is directly present before you but pass on to another perception when a new perception comes or the old one fades. This "hold and let go" approach sees life as a cinema show, a series of passing frames, a kaleidoscope of ever-changing patterns. (130)

And it should be recalled that Buber's concept of "presence" entails a simultaneous embracing of the dignified other (as Thou) and letting slip away of the objectified other (as It): "True beings are lived in the present, the life objects in the past" (1958:13).

But perhaps it would be most useful for Buber scholars to consider how the text of *Chuang Tzu* has actually functioned as a manual for meditation in Taoist monastic communities, information that is becoming increasingly available thanks to Michael Saso's field work among the Cheng-i tz'u-t'an Taoists of northern Taiwan. In this tradition, each of the seven "Inner Chapters" corresponds to a particular stage of meditative practice. The entire process involves a number of esoteric techniques, all of which are directed toward the goal of "union with the tao by the exorcising or sending out of selfish desires, glory, and good name, as well as externalizing the spirits and demons of the popular religion" (Saso 1983:154). And though the articulated goal may not appear directly relevant to Buber's dialogical philosophy, the sequence does include two interesting variants of the phenomenon of fasting. On the one hand, this tradition characterizes the fasting of the heart-mind as "a practice which will lead to the ability of listening for primordial breath with the ears of the heart" (146). And on the other hand, it introduces the practice of "fasting from discourse on the world of multiplicity," a technique whereby "the novice must be taught to abstain from discursive reasoning, debate, philosophy, and the pursuit of knowledge for self-aggrandizement or fame" (143). It is important to note that the problem is not with the world of multiplicity itself, but with the fundamental orientation of "discourse" toward that world. And for Buber: "The world has no part in the experience. It permits itself to be experienced, but has no concern in the matter. For it does nothing to the experience, and the experience does nothing to it" (1958:5).

Of course, these speculations about meditative techniques represent only one avenue within a wide range of possibilities. Moreover, just as there is continuity (rather than identity) between Buber's proto-dialogical position in the Taoist volume and the mature dialogical philosophy in *I and Thou,* so too the methods introduced by Chuang Tzu may resonate with (rather than define) the quest for relation. The key point here is that a comprehensive understanding of the life of dialogue is contingent upon some appreciation of the Taoist philosophy that partially informed it; and in turn, this understanding of Chuang Tzu's philosophy is predicated upon some familiarity with its Chinese contexts. Indeed, here is an important case where the intellectually responsible scholar in Jewish studies will look to material that at first appears temporally and spatially disconnected from his or her topic of inquiry.

The Mysticism Issue: The Rehabilitation of Comparative Study

Because so much of this project amounts to arguments and conclusions that might be considered "comparative" in nature, its most important implications may lie in the challenges it brings to the modern study of mysticism, a discipline that is becoming increasingly dominated by a methodology that is sometimes labelled "particularist" or "contextualist." This new particularism, identified most with Steven Katz, though owing an obvious debt to Gershom Scholem, is largely a conscious response to the previous dominance of adherents to "the perennial philosophy" or simply "perennialism," which puts forth, according to one of its most ardent critics, "the view that mysticisms are essentially the same, that summons up the dark night in which all cats are gray" (Gimello 1990:10). In truth, perennialism, at least Huston Smith's variety of it, is not quite so nihilistic, but instead proceeds from the assumptions that ultimate truth is singular, that there are certain archetypal cross-cultural phenomena which express that truth, and that these archetypes establish conceptual centers around which comparative study can be based. Nevertheless, Robert Gimello contends that this approach has historically lent itself to "affectation of an aristocratic spiritual individualism," where many of its proponents have the ulterior yearning "to join an imagined company of mystical illuminati, a trans-cultural and trans-historical brotherhood of 'seers' and spiritual heroes who were thought to feed . . . only on the distilled 'essence of all religions,' an elixir of 'pure . . . mystical experience'" (1990:2). Such comments are not only playful entries in an exaggerated polemic, they are also indicative of how fiercely suspicion is cast on those who still strive academically to find commonality among traditions or practically to draw without restriction from multiple traditions:

Such attitudes have not vanished, by the way. They are still very much in the air—in the works by the likes of Frithjof Schuon, for example, whose theory of "the transcendental unity of religions" the great theologian and historian of religion Henri de Lubac rightly called "esoterically pretentious." Much the same might be said of the too many works by the insufferable Joseph Campbell, and of the current epidemic of enthusiasm for the "new age." (2)

On the other hand, the particularists begin from the view, quite reasonable by today's standards, that mystical insights and experiences are historically and culturally specific phenomena—i.e., "constructed" by their contexts—and that any rigorous study should situate them squarely in those contexts. "Mysticism," Gimello writes, "is inextricably bound with, dependent upon, and usually subservient to the deeper beliefs and values of the traditions, cultures, and historical milieux which harbour it" (1983:63). But while this approach has rescued the study of mysticism from sometimes blatant ahistoricism, it too lends itself to two overly severe corollaries: that mysticism does not exist as a sui generis category and, consequently, that an understanding of a particular historical occurrence of mysticism has no a priori bearing on understanding a separate occurrence. Taken together, these two points render somewhat suspect the entire enterprise of a "comparative" study of mysticism, for there is now no basis to expect that an accumulation of cross-cultural data will produce either generalizations about the nature of mysticism itself as a singularly conceived phenomenon or enhanced understandings of each of the specific mystical phenomena. Stated simply by Scholem, "There is no mysticism as such, there is only the mysticism of a particular religious system, Christian, Islamic, Jewish mysticism and so on" (1941:6).

However, the study in this volume poses an important challenge to the particularist school, as it demonstrates that Buber's dialogical principle is a valid interpretive lens for interpreting Chuang Tzu's intraworldly mysticism, while also laying the theoretical and historical groundwork for exploring how Taoist philosophy and practice can help one better to understand or realize the I-Thou relation. Moreover, the implicit typological connection established serves to caution the academy against too soon dismissing mysti-

cism as a conceptual category. What is most significant about this
study is how it is not simply an arbitrary block of comparisons of
themes wrenched from their contexts; rather, it is a rigorous interpretive project grounded in both the historical evidence of Buber's
encounter with *Chuang Tzu* (particularly *Reden und Gleichnisse*)
and the methodological cornerstones of hermeneutic theory. Thus,
the conclusions are generated not from a perennialist perspective,
but from the same concern for context that so preoccupies Katz and
his allies, where the entire issue of what exactly is meant by "context" is called into question at the same time. The subject is an
important one, because it is not unusual for scholars to define
context in such a way that it shuts inconvenient or undesirable
topics out of a discourse, because of unexamined epistemological
assumptions or political motivations. Certainly, the most salient
example is the argument summarized in the second hermeneutic
chapter that comparison or dialogue between Hasidic mysticism
and Buber's I-Thou relation is inappropriate, on the basis that the
two are contextually discontinuous, that the former conforms to a
predetermined definition of true Jewish mysticism while the latter
represents a renegade existentialism. Still, some of the particularists are well aware that the question of context can produce a
range of possibilities:

When I speak of mysticism as something that can be
understood only within its contexts—when I go further to
suggest that mysticism is always conditioned by, born of, or
constituted by, those contexts—I am not only referring to
entirely mundane contexts. Language, literature, art, culture
generally, institutions, methods of practice, codes of behavior,
arrays of symbols—all of these things which I have particularly
in mind when I speak of contexts are *not*, so the religions that
foster them claim, merely human contrivances. They are also
vehicles for the transmission of what might be called the
influence of the transcendent. When I speak, for example, of
the discursive, literary, and scriptural contexts or determinants
of mystical experience I am not speaking of "the prison house
of language" that a modern Marxist literary theorist like
Frederic Jameson might have in mind; nor am I speaking of
the mad-house, or the fun-house of mirrors, out of which

Derrida and the deconstructionists seem unable to find their way. Rather, I am speaking of such things as *verbum Dei* or *buddha-vacana*, and of such human discourse as is inspired thereby. (Gimello 1990:17–18)

I would take Gimello's point one step further by arguing that if one accepts Hans Penner's point that mysticism as a conceptual category is an "illusion . . . the result of an abstraction which distorts the semantic or structural field of a religious system" (1983:96), then one should also reach the same conclusion about such categories as "religious system" and "cultural context." That is to say, if the purpose of the new methodological particularism is to rescue the study of mysticism from the entropy of philosophical speculation and return it to its rightful place as a topic within the "history of religions," then it is essential to recall Wilfred Cantwell Smith's landmark observation that these "religions" should be thought of not as discrete, easily compartmentalized entities, but as living historical complexes that are in constant interaction with one another, often overlapping in unusual and unanticipated ways.[2] Once again, it should be noted that this formulation augments, rather than undermines, the particularist view, as it shares the assumption that it is appropriate to "regionalize" the study of mysticism, but also stresses that a tremendous number of factors are involved in informing and determining each "region." And part of this determination, particularly in this modern era of widespread literacy and intellectual exchange, is the historical role of interpretation, either textual or otherwise. As this study demonstrates, Martin Buber and the text of *Chuang Tzu*, which superficially appear so historically disjoint from each other so as not to allow for meaningful comparison, are now actually part of each other's hermeneutic-historical contexts. Bringing them into a disciplined comparative study is not merely possible, but ultimately necessary in order to obtain a complete picture.

It is thus premature to discard a comparative study of mysticism, even within the particularistic paradigm; in fact, this project establishes some workable parameters by which such a study may be conceived. Consequently, it is also premature to dismiss the concept of mysticism in and of itself. Perhaps this book will provide further impetus to scholars interested in various forms of mysticism to continue undertaking comparative work without fear that doing so necessitates conflating their subjects and sacrificing historical integrity. They may soon discover some remarkable connections in highly unlikely places.

✿-NOTES-✿

Preface

1. The compendium of folk tales, entitled *Chinesische Geister- und Liebesgeschichten (Chinese Ghost and Love Stories)*, is a selective translation of P'u Sung-ling's *Liao-chai chih-i*, a massive collection of fables and fantastic stories. The unpublished essay, "Besprechungen mit Martin Buber in Ascona, August 1924 über Lao-tse's Tao-te-king" ("Discussions With Martin Buber on Lao Tzu's Tao Te Ching, in Ascona, August 1924"), which was drawn from lectures held over a three-week period, is on file at the Martin Buber Archive, Jewish National and University Library (JNUL), Jerusalem, Arc. Ms. Var. 350/2–45. To date, the most informative, though by no means complete, study of Buber's unpublished essay on the *Tao Te Ching* (as well as Buber's 1942 Hebrew translation of eight chapters) is found in Eber 1994.

2. As just one example, Buber cites a passage from *Chuang Tzu* in the 1956 essay, "Dem Gemeinschaftlichen folgen," later translated by Maurice Friedman as "What Is Common to All." See Buber 1956, Buber 1958a.

3. I learned this through a telephone conversation with Professor Page, in the fall of 1990.

Introduction

1. For example, Livia Kohn speculates about their content based on materials extant in a Japanese temple, and Harold Roth reports that several passages have been tentatively located in the *Huai-nan Tzu*. It should be noted that many of Kohn's early works are listed under the author's unmarried name, Livia Knaul; in order to avoid confusion, I hereafter refer to her as Livia (Knaul) Kohn, regardless of how the particular article or text is indexed. See Kohn 1982: 53–79; Roth 1991:116.

2. Of course, one should be advised to accept the premise of a "final" recension cautiously, as it has been noted by John B. Henderson that chunks of commentary by Kuo Hsiang and later interpreters may have "crept into the text even in post-T'ang (618–906 C.E.) times." Furthermore, alternative arrangements of the text were suggested well into the second millennium C.E., although the Kuo Hsiang edition has remained more or less orthodox. See Henderson 1991:69; Roth 1991:80.

3. The "mystical" interpretation reflects that of Kuo Hsiang's edition and commentary, which has been accepted as standard by the majority of Chinese thinkers since then. For information on the individualistic interpretation—which Kohn suggests was represented by the commentaries and textual arrangement in lost editions by Ts'ui Chuan and Hsiang Hsiu, both of which slightly predated the Kuo Hsiang edition—see Kohn 1992: 69. On the subject of freedom, see Watson 1968:3 and Kohn 1985a:71–79. On language and epistemology, see Hansen 1991: 179–208. On asceticism, see Kohn 1985a:80–81. On landscape painting, see Chang 1963:199–238, and Shaw 1988:183–206. On poetry, see Chang 1963:169–198, and Lynn 1970:228–229. On Ch'an Buddhism, see Kohn 1986:411–428. On immortality cults, see Kohn 1992:81–95. On class conflicts, see Louie 1986:119. On meditation, see Saso 1983:140–157.

4. Graham (1981) includes translations of about eighty percent of the text. Wu (1990) includes translations of the first three chapters. A new version by Victor H. Mair is the first complete English translation in nearly thirty years. Mair's stated intention—"to present Chuang Tzu as a preeminent literary stylist and to rescue him from the clutches of those who would make of him no more than a waffling philosopher or a maudlin minister of the Taoist faith"—perhaps suggests an implicit rebuke of Graham and Wu respectively. See Mair 1994:xii.

5. A new and rigorous study by Liu Xiaogan challenges Graham's documentary hypothesis in some interesting ways, grouping chapters into slightly different blocks and assigning different labels to the hypothetical authors. However, Liu's new textual arrangements do not in any significant way effect the connections drawn here. See Liu 1994.

6. While Wang's contributions to the Taoist volume are unclear, he is specifically credited as a contributor to *Chinesische Geister- und Liebesgeschichten*. Buber 1911:9.

7. Before leaving Germany in 1911, Wang wrote *Die Staatsidee des Konfuzius and ihre Beziehung zur konstitutionellen Verfassung*, a conservative study of the challenges facing traditional Confucian ethics in the

emerging Chinese republic. The text was not published until 1913 (appearing as both an essay in *Mitteilungen des Seminars für Orientalische Sprachen* and an independent monograph), although an English translation *(Confucius and New China: Confucius' Idea of the State and its Relation to Constitutional Government)* was issued in 1912 by Shanghai's Commercial Press. Because of the arbitrary fashion by which Chinese names had been romanized, as well as the paucity of relevant documents, there is no certainty as to the characters or even the actual pronunciation of Wang's name. His letters to Buber, as well as other documents bearing his signature, were usually signed "Chingdao Wang," "C. Wang," "Ch. Wang," or, rather oddly, "C. H. Wang." And though the German article was published under the name "Ching Dao Wang," most current bibliographies, including the Library of Congress, for no explicit reason list the author as "Wang Ching-t'ao." This is also the name of the author of a 1927 Chinese publication, *Min-sheng-chu-yi yü Jen-k'ou Wen-t'i (The People's Livelihood and the Population Problem)*, which addresses an economic issue from the perspective of the Kuomintang. Given the coincidence in the names and the similarity in traditionalist-nationalist ideology, Wang Chingdao may be tentatively identified as Wang Ching-t'ao, although there is, as of this writing, still no definitive proof of this. In the introduction to *Chinese Tales,* Irene Eber refers to him as "Wang Jingdao"; in an expansion of this essay for a journal article, she accepts the plausible connection and refers to him as "Wang Ching-t'ao." See Eber 1991, 1994.

8. The original manuscript of only the first half of the completed essay, which makes but a single passing reference to Chuang Tzu at the very end, still exists at the Buber Archive. This suggests that Buber may have later appended the section specifically addressing Chuang Tzu for the purpose of making the essay directly relevant to the translation. JNUL, Arc. Ms. Var. 350.

9. See von Strauss 1870. Mystic and sinologist von Strauss is, unfortunately, best remembered as one of the most recent scholars to seek a correspondence between three Chinese characters used to describe Tao and the Hebrew tetragrammaton. His approach to the *Tao Te Ching* is discussed in some detail in Eber 1994.

10. *The Classic of Purity and Rest* is one small entry in the Taoist Canon; its complete title is *T'ai-shang Lao-chün Shuo-ch'ang Ch'ing Cheng Miao Ching (The Most Revered Lao-chün's Secret Classic of Eternal Purity and Rest).* Lao-chün is, of course, an epithet for Lao Tzu. *Lieh Tzu* is widely recognized as a third century C.E. forgery that bears the name of a possibly historical Taoist sage who is a frequent character in *Chuang Tzu.*

He appears here in two segments translated by Buber, sections XXI (pages 38–39) and XL (page 56).

11. Irene Eber notes that in the years immediately prior to this final edition, Buber exchanged correspondence with sinologist Willy J. Tonn (who appended a brief pronunciation guide to this volume) with regard to possible revisions. In light of the pains that Buber took in revising the two later editions, Eber's claim that Buber had apparently lost interest in Chuang Tzu well before the third edition is somewhat puzzling. See Eber 1991:xi–xii; Eber 1994:456.

12. The original manuscript of Friedman's translation—typed, with handwritten corrections—indicates that most of these deletions had not yet occurred. In a letter to Friedman dated November 17, 1956, Buber states that six pages of remarks on the manuscript were to be sent under separate cover. Unfortunately, this correspondence is presently lost or unfindable. Nevertheless, it is Friedman's recollection that Buber's comments on translated texts tended to address the choice of language rather than substantive changes in the material. Moreover, Buber had stated only five years before, in the preface to the final edition, that the essay "should not be altered" (see page 15).

Text Translation

Preface to the 1951 Edition

1. This is poet Hugo von Hofmannsthal (1874–1929).

I. The Inactive Man

1. The 1910 edition reads, "I heard Chieh Yü expressing something immoderate, which was of an illicit foolishness and had neither sense nor intelligibility."

2. Buber liberally translates a number of different words and phrases as *Geist, geistige,* or *geistergleich,* and he sometimes employs these terms for fairly loose paraphrases. The Chinese behind "spirit-like man" is *shen-jen,* and many modern translators are comfortable rendering *shen* as "spirit" or "spiritual." However, Graham suggests that "daemonic" (as used by

Goethe) or "numinous" (as used by Rudolf Otto) would be most appropriate for capturing that unique power or presence that falls outside the realm of rational experience. In the cases where *Geist* is evidently a translation of "spirit" and the Chinese is indeed *shen*, I retranslate it as "spirit" (or "spiritual," if appropriate); in the instances where it is evidently a translation of "mind" and the Chinese is *hsin* (literally "heart-mind"), I retranslate it as "mind." In all other cases, its usage is noted. See A. C. Graham 1981:36.

3. Buber's text contains an inconsequential footnote explaining that the "four seas" include that which is beyond the frontiers of the terrestrial world, a paraphrase from the body of Giles's translation. See Giles 1889:7.

4. This sentence, nearly a direct translation from Giles, is an apparent gloss of *ch'i shen ning* ("his spirit is concentrated"), considered by Wang Yü, an eleventh century interpreter, to be one of the most important phrases in the entire text. See Ch'ien Mu 1951:5.

5. Buber employs the word *Seelen* in a number of different places, though it here appears to be his own gloss; the Chinese is *chih*, translatable as "knowing," "knowledge," "perceiving," or "perception."

6. A more plausible translation of the Chinese would read, "This man, through his power/virtue, will embrace the ten thousand things and deem as one."

7. The German *Umgestaltung* is one of three words used by Buber that are best translated as "transformation," though he consistently employs *verwandeln* for the verb form. These terms—*Umgestaltung, Änderung, Wandlung*—are each employed in very specific circumstances, and all appearances of them are noted hereafter. Despite the translation, the Chinese in this instance does not include the very important character *hua;* rather, it reads *shih ch'i hu luan*, "the age leans toward chaos."

III. The Organ-Playing of Heaven

1. Before 1951, the chapter is entitled "The Music of Heaven."

2. The Chinese translates literally as ". . . as though he had lost his mate." Buber translates directly from Giles, whose rendering is in accord with the suggestion of Ssu-ma Piao, that "mate" refers to the relation between body (*shen*) and spirit (*shen*). See Giles 1889:12; Ch'ien Mu 1951:8.

3. The Chinese includes the fairly often discussed phrase *ta-k'uai yi ch'i*, translated as straightforwardly as possible by Graham as "that hugest clumps of soil blows out breath," personified by Watson as "the Great Clod belches out breath." As for Buber's sources, Giles rendered it as "breath of the universe," Legge as "breath of the Great Mass (of nature)," and Balfour as "breathing of the immaterial energy in Heaven and Earth (nature)." This phrase also includes the very problematic character *ch'i*, which has been variously translated as "breath," "energy," "psychophysical stuff," "vital force," and so forth. Because *ch'i* has virtually entered modern Western vocabulary through its place in acupuncture, martial arts, and New Age literature, I hereafter leave this term untranslated. See A. C. Graham 1981:48; Watson 1968:36; Giles 1889:12; Legge 1891:225; Balfour 1881:10.

4. Graham suggests that the true conclusion to this dialogue is misplaced in a later chapter of the text, and that what follows is actually a separate discussion. The original text for much of the remaining portion is written not in prose, but in poetry, a fact ignored by Buber's main sources; the uncomfortable and sometimes unintelligible prose in Buber's translation reflects the confusion of Giles et al. See A. C. Graham 1981:49–50.

5. Buber appears to arrive at *geist* by translating from Giles, who rendered it as "mind," though it may in fact be from Legge or Balfour, who both rendered it as "soul." The Chinese is *hun*, the aspect of the soul that ascends up into the aether after a person's death. The complete phrase translates more plausibly as "In sleep the souls interweave, when awake the bodies open." See Giles 1889:14; Legge 1891:226; Balfour 1881:11.

6. The Chinese translates more plausibly as ". . . the heart-mind that nears death cannot be made to return to *yang*." Even more so than ch'i, the terms *yin* and *yang*, the female and male principles, have found their way comfortably into the English language and remain untranslated hereafter.

IV. The Conditioned and the Unconditioned

1. Buber omits a brief part of this exchange, where the two characters playfully express some confusion about consciousness of one's capacity to know or not to know.

2. The Chinese refers not to "good and bad" but to *jen* and *yi*, the two principal Confucian virtues of "benevolence" and "rightness"; not ex-

actly to "yes and no," but to *shih* and *fei*, best translated by Graham as "that's it" and "that's not." See A. C. Graham 1981:58.

3. The 1910 edition reads, "If the Milky Way froze ..."

V. Antitheses and Infinity

1. The German text actually reads "Fu-tse" ("Kung-Fu-Tse" before 1951). The 1951 edition also includes a footnote explaining that this is, in fact, Confucius.

2. Before 1951, the text reads, "... the true sage ..."

3. This is the first appearance of the central term *Tao* in the text translation. Buber includes a brief footnote, explaining that Tao is the path (*die Bahn*), the primordial foundation (*Urgrund*) and primordial sense (*Ursinn*) of existence. The prefix "*Ur-*," which Buber uses frequently, is here translated as "primordial" for all words that do not have a conventional English equivalent. So as not to conflate *Sinn* and *Geist*, I translate the former as "sense" whenever possible.

4. Buber's text contains an inconsequential footnote, basically a paraphrase of Giles, discussing the Yellow Emperor's legendary status and relation to Lao Tzu. See Giles 1889:29.

5. Before 1951, "... the sage ..."

6. Graham suggests that this marks the end of the dialogue, and that the remainder is actually a separate essay (Graham 1981:60).

7. This is a paraphrase of Giles, who was in accord with Chu Kuei-yao's reading of the phrase *he chih yi t'ien-ni*, "harmonize them by way of Heaven's equality." However, there is much discussion over the meaning of the character *ni*; Graham, for example, renders *t'ien ni* as "the whetstone of Heaven," following Lu Te-ming's *Ching-tien shih-wen*. See Giles 1889:31; Graham 1981:60; Wu 1990:169.

8. This is where an interesting fragment of the essay, a continuing discussion of disputation, is omitted. There is much debate as to whether this portion is mislocated, and Buber evidently found it either spurious or unintelligible.

9. The Chinese translates more plausibly as "... forget years, forget rightness."

10. Before 1951, the text reads, "Step into the realm of the infinite, in your chosen repose." The Chinese translates more plausibly as, "Be shaken by the limitless, and thus lodge things in the limitless."

VI. The Butterfly

1. Before 1951, the text reads ". . . in all intents and purposes a butterfly. I knew only that I followed my moods like a butterfly, and was unconscious of my humanity."

2. The German is *Wandlung,* the second and most interesting word employed by Buber for "transformation." The Chinese reads *wu-hua,* literally "transformations of things." Although Buber may be translating from Legge, who rendered it as "Transformation of Things," or Balfour, who rendered it as "metamorphosis," the language throughout this essay suggests that he is, in fact, translating from Giles, who translated *wu-hua* with the very problematic "Metempsychosis." Thus, Buber may have chosen *Wandlung* for its theological implication (as "transubstantiation"); his other applications of this term in the translation may lend some credence to this hypothesis. See Legge 1891:245; Balfour 1881:31; Giles 1889:32.

VII. The Cook

1. The Chinese translates more plausibly as, "When senses know to stop, but the spirit desires to carry it out, I trust in Heaven's patterning."

2. The Chinese *yang-sheng* ("tending" or "nurturing life"), a phrase from the original chapter title, is the central principle in the thought of Yang Chu, possibly Chuang Tzu's senior or contemporary. It has been suggested by Lee Yearley that Chuang Tzu may have once been an advocate of the Yangist school of body nurture, and that one story in the text (not included in Buber's translation) gives partial testimony to his disaffection and subsequent "conversion" to the cult of spontaneity. As noted in the introduction, though *Chuang Tzu* includes several chapters penned by "Yangist" authors, Buber selects none for his translation. See A. C. Graham 1981:172.

VIII. The Death of Lao Tzu

1. Chuang Tzu occasionally employs the older term *Ti* to depict Heaven anthropomorphized; Giles's translation, "God," is common and

serviceable. The Chinese phrase literally translates as "God's loosening of the region," although it is commonly read as something closer to "God's loosening of the reins." See Giles 1889:37.

IX. With Men

1. Buber's text contains a short footnote explaining that Yen Hui was the favorite disciple of Confucius.

2. The 1910 edition reads, "The therapeutics comprise various and multifarious illnesses."

3. The Chinese translates more plausibly as, "Tao desires not to be made a mixture; if a mixture, then it becomes many; if many, then there is a disturbance; if a disturbance, then there is sadness."

4. The Chinese includes no mention of Tao, but translates as, "The perfect men of antiquity first obtained in themselves, and then obtained in others." Before 1951, the passage reads, "The sages of antiquity . . ."

5. Though the Chinese text simply reads *chih*, translated adequately by Giles as "Wisdom," Buber notes that in this instance Chuang Tzu appears to be talking pejoratively about ordinary cognition; thus, he translates it as *Klugheit*. See Giles 1889:39.

6. Giles, like many other translators, sometimes rendered *hsin* as "mind" and sometimes as "heart." Unless otherwise noted, the term "heart" is a retranslation of *Herz* as a rendering of *hsin*.

7. There is a large section of the essay omitted here, including more hypothetical discussion of the types of tyrants Yen Hui may encounter and historical examples of self-aggrandizing altruists whose good intentions were not met warmly.

8. This sentence is especially noteworthy only because in it Buber employs two terms, *Wesen* and *Haltung*, both of which would later appear in his dialogical philosophy. The somewhat ambiguous Chinese translates loosely as, "What can be discerned in the appearance is not stable." Buber paraphrases from Legge ("His feelings are not to be determined from his countenance"), who apparently followed Kuo Hsiang's suggestion that this phrase refers to how the motivations of the prince of Wei cannot be seen in his face. For the most part, I translate *Wesen* as "being," though in a few places it is more appropriate to render it as "essence." See Legge 1891:254; Watson 1968:56.

9. The Chinese translates more plausibly as, ". . . one who is a follower of Heaven."

10. Before 1951, all references to "antiquity" instead read "the sages of antiquity."

11. The Chinese reads *hsin-chai*, "heart-mind fasting."

12. The Chinese translates more plausibly as, "This is not listening with the ears, but listening with the heart-mind. This is not even listening with the heart-mind, but listening with ch'i."

13. The Chinese translates more plausibly as, "When the ch'i is made tenuous, it is in wait of things. Only Tao gathers together the tenuous; as for this attenuation, it is the fasting of the heart-mind."

14. The 1910 edition reads, "If you can enter into this man's realm without injuring his self-love, cheerful when he hears you, unmoved when he does not, without skill, without medicine, simply living within the state of perfect equanimity—then you will be near success."

15. The Chinese translates more plausibly as, "To be an envoy on man's behalf, it is easy to be taken as artifice; to be an envoy on Heaven's behalf, it is difficult to be taken as artifice."

16. The Chinese translates as, "Ghosts and spirits will come and dwell."

17. The Chinese translates as, "This is the transformation of the ten thousand things."

X. Training of Princes

1. The Chinese translates more plausibly as, "In form, nothing compares with approaching; in heart-mind, nothing compares with peace."

2. The 1910 edition also includes the phrase "will plunge to the ground."

3. The 1910 edition reads, "If he puts down all sense of decency, so you must also put it down."

4. The 1910 edition reads, "Thus you will meet him without injuring him."

5. Buber's text contains an inconsequential footnote that describes the praying mantis.

6. The 1910 edition reads, "Those who love horses surround them with a multitude of conveniences."

XI. The Holy Tree

1. The Chinese actually refers to a tree beside a local earth-god shrine.

2. The 1910 edition reads, "Is a worthless man whose time of dangers are not yet over the right person to talk about a worthless tree?" Moreover, this is not the actual end of the essay; Buber omits the section where the carpenter wakes, reports the dream to his apprentice, and discusses the limitations of conventional standards for judging such a tree.

XII. The Mutilated Man

1. Before 1951, the text reads, ". . . a sage."

2. The Chinese translates more plausibly as, ". . . he refuses to alter with them."

3. The Chinese translates more plausibly as, ". . . he does not shift with things."

4. Here, Buber's rendering of *hua* is *Anderung*. The 1910 edition reads, ". . . yet he preserves his being untouched." The Chinese translates more plausibly as, "He decrees the transformations of things and holds to his ancestors."

5. The Chinese translates more plausibly as, ". . . roams his heart-mind through the harmony of power/virtue."

6. This is an unfortunate abridgment. The Chinese translates more plausibly as, ". . . by his knowing he obtains his heart-mind, by his heart-mind he obtains his constant heart-mind."

7. The expressions *die Gnade der Erde* and *die Gnade Gottes* are direct translations from Giles. The Chinese translates more plausibly as ". . . that which receives its decree from earth . . ." and ". . . that which receives its decree from Heaven." See Giles 1889:58.

8. Buber's text contains a short footnote describing Yao and Shun as two great emperors circa 2400 B.C.E.

9. The 1910 edition reads, "Through nourishment of bodily courage . . ."

10. The Chinese translates more plausibly as, ". . . makes a palace of Heaven and Earth, makes a storehouse of the ten thousand things."

11. The Chinese translates more plausibly as, "... makes into one that which knowing knows, and the heart-mind has never died."

12. The 1910 edition reads, "He waits for the commanded hour ..."

XIII. Shu-shan No-Toes

1. The Chinese translates as, "... men of complete power/virtue."

2. Before 1951, the text reads, "Is Confucius a sage or is he not? How is it that he has so many students?"

3. The 1910 edition reads, "... as the fetters of a criminal."

4. This is indeed the end of the essay, as it appears in the text. However, Graham suggests that a misplaced moral to the story appears in a later chapter (see Graham 1981:79).

XIV. The Leper

1. The 1910 edition reads, "He possesses no force through which he could protect the bodies of the people. He has no administrations to give away through which he could gladden their hearts."

2. This line does not appear in the 1951 edition.

3. The 1910 edition reads, "Perhaps I was not good enough for him."

4. A considerable piece of the essay is omitted here, discussing how context shapes one's needs; a dead man does not need medals, an amputee does not need shoes, an empress does not need a commoner's trappings.

5. The Chinese translates more plausibly as, "... he must be one whose raw materials are complete, but his power/virtue does not take form."

6. The Chinese translates more plausibly as, "... the alternations of affairs, the phases of destiny."

7. This is still another use of *Geist*; the Chinese reads *ling fu*, literally "spiritual storehouse" or "magical storehouse." In some cases, *ling* appears to be used almost interchangeably with *shen*, though while the latter tends to refer to discrete beings (ancestors, local deities), the former

tends to refer to a quality internal to the person. Interestingly, in later Buddhist thought in China, the term for personal soul is *shen-ling*.

8. This is a severe gloss of a passage where the language is problematic and subject to several possible readings. Graham translates, "To maintain our store in peace and joy, and let none of it be lost through the senses though the channels to them are cleared, to ensure that day and night there are no fissures and it makes a springtime it shares with everything, this is to be a man who at every encounter generates the season in his own heart. This is what I mean by his stuff being whole." Watson translates, "If you can harmonize and delight in them, master them and never be at a loss for joy, if you can do this day and night without break and make it be spring with everything, mingling with all and creating the moment within your own mind—this is what I call being whole in power." Mair translates, "To make the mind placid and free-flowing without letting it be dissipated in gratification, causing it to have springtime with all things day and night uninterruptedly, this is to receive and engender the seasons in one's mind. This is what I mean by the wholeness of one's abilities." See Graham 1981:80; Watson 1968:74; Mair 1994:48.

9. This is *vollkommener Mensch,* another translation of *chih-jen.*

XV. Pure Men

1. Graham claims that this last sentence is a parenthetical note, perhaps added by a later commentator. Buber seems to have partially discerned this, because there is actually one more extraneous sentence in the text which he does choose to omit. See Graham 1981:84–86.

2. The 1910 edition reads, "To come quickly, to go quickly, . . ."

3. The Chinese translates more plausibly as ". . . not to use the heart-mind to salute the way, not to employ man to assist Heaven." Buber paraphrases Giles, whose rendering was in accord with the suggestion of Chu Kuei-yao; thus, the phrase would read "not to use the heart-mind to reject the way." See Giles 1889:70; Ch'ien Mu 1951:48.

4. This is a serviceable translation of *hsin chih,* reflecting a literal reading; however, the most recent translations, those of Watson, Graham, and Mair, follow the suggestions of Chiao Hung, Wang Mao-hung, and others, reading *chih* as *wang*; thus *hsin chih* would be translated as "the heart-mind forgets." See Ch'ien Mu 1951:48; Legge 1891:286–287; Watson 1968:78; Graham 1981:85; Mair 1994:52.

5. The Chinese translates more plausibly as, "Thus the sage may make use of armies and destroy the kingdom but not lose men's hearts-minds; his benefits are bestowed upon the ten thousand ages, but he is not one who loves men." Note that the subject of the discussion abruptly changes from "the pure man" to "the appointed man" (before 1951, "the accomplished man")—in actuality, from *chen-jen* to *sheng-jen*—and that there seems to be a lapse in thematic continuity. Graham suggests that these next two paragraphs are, in fact, not part of this essay. Interestingly, the essay does return to a discussion of "the pure man," but Buber does not include this part. See Graham 1981:85.

6. The 1910 edition reads, "Whoever shows love to man is not one who loves." The Chinese here is the Confucian virtue *jen*.

7. The Chinese reads *hsien*, "a worthy;" before 1951, "a sage."

8. The 1910 edition reads, "Whoever does not conduct intercourse with good and evil is not a superior man."

XVI. Steps

1. 1910: "I have learned Tao."

2. Before 1951, the references throughout this essay were not to the "appointed man," but to the "sage," which is more faithful to the Chinese.

3. This passage, without question, contains the most extraordinary gloss in the text. The key phrase in Chinese translates plausibly as, "After nine days he was able to externalize life; once externalizing life, he was able to penetrate morning; after penetrating morning, he was able to see the one." The last phrase in the German reads *"er schaute das Wesen, sein Ich, von Angesicht zu Angesicht,"* translated loosely from Legge, who wrote, "and after this he was able to see his own individuality," adding the footnote, "Standing by himself, as it were face to face with the Tao." Here, Buber is conflating "the one" with "being," and is describing the experiential insight as a "countenance to countenance" meeting of "being" with "his I." This clearly suggests an early incarnation of the dialogical principle, which, ironically, would be partially expunged for the 1951 edition, when *"sein Ich"* is deleted. As Buber could have simply translated "face" as *Gesicht*, the English rendering of this passage follows Walter Kaufmann's convention of translating *Angesicht* as "countenance." Unless otherwise noted, all citations from *I and Thou* are from Ronald Gregor Smith's translation. See Legge 1891:294; Buber 1970:92.

4. The Chinese, which does not include explicit mention of Tao, translates more plausibly as, "The thing it is, it never does not take hold, it never does not welcome, it never does not destroy, it never does not complete."

5. Buber omits the essay's conclusion, where Nü-yü explains the chain of transmission of this teaching.

XVII. The Four Friends

1. The 1910 edition reads, "Four men were speaking to one another, and this resolution was put forward: "Whoever can make 'nothing' as the head, life as the spine, death as the tail of existence, he should be permitted our friendship."

2. The Chinese reads *tsao-wu che,* "maker of things" (or possibly "makers of things"). Throughout the 1910 edition, the text refers not to "the creator," but to "God."

3. The 1910 edition reads, "My back is so curved that my bowels are solidly at my upper body. My cheeks are in the same hole as my navel. My shoulders sit over the nape of my neck."

4. The Chinese translates more plausibly as, "The ch'i of yin and yang are awry. His heart-mind was at ease and there were no concerns."

5. The 1910 edition reads, "What should I fear? Soon I will be carved up. My left shoulder will become a cock, and I will announce the approaching morning. My right shoulder will become a crossbow, and I will chase down wild ducks."

6. The Chinese reads *shen,* "spirit."

7. Before 1951, the text reads, "God is great." The Chinese translates more plausibly as, "How extraordinary, the processes of creation and transformation!"

8. The 1910 edition includes a footnote, taken from Giles, explaining the popular belief of the Chinese that a rat has no liver. See Giles 1889:82.

9. Buber's text contains a brief footnote explaining yin and yang as the negative and the positive, the passive and the active, the dark and the light elements, out of whose interactions all things arise. The 1910 edition reads, "Yin and yang are man's elders."

10. These last two sentences appear only in the 1910 edition. The Chinese refers not to "Tao," but to *ta-k'uai*. See "The Organ-Playing of Heaven," note 3.

11. The 1910 edition reads, ". . . to awaken, unaware of what has been, as a man wakes out of dreamless sleep."

XVIII. The Death Song

1. The Chinese translates more plausibly as, ". . . those who wander outside the limits."

2. The 1910 edition reads, "They look upon themselves as God's companions and do not divide human and heavenly." The Chinese translates more plausibly as, ". . . to become fellow with the maker of things, to wander with the single ch'i of Heaven and earth."

3. The Chinese translates more plausibly as, ". . . persons direct one another toward Tao."

4. The 1910 edition reads, "Fish are born in water. Man is born in Tao. If fish obtain a pond to live in, they thrive. If a man obtains Tao to live in, he can complete his life in peace."

5. The Chinese translates more plausibly as "Fish forget one another in rivers and lakes, persons forget one another in the arts of Tao."

6. In this and in the previous paragraph, "superior men" is a rendering of *chi-jen*, literally "extraordinary men." The Chinese here translates as, "The extraordinary man is extraordinary among men, but ordinary with Heaven."

7. The Chinese translates more plausibly as "The petty man of Heaven is man's gentleman; man's gentleman is the petty man of Heaven."

XIX. The Way

1. The Chinese reads *tso-wang*, literally " to sit and forget." This is a central practice of Taoist meditation.

2. The 1910 edition reads, ". . . I have become one with the infinite." The Chinese translates more plausibly as, "Since I have let my body fall away, dismissed apprehension and clarity, departed from form and let go of knowing, I share in the great passageway."

3. The Chinese translates more plausibly as, "Thus sharing in it, there is no devotion to anything; thus transformed, there is no constancy."

4. The 1910 edition reads, "Since you have entered into the infinite, in reality you no longer have beginning and end. And if in reality you have attained this, so I ask if it is permitted for me to tread in your footsteps."

XX. To Rule the State

1. The Chinese translates more plausibly as, "Roam your heart-mind to the insipid, bring together your ch'i with the indifferent, spontaneously in accord with things do not permit the private, and all-under-Heaven will be ordered."

XXI. The Magician and the Accomplished Man

1. Before 1951, the title of this passage is "The Magician and the Redeemed Man."

2. Buber's *Zauberer* is an adequate rendering of *shen-wu*, literally "spiritual wizard" or "spirit shaman."

3. The Chinese makes no explicit mention of Tao; rather, it juxtaposes the concepts of *wen* and *shih*, the latter term more easily translatable as "reality." As for the former, Wu Kuang-ming notes that its original use was "non-metered writing" in contrast to the *shih* poetic form; Graham elects to translate it as "scriptures." The term eventually comes to refer to the entire cultural legacy preserved in the classical tradition; in the Taoist philosophical texts, this carries the pejorative connotation of artifice. See Wu 1990:487; Graham 1981:96.

4. The Chinese translates more plausibly as, "It was only that he saw me close off the motions of power/virtue."

5. Here, Buber translates from Giles, who was in accord with Lu Te-ming's reading. The Chinese translates more literally as, "Your teacher does not fast," as in the "fasting of the heart-mind." See Giles 1889:96; Ch'ien Mu 1951:64.

6. The Chinese translates more plausibly as, "I made manifest by way of ultimate vastness and no foreboding." Buber's source for this section is Giles, who neglected to translate the next phrase, which translates as, "It was only that he saw me level the motions of ch'i." Graham suggests

that the remainder of this paragraph is extraneous to the essay and is actually a misplaced fragment belonging to an earlier essay, which is here translated as section XIV, "The Leper." See Giles 1889:96.

7. Buber's text contains an inconsequential footnote, paraphrased from Legge, discussing the "mermaid." See Legge 1891:313.

8. The Chinese translates more plausibly as, "I made manifest as I had not yet come forth from my ancestors, with him I was tenuous, and like a snake," the latter phrase translated by Graham as "wormed in and out," by Watson as "wriggling and turning," by Mair as "intertwined with it." See A. C. Graham 1981:97; Watson 1968:97; Mair 1994:70.

9. The 1910 edition reads, "He did not know who I was. Then he lost his composure. He became confused."

10. The 1910 edition reads, "Like a clump of earth he stood in his corporeal presence."

XXII. The Boring

1. Before 1951, this chapter is entitled "Senses."

2. Buber's text is footnoted that Shu means "volatile" and that Hu means "sudden." In the 1910 edition, the footnotes explain Shu as "sudden" and Hu as "heedless," a garbling of the explanations from Legge 1891:314–315.

3. Buber's text is footnoted that Hun-tun is chaos, undifferentiated primordial being. In the 1910 edition, it is also described as "aether."

XXIII. The Strong Thief

1. In an interesting bit of synchronicity, this is also the title of a snippet that Buber would later include in a compendium of Hasidic tales. See Buber 1947:104–105.

2. This is only a fragment of a much longer essay.

XXIV. Over-Indulgence and Non-Doing

1. This portion picks up in the middle of a much longer essay.

2. The Chinese translates more plausibly as, ". . . the essentials of nature and destiny," a common phrase for the "Primitivist" author.

3. The 1910 edition reads, "Nevertheless, the world honors and loves them and thereby increases enormously the quantity of human error."

4. This is paraphrased directly from Giles, who makes a significant error in translation. The Chinese translates more literally as, "To esteem one's person as he does all-under-Heaven, only then may he be entrusted with all-under-Heaven; to love one's person as he does all-under-Heaven, then he may be entrusted with all-under-Heaven." Also, the 1910 edition translates as "body" rather than "self." See Giles 1889:122.

5. In the 1910 edition, this entire paragraph is stated in the first person; in addition, it refers not to "movement," but to "transformation" of the will. The Chinese translates as, ". . . the spirit moves, and Heaven follows."

XXV. The Heart of Man

1. The 1910 edition reads, ". . . be kept in order?"

XXVI. Immortality

1. The Chinese simply reads *wu chih chih*, "the disposition of things."

2. The Chinese reads *chih-tao chih ch'ing*, translated well by Graham as "the quintessence of the utmost Way." All translation of the remainder of this paragraph and of the subsequent four paragraphs is problematic; most of the Chinese is obscure and structured in poetic form, a fact that Buber does not realize. See Graham 1981:178.

3. The Chinese translates more plausibly as, "With no looking, with no listening, embrace the spirit and by that be still; the body will become correct of itself."

4. The Chinese translates more plausibly as, ". . . your spirit will preserve your body, your body will thus live long."

5. The two expressions, *der treibenden Urgewalt* and *der hemmenden Urgewalt,* are both paraphrases of Giles; the Chinese translates as "the source of the utmost yang" and "the source of the utmost yin." See Giles 1889:127.

6. The 1910 edition reads, "These powers are the rulers of Heaven and Earth, and each of the two contains the other in itself." The Chinese translates more plausibly as, "Heaven and earth possess palaces, yin and yang possess treasuries."

7. The problematic Chinese translates more plausibly as, "Care for and preserve your person, and things will be strong of themselves; I preserve the one, and by this abide in its harmony; thus, I have cultivated my person for twelve hundred years, and my body has not yet declined."

8. Buber is following Giles here, though the Chinese refers simply to "things," not to the "self." See Giles 1889:128.

9. The Chinese translates more plausibly as, ". . . enter the gates of the limitless, and by this roam in the limitless spaces.

XXVII. The Cloud Prince and the Primordial Mist

1. The characters in the 1910 edition are "The Cloud Spirit and the Life Whirlwind;" in the 1918 edition, they are "The Cloud Spirit and the Primordial Whirlwind."

2. In the 1910 edition, "lifted his gaze" does not appear.

3. The 1910 edition reads, "The relation of Heaven and Earth has turned out of joint." (The word *Beziehung* would be replaced in later editions.) The Chinese translates more plausibly as, "Heaven's ch'i is not in harmony, the earth's ch'i is grieved."

4. The Chinese translates more plausibly as, ". . . to harmonize the quintessence of the six ch'i, and by this nourish all that lives." Buber's text contains a footnote taken from Giles, explaining that the "six influences" are the positive and negative world elements, wind, rain, light, and darkness. See Giles 1889:129.

5. The 1910 edition reads, "I stroll along for myself in this ecstatic state and await the events." The 1918 edition reads, "I stroll along for myself in this frolicsome state, and watch how all things go their way."

6. The 1910 edition reads, ". . . but the people depend on my movements. So I am unavoidably called to power."

7. The Chinese simply reads *hsin-yang*, literally translatable as "heart-mind nurture," rendered by Watson with the adequate but ambiguous "mind-nourishment." With this wording, it is unclear whether the author

is advocating the nurture of the mind or using the mind to nurture. Before 1951, Buber's translation (straight from Giles, in accord with the interpretation of Wang Hsien-ch'ien) reads, "Feed then your people . . . with your heart." See Watson 1968:122; Giles 1889:131; Ch'ien Mu 1951:85.

8. The 1910 edition reads, "Cast off yourself. Spit out intelligence. Forget all discrimination. . . . Let all things return to their original nature." The phrase "original nature" remained in the 1918 edition. The Chinese translates more plausibly as, "Follow and dwell in non-doing, and things will transform of themselves; let fall your body, spit out perception and illumination; in relation to things, forget; greatly share in the vast obscurity; disperse your heart-mind, unloose your spirit; be so through nothing, without 'soul'; as for the ten thousand things, each returns to the basis."

9. Here, *te* ("power/virtue") is rendered as *Macht*.

XXVIII. The Pearl

1. The Chinese is *wang*, "nothing" or "there is not." In the 1910 edition, the four characters are "Reason," "Beholding," "Word," and "Nothing." In the 1918 edition, the first character is "Knowledge" and the third character is "Speech-power."

XXIX. Cosmogony

1. The German commences with *Im Uranbeginn*, probably translated from Giles, whose rendering of "at the beginning of beginning" is a plausible rendering of *t'ai-ch'u* ("ultimate beginning"). Before 1951 the text reads, "In the primordial beginning was the nothing." See Giles 1889:143.

2. The 1910 edition reads, "When the one stepped into existence, there was the one, but it was formless. When things obtained that through which they stepped into existence, it was known as their virtue But that which was formless divided, it was nevertheless without breach, became known as fate." In 1918, the second sentence is changed to, "When things stepped into existence, they obtained what was known as their virtue."

3. The complicated Chinese translates plausibly as, "The forms embodied guard the spirit, each having its own deportment, this is known as the nature; with the nature cultivated, one returns to power/virtue;

when the power/virtue is fulfilled, one shares in the beginning; to share, one thus attenuates; tenuous one thus becomes great."

4. The 1910 edition reads, "This is harmony with Tao." The Chinese translates more plausibly as, ". . . this is known as mysterious power/virtue, to share in the great course."

XXX. The Gardener

1. The Chinese is translatable as either "spiritual life is not secure" or "spirit and life are not secure."

2. The 1910 edition reads, ". . . in order to set themselves over the rest of humankind; who play in a key that no one else can sing. If you could forget the egotism and strip off the fetters of the flesh . . ." The last phrase of the Chinese translates more plausibly as, ". . . forget the ch'i of your spirit, let fall your flesh and bones."

3. This is not the actual end of the essay; in the omitted portion, Tzu-kung leaves the gardener, and converses with a disciple and with Confucius on the characteristics of the enlightened man.

XXXI. Three Types

1. Buber's text contains an inconsequential footnote, suggesting that the names of the two characters are allegorical. In the 1910 edition, the note echoes Giles's uncertainty about what the characters represent; in later editions, it is suggested that they may represent the "east wind" and the "primordial incipient power" (*Urkeimgewalt*). See Giles 1889:150.

2. Before 1951, the text reads, "But do you not have anything in mind about man?"

3. The 1910 edition reads, "The talent is sure to be employed. The voices of the people are heard before one acts. Each man's talking and doing is his own matter. The kingdom is in peace." The Chinese translates more plausibly as, ". . . speech occurs of itself and all-under-Heaven transforms."

4. The 1910 edition reads, ". . . the man of perfect virtue . . ."

5. The Chinese translates more plausibly as, "The ten thousand things return to the essential."

XXXII. The Prayer

1. This is actually a small portion of a larger essay, where the Syncretist narrator extols the virtues of ancient sage kings and advocates spontaneity. To illustrate the qualities of "those who are in harmony with Heaven," the narrator here quotes the "Inner Chapters" 18/6/87–89 from a speech attributed by Chuang Tzu to Hsü Yu. The final phrase—"this is the bliss of Heaven"—is tacked on by the Syncretist. Neither of the appearances of this passage in the original text gives any indication that it is a "prayer."

2. This is how it reads in the 1910 and 1951 editions. In 1918, it reads, "Oh, my master!"

3. The Chinese here is the Confucian virtue, *jen*.

4. Before 1951, the text reads, ". . . primordial time." The Chinese translates more plausibly as, "high antiquity."

XXXIII. Books

1. Before 1951, this chapter is entitled "The Wheelwright."

XXXIV. The String-Music of the Yellow Emperor

1. This segment of Buber's translation contains some of the most problematic prose and least intelligible discussion. This is, no doubt because the Chinese is quite complex (and actually includes a good deal of poetry) and Buber's main sources were all apparently baffled by it. Graham's explanation is that this episode is part of a cycle of stories, the purpose of which is to demonstrate the limitations of language when discussing certain profound matters: "In these to speak articulately about the Way is enough to show that one has not grasped it; the proof of insight is that you refuse to speak, or try but forget what you meant to say, or fall into a trance while you are being told, or see in a flash stimulated by some aphorism which on reflection seems meaningless, or burst into improvising song, or are moved by music without understanding what it is doing to you." With this in mind, Buber's second-hand translation is particularly tenuous here. See Graham 1981:158.

2. The Chinese translates more plausibly as, "I play it toward man, but summon it toward Heaven, carry it out in ritual and rightness, establish it in ultimate clarity."

3. The German *Selbsttatigkeit* captures the spirit of the Chinese better than does the English "spontaneity"; the Chinese *tzu-jan* literally translates as "of itself, so."

4. The Chinese reads *kuei-shen*, "ghosts and spirits."

5. Before 1951, the text reads, ". . . the sage."

6. Buber's translation, *von-Sinnen-geraten*, is a paraphrase of Giles, who gave the rendering, "absence-of-sense," in accord with the suggestion from the commentary of Hsüan Ying. The Chinese translates more plausibly as ". . . moved emotionally, thus foolish." See Giles 1889:179; Ch'ien Mu 1951:115.

XXXV. The Ways of the World

1. Before 1951, the text reads, ". . . peacemakers and teachers of men who wish to undertake journeys in pursuit of wisdom." The 1910 edition reads "frugality" instead of "selflessness and friendly behavior."

2. The Chinese translates more plausibly as, ". . . the people who nurture the body."

3. The Chinese translates literally as ". . . adepts at guiding and pulling," an esoteric Taoist breathing technique.

4. The Chinese translates more plausibly as, ". . . the power/virtue of the sage," which is more correctly translated in the 1910 edition, which reads, "the virtue of the sage." The remainder of the essay, not included by Buber, continues its discussion of the enlightened man, his relation to Heaven's power, the nurture of the spirit, and qualities of stillness and calmness.

XXXVI. The Spirit of the Sea and the River Spirit

1. A small portion, where the master of the river compares his own wisdom to that of past sages, is omitted here.

2. The Chinese reads *ta-li*, "the great patterning."

3. The Chinese translates literally as, ". . . received ch'i from yin and yang."

4. Another small portion containing historical references is omitted.

5. The Chinese reads *fen wu ch'ang*, literally "divisions have no constancy," though Legge, Buber's source for this passage, was in accord with Ch'eng Hsüan-ying's suggestion to read *ming* ("fate") in place of *fen*. See Legge 1891:425; Ch'ien Mu 1951:129.

6. The Chinese reads *ta-chih*, "great knowing" or, by implication, "a person of great knowing."

7. Here there is a fairly large omission, a continuing discussion of relation and perspective. In addition, Graham claims that the next two paragraphs are mislocated fragments from the conclusion to this essay. See Graham 1981:149–150.

8. In this and the next paragraph, "the accomplished man" is a rendering of *ta-jen,* "the great man."

9. The Chinese is the Confucian virtue, *jen.*

10. The Chinese translates more literally as, "To see them by way of Tao, things have no nobility and baseness; to see them by way of things, oneself is noble and the others base; to see them by way of the customary (or 'the vulgar'), nobility and baseness do not exist in oneself." Buber's translation is based largely on Giles, whose rendering reflected the interpretation of Ma Ch'i-ch'ang, but also sacrificed the parallel structure of the sentences. See Giles 1889:205–206; Ch'ien Mu 1951:131.

11. This is *Verhältnis*, which I have chosen to render as "comparison" rather than "relation," so as not to confuse it with *Beziehung*, perhaps the most important word in *I and Thou*, which appears in the next paragraph. The Chinese translates more plausibly as, "to regard them by way of difference," implying relativity more than relation, a kind of relationality based on separation rather than on connection.

12. This is *Beziehung*, an extremely interesting gloss of Buber's own. The Chinese—which translates more plausibly as "to regard them by way of achievement"—and Buber's sources—Giles ('function"), Balfour ("efficacy"), Legge ("services they render")—do not give any clues to Buber's interpretation. Except for insignificant appearances in sections XXVII and XXXV, this paragraph contains the only times that *Beziehung* appears in Buber's text translation. See Giles 1889:206; Balfour 1881:201; Legge: 1891:428.

13. The Chinese translates more plausibly as ". . . to regard them by way of inclination."

14. Still another portion of this essay, more discussion of relativism and historical examples, is omitted.

15. The Chinese translates more plausibly as, "... they are those who have illumined neither the patterning of Heaven and earth nor the essentials of the ten thousand things."

16. The last phrase of this sentence does not appear in the 1910 edition.

17. The Chinese refers to an earth-god; see section XI, "The Holy Tree," note 1.

18. This is, in actuality, not the end of the essay. The omitted portion contains a direct discussion of Tao and of the differences between Heaven and man. Further, Graham suggests that a fragment of a much later chapter is actually part of the true conclusion to this essay. See Graham 1981:149.

XXXVIII. When Chuang Tzu's Wife Died

1. The Chinese translates more plausibly as, "Mixed into the muddled spaces, a change occurred and there was ch'i; the ch'i changed, and there was form; the form changed, and there was life." The word translated throughout this paragraph as "transformation" is *Wandlung* (*Wandel* in the 1910 edition).

XXXIX. The Dead Man's Skull

1. The 1910 edition reads, "... and went down in rebellion?"

2. The 1910 edition reads, "... to the friends of your youth ..."

XL. In Tao

1. The 1910 edition reads, "... ascends the height without fear and peril."

2. The Chinese translates more plausibly as, "... the preservation of the pure ch'i."

3. The Chinese translates more plausibly as, "He roams at the end and beginning of the ten thousand things, unifies his nature, nurtures his ch'i, harmonizes his power-virtue, and by this reaches through that which things create; it is as if his Heavenly preserves the whole, his spirit is without decline, how could things of themselves penetrate therein?"

4. The Chinese translates more plausibly as, ". . . his spirit is whole."

5. Graham suggests that this is indeed the end of the essay, although the 1910 and 1918 editions include the following: "An avenger does not shatter the sword that has murdered; the irascible one does not let his displeasure out at the tiles that fall on his head. Regulated under this maxim, the kingdom would be at peace; thus there would be no more disturbance of war, no more punishment of death." Furthermore, the 1910 edition ends with the following: "Display not what you have of man, but what you have of Heaven. Out of this comes virtue, out of the former cunning. Whoever does not evade Heaven, who does not find man sufficient, is near to the completion." See Graham 1981:137

XLI. The Cicada-Catcher

1. The essay is entitled "The Cricket-Catcher" in the 1910 edition.

2. The Chinese, in poetic form, translates more plausibly as, "To make use of intent not divided, thus concentrates the spirit."

XLIII. The Priest and the Pigs

1. The 1910 edition reads, ". . . and escape from the slaughterhouse . . ."

XLV. The Chimepost

1. The Chinese translates literally as ". . . like ghosts and spirits." Giles, Buber's source, followed the interpretation of Kuo Hsiang. See Giles 1889:240; Ch'ien Mu 1951:150.

2. The Chinese translates more plausibly as, "I never dared to squander my ch'i, must fast, and, by this, still the heart-mind."

3. The Chinese translates more plausibly as, "Thus I harmonized Heaven by way of Heaven; the mistaking of the implement as a spirit, is this why?"

XLVI. The Beautiful Woman and the Ugly Woman

1. The 1910 edition reads, "He loved the ugly one; he hated the beautiful one."

2. The brief moral to the story, an address by Yang Tzu to his disciples warning against self-glorification, is omitted.

XLVII. Silence

1. This passage is the final segment of a longer account of Wen-po Hsüeh-tzu and his diatribes against Confucian learning. The Chinese makes no explicit reference to Wen-po Hsüeh-tzu as a "sage" or any other special kind of being; Buber evidently found the word in a parenthetical note from Giles 1889:262.

XLVIII. The Perpetual Dying

1. The 1910 edition reads, "There is no place that it has not illumined; and all that have eyes and feet depend on it in order that they may see and go."

2. The Chinese, with no reference to a "sun-mind," translates more plausibly as, "The ten thousand things are indeed so; there is something for which they wait, and thus they live; there is something for which they wait, and thus they die." Buber's unusual term *Sonnegeist* comes from combining Giles's translation ("And every human being has that upon which he depends for death or for life") and his comment on this reference ("Mind, which rises with life and sets at death"). See Giles 1889:265.

3. The Chinese translates more plausibly as, "I one time received this completed form, but am not transformed and wait for the end." The German is *lebenerneuernde Wandlung*.

4. The Chinese translates more plausibly as, "Although I have forgotten this longstanding 'I,' I possess in existence that which is not forgotten." Again, Buber's rendering comes from combining Giles's translation ("Although my old self is constantly passing away, there remains that which does not pass away") and Giles's subsequent comment ("The mind, which feeds and thrives upon change"). The 1910 edition reads, "Look, what I love in you is the changeable." The subsequent sentence does not appear. See Giles 1889:266.

XLIX. The Three Answers

1. A sizeable portion of the essay is omitted here; the excised piece includes an explanation of Confucian virtues as differentiations of Tao (nearly identical to a similar passage from the *Tao Te Ching*), a brief discussion that relates non-doing to the return to Tao, and a continued discourse on relativism.

LI. The Place of Tao

1. The Chinese here is not *hsin*, but is *chih*, "intentions."

LIII. Of Dogs and Horses

1. The Chinese translates more plausibly as, ". . . as if they had lost their one." Giles, Buber's source here, was in accord with the suggestion of Lu Te-ming. See Giles 1889:312; Ch'ien Mu 1951:195.

2. The 1910 edition reads, ". . . a pure man . . ."

Commentary

1. This is *der morgenlandische Geist,* which Maurice Friedman, in "The Teaching of the Tao," inadvertently translates as "the spirit of the West." In good humor, Friedman writes, ". . . a simple error, if an egregious one, as I, who live on the Pacific, know all too well from watching the sun go down in the West night after night!" From personal correspondence, January 3, 1991. See Buber 1957:31.

2. Friedman translates *Sein* as "the 'is'," which superimposes an emphasis and intent not evident in the text. In accord with the preceding text translation, I continue to translate *Sein* as "existence." See Buber 1957:32.

3. Similarly, Friedman translates *Sollens,* as "an 'ought.'" Buber 1957:32.

4. This is *das Eine, das not tut,* which Friedman translates as "the one thing needful." Buber 1957:32.

5. So as to distinguish this from *das Eine, das not tut,* I translate *das Notwendige* as "the needful."

6. Friedman's version omits one complete line from the German, rendering the puzzling translation, "Science rests upon the duality of demand and deed." However, this error had not been made in the original manuscript of the translation, and there is obviously no reason why Buber would have directed such an unintelligible change. This lends credence to the hypothesis that many of the deletions in the English translation can be traced neither to Buber nor Friedman, but to the publisher. Buber 1957:33.

7. This entire sentence is omitted in Friedman's translation, and it does not appear in the original manuscript of the translation. In a personal correspondence (January 3, 1991), Friedman writes: "An essential sentence. I cannot imagine that Buber would have asked me to omit it, and I cannot imagine how I could have overlooked it!" Buber 1957:35.

8. This sentence contains the only appearances of the word *Beziehungen* in this essay; in a few instances, Buber uses the word *Relation,* which is here translated the same way.

9. The phrase *als eines Seienden* is omitted from Friedman's translation, though it does appear in the original manuscript. Buber 1957:37.

10. The German is *Urchristentum.*

11. This parenthetical note does not appear in the 1951 edition or Friedman's 1957 translation. Buber 1957:38.

12. Since Buber does not footnote any quotations in the essay, it is difficult to tell whether or not he is intending to represent this as a passage from Lao Tzu; it is, of course, from the New Testament (Matthew 5:17).

13. LT, 42:97.

14. The phrase *In Ihrer höchsten Wahrheit,* which begins the sentence, is omitted from Friedman's translation, though it does appear in the original mansucript. Buber 1957:39.

15. All biographical quotations concerning Chuang Tzu and Lao Tzu are from the sixty-third chapter of the *Shih Chi.* The first line of the Chinese translates more plausibly as, "His teaching was, by way of self-concealment, to be without name, without attention." For an English translation of the biography of Lao Tzu, see the introduction to Lao Tzu 1963:8–10.; for that of Chuang Tzu, see Giles 1889:vii–viii.

16. The phrase *bis sie verschwunden ist* is omitted from Friedman's translation, though it does appear in the original manuscript. Buber 1957:41.

17. This passage is from the *Maha-Parinibbana-Sutta*. Buber may have encountered it in T. W. Rhys David's complete English translation, which appears in *The Sacred Books of the East, Buddhist Suttas* (Vol. 11).

18. LT, 28:63. This passage and the one cited just below (see note 20) are part of the same verse and are in parallel structure. In context, the Chinese translates more plausibly as, "Knowing one's whiteness, preserving one's darkness, one becomes the model of all-under-Heaven; having become the model of all-under-Heaven, one does not stray from constant virtue and again returns to the limitless." Here Buber includes a footnote explaining that the verse citations from Lao Tzu are taken directly from von Strauss, while all others are in his own words. Nevertheless, all citations are, at best, rearrangements of the words from von Strauss.

19. LT, 73:179. This verse enumerates several qualities of "Heaven's way," including that it "does not speak, but is adept at response."

20. LT, 28:63. In context, the Chinese translates more plausibly as, "Knowing one's maleness, preserving one's femaleness, one becomes a valley of all-under-Heaven; having become a valley of all-under-Heaven, one does not distance constant virtue, and returns again to infancy." See note 18.

21. The phrase *zum Gleichnis* is omitted from Friedman's translation, and it does not appear in the original manuscript. Buber 1957:42.

22. LT, 56:128.

23. In Friedman's translation, Buber adds the footnote, "I cannot agree with the late dating of Lao-tzu that is recently gaining ground." This does not appear in any of the German editions. Buber 1957:43.

24. The phrase *den Dingen* is omitted from Friedman's translation, though it does appear in the original manuscript. Buber 1957:43.

25. "School of Chuang Tzu" 90/32/48–49.

26. "Primitivist" 24/10/19.

27. "Primitivist" 24/10/19.

28. "Primitivist" 32/12/91–93. Buber is here following Giles, who, by not following the suggested textual rearrangement of Lu Te-ming, is clearly struggling with the obscure language of the passage. The actual Chinese translates more plausibly as, "Great sounds do not enter the villagers' ears; but if it is 'Breaking the Willow' or 'Bright Flowers', then they laugh

and smile. That is why lofty words do not reach the heart-mind of the multitude. The utmost words do not go out, the customary (or 'vulgar') words overcome them. Two hanging bells are uncertain, and their harmony is not obtained. And now, as all-under-Heaven is uncertain, though I have offered guidance, how can they obtain it?" See Giles 1889:154; Watson 1968:140.

29. "School of Chuang Tzu" 41/16/12–13. This brief quotation is the only passage in either the translation or the commentary taken from the *Shan Hsing* ("Mending Nature") chapter. Graham writes: "It is an apology for the hermit's life by an author of uncertain date, not recognisable anywhere else in the book. His style is pedestrian, but he is interesting as the first documented instance of a true anarchist in China, in the sense that he conceives the ideal community as living in a spontaneous oneness without any ruler at all." In context, the Chinese translates plausibly as, "The age has lost Tao, Tao has lost the age; the age and Tao are mutually lost. By what means can the man of Tao rise up in the age? Indeed, by what means can the age cause Tao to arise? Tao has no means to rise up in the age; the age has no means to cause Tao to arise. Although the sagely man does not live in the midst of mountains and forests, his virtue is obscured. When obscured, it is thus not obscured of itself." See Graham 1981:170.

30. "Syncretists" 91/33/13. Because Buber translates and glosses loosely, his single-phrase citations containing no distinct jargon present special problems for conclusively locating the sources. This phrase is tentatively identified with one appearing in the text's final chapter, *T'ien-Hsia* ("Under Heaven"), where the Syncretist author laments that the world has broken into the "Hundred Schools," contending specialists who "reify the patterns of the ten thousand things." The German is *zugrunde liegt,* which, given the context of the essay, is probably a rendering of part of Giles's phrase, "the principles which underlie all creation." See Giles 1889:439.

31. LT, 21:49.

32. LT, 1:1.

33. "School of Chuang Tzu" 73/25/79–80. This brief citation is drawn from an extended reflection on what appear to be competing cosmogonic theories, put forth by two rival philosophers of the Chi-hsia Academy, an important intellectual center during the latter half of the "Hundred Schools" Period. Chi Chen advocated *mo wei* ("nothing does it), while Chieh Tzu advocated *huo shih* ("someone caused it"). The citation is the first part of a couplet, the second part of which is subject to different interpretations. The Chinese translates literally as, "As for Tao there can be no 'there is';

as for 'there is' there can be no 'there is not.' " However, neither of Buber's sources was aware of suggestions from Yen Fu and Ma Ch'i-ch'ang to read *you* ("there is") as *you* ("also"). The more common contemporary rendering would be: "As for Tao there can be no 'there is'; there can also be no 'there is not." Either way, Buber loses the ambiguity of the original.

34. "Inner Chapters" 4/2/24–25. This citation is a fragment of a passage that concludes with a line cited below (see note 67). The complete portion translates plausibly as, "How can Tao be obscured that there is truth and artifice? How can words be obscured that there is affirmation and negation? How can Tao go that it does not exist? How can words exist that they are unallowable? Tao is obscured by small becoming. Words are obscured by luster and flowers. Thus, there are the affirmations and negations of the Confucians and Moists, by which one's affirmation is the other's negation, and one's negation is the other's affirmation. If one wishes to affirm their negation and negate their affirmation, then nothing compares with illumining."

35. "Inner Chapters" 5/2/42–44. This is another instance where Buber decontextualizes material that gave Giles much difficulty. Still, Buber does correctly note that Chuang Tzu is regarding conventional human knowledge, the partial or flawed apprehension of Tao, as the product of ephemeral, existential fluctuations. The Chinese translates plausibly as, "Is there, in fact, completion and deficiency? Is there, is fact, no completion and deficiency? If there is completion and deficiency, then it would be like Mr. Chao playing the lute. If there is no completion and deficiency, then it would be like Mr. Chao not playing the lute." See Giles 1889:21–22.

36. "School of Chuang Tzu" 27/11/35. The citation appears to be a gloss of one appearing in the text translation (42). This entire sentence, including the quotation, is omitted from the 1951 edition and Friedman's translation. See Buber 1957:46.

37. LT, 62:146. This fragment and one cited below (see note 57) form a complete phrase. The Chinese translates more plausibly as, "Is it not said that by seeking one obtains; when having guilt, by this one is released?"

38. The Chinese translates more plausibly as, "Only one who obtains it in silence and by nature completes it, obtains it."

39. "School of Chuang Tzu" 58/22/32–33.

40. LT, 39:85. The Chinese translates more plausibly as, "Heaven obtains the one, and by it translucence; Earth obtains the one and by it

serenity; spirits obtain the one and by it spirituality; valleys obtain the one and by it fullness; the ten thousand things obtain the one and by it life; lords and kings obtain the one and by it become the upright of the world."

41. "School of Chuang Tzu" 60/22/75–76. Again, Giles added some severe glosses to this passage. The paragraph in Chinese, which makes no explicit mention of "Tao," translates more plausibly as, "One does not make death life by way of life; one does not make life death by way of death. Do death and life lie in wait? As for them both, there is something of which there is one body. Is that which precedes Heaven and Earth a thing? That which deems things as things is not a thing. The going out of things cannot precede things. It is as if it has things; to be like having things, this is without end." See Giles 1889:291.

42. The original Chinese is written in the terse style that is common to its period, and there is some ambiguity as to how some of the characters should be read; for example, the word *sheng* could mean "to engender," "to arise," "to live," or simply "life." The key passage is translated by Graham as, "To be born normally, coming from nowhere, is the Way. When a man follows a course consistent with life, and lives, so that although he dies when his term is up he does not perish before his time, this is normal; to follow a course consistent with life and perish before his time is misfortune. To die normally, in accordance with your manner of life, is also the Way. When a man follows a course which leads to death, and dies, so that he perishes by his own fault even before his term is up, this is also normal; to live after following a course which leads to death is good luck." Graham 1960:83.

43. "School of Chuang Tzu" 46/18/19. This fragment is lifted from the text translation (55).

44. Graham suggests that this is from a misplaced fragment of the "Inner Chapters," 63/23/57–58. In context, the Chinese translates plausibly as, "There is somewhere from which occurs engendering; there is somewhere to which occurs dying; there is somewhere from which occurs emerging; there is somewhere to which occurs entering. Entering and emerging, but without seeing its form, this is called Heaven's gate. As for Heaven's gate, there is no 'there is'. The ten thousand things emerge from where there is no 'there is'. A 'there is' cannot become a 'there is' by means of a 'there is'; it must emerge from that where there is no 'there is'; and what is without a 'there is' is always without a 'there is'. The sagely man is hidden away in there." See Graham 1981:103.

45. "Inner Chapters" 5/2/52–53. This line is actually the conclusion to the paragraph that includes a citation below (see note 63).

46. "Syncretists" 29/12/12–13.

47. "Inner Chapters" 16/6/29. This line is part of a longer discussion of Tao that also includes a citation below (see note 54).

48. The Chinese translates more plausibly as "If man is able constantly to abide in purity and rest, Heaven and Earth both return." Buber's gloss of "undifferentiated existence" is inspired by Legge, who, though admitting to be baffled by the line, adds the parenthetical gloss "to non-existence." Buber's gloss of "to Tao" is entirely his own. See Legge 1891:692–693.

49. This parenthetical note is omitted from *Hinweise* and, thus, from Friedman's translation; as the sources of the Taoist Religion are becoming more available, few scholars still hold to this chauvinistic attitude. Buber 1957:49.

50. "Inner Chapters" 5/2/59. This line is the first from a sequence of paradoxes. The Chinese translates more plausibly as, "The greatest Tao is not cited."

51. LT, 25:58. In context, the Chinese translates plausibly as, "Man patterns after Earth, Earth patterns after Heaven, Heaven patterns after Tao, Tao patterns after what is of itself so."

52. LT, 1:2.

53. LT, 6:17.

54. "Inner Chapters" 16/6/29. The Chinese translates more plausibly as, "As for Tao, there is actuality, there is reliability; there is no doing, there is no form." See note 47.

55. LT, 37:81. This rendering is not implausible, but it is the result of some confusion about the use of negatives in the literary Chinese. A more likely translation is, "As for Tao, constantly there is no doing, yet there is nothing not done."

56. LT, 25:56.

57. LT, 62:146. See note 37.

58. The phrase *in der Welt* is omitted from Friedman's translation, though it does appear in the original manuscript. Buber 1957:50.

59. "Inner Chapters" 18/6:67. The phrase "God's companions" appeared in the 1910 edition of the text translation, later replaced by "companions of the creator" (36). When Buber made the change for later editions, he neglected to correct this citation in the commentary.

60. LT, 16:37. In context, the Chinese translates more plausibly as, "Attaining the limit of the rarified, preserving the genuineness of stillness, the ten thousand together arise; by this I view the return, things abounding, each again returning to its root; returning to the root means stillness; this is called returning to destiny; returning to destiny is called constancy; knowing constancy means illumining."

61. The phrase *wird die Ewigkeit* is omitted from the 1951 edition and Friedman's 1957 translation. Buber 1957:50.

62. *Verhältnis* is throughout this essay rendered as "comparison" or "liaison," so as to distinguish it from *Beziehung*.

63. "Inner Chapters" 5/2/51–52. See note 45.

64. "Inner Chapters" 1/1/6–9. This line, though not presented as a direct citation, is the moral that Buber infers from the very first episode in *Chuang Tzu*.

65. "Inner Chapters" 5/2/52.

66. "Inner Chapters" 1/1/10–11. Though not attributed, the last part of this sentence is a direct quotation from Giles's translation; it too is drawn from the first story in the text. See Giles 1889:3.

67. "Inner Chapters" 4/2/26–27. See note 34.

68. LT, 47:106.

69. "Inner Chapters" 3/2/4. This phrase is changed to *Orgelspiel des Himmels* in the 1951 edition and Friedman's 1957 translation; the Chinese is *t'ien lai*, "Heaven's piping." This and the next citation appear in the same segment of the text translation (17–18).

70. "Inner Chapters" 3/2/7–8. See note 69.

71. Although the verb *erkennen* is translated throughout as "to know," there is a clear distinction made between *Erkenntnis* and *Wissen*. Thus, I translate the former as "cognition" or "perception," depending on the context, and the latter as "knowledge."

72. This is clearly a reference to the beginning of the "Webbed Toes" chapter of the text. "Primitivist" 21/8/1.

73. "School of Chuang Tzu" 39/14/57–58.

74. "School of Chuang Tzu" 38/14/51–52.

75. LT, 71:173.

76. LT, 41:91. The translation that Buber borrows from von Strauss is plausible, though the parallel structures in the Chinese suggest that an alternative—"illumined Tao appears dark"—is more likely.

77. LT, 2:6.

78. "Syncretists" 33/13/2–3. The Chinese translates more plausibly as, "As for the stillness of the sage, it is not that it is said 'stillness is good' and thus he is good; as for the ten thousand things, none is sufficient to disturb his heart-mind."

79. Compare *"Diese Tun, das 'Nichttun,' is ein Wirken des ganzen Wesens"* with *"Das Grundwort Ich-Du kann nur mit dem ganzen Wesen gesprochen werden"* from the first page of *Ich und Du.*

80. "Primitivist" 26/11/15–16. This citation appears in the text translation (41).

81. LT, 55:125.

82. LT, 5:14.

83. LT, 49:111. The Chinese translates more plausibly as, "As for the good, I treat them well; as for those not good, I also treat them well; for virtue is goodness; as for the trustworthy, I trust them; as for those not trustworthy, I also trust them; for virtue is trusting." Buber's source, von Strauss, is not aware of or does not accept the standard suggestion to read *te* ("virtue") as *te* ("obtain"), which would change the two phrases to "I obtain goodness" and "I obtain trust."

84. LT, 64:156. In context, the Chinese translates more plausibly as, "That is why the sagely man desires not to desire, does not esteem goods that are difficult to obtain, learns not to learn, and makes good the transgressions of the multitude; by this he helps that which for the ten thousand things is of itself so, but does not presume to do."

85. LT, 56:129. The Chinese passage, which is sometimes interpreted as an evocation of esoteric physical practices, translates more plausibly as, "Block the paths, obstruct the doors, blunt the sharpness, disperse the distinctions, harmonize the luster, bring into accord the dust; this is called the 'primordial accord'."

86. LT, 29:56.

87. LT, 57:133. This passage is actually the conclusion to the next one cited.

88. LT, 57:132. See the previous citation.

89. LT, 75:181.

90. LT, 78:188.

91. LT, 17:41.

92. LT, 25:57.

93. Buber's footnote reads, "The teaching of the kingdom, which I have explained last, already stands firm even in the stamp of Lao Tzu's words."

94. This is *Fioretti Di San Francesco (The Little Flowers of St. Francis)*.

95. In Friedman's translation, it is specified that *Stirb und werde* is indeed the work by Goethe. Buber 1957:58.

Postscript to the 1910 Edition

1. Buber is referring to Paul Carus, who translated "Lau-tsze's Tau-teh-king: The Old Philosopher's Classic of Reason and Virtue," in *The Monist*, 7:4 (1896), 571–601. This was reprinted two years later in book form as *Lao-tse's Tao-teh-king*, (Chicago: Open Court, 1898).

Glossary

1. The title of this section was changed to "The Magician and the Accomplished Man" in the 1951 edition, though Buber neglected to change it for the glossary. See pages 38–39.

2. Hu Tzu's biography in the 1951 edition ends here.

3. See p. 56.

4. "Syncretists" 92/33/55. The Chinese translates more plausibly as, "If there is no abiding in one's self, things taking shape manifest of themselves." See also Graham 1960:90.

5. See p. 41–43.

6. These quotations appear in English in Buber's text. The Balfour quotation is actually the title of a chapter from Balfour 1887.

7. See de Harlez 1891. Lieh Tzu's biography in the 1951 edition ends at this point.

8. This parenthetical note appears only in the 1910 edition.

9. See p. 62.

10. See p. 56.

11. See p. 57–58.

12. See p. 57.

13. See p. 38–39.

14. See p. 59.

15. See p. 58–59.

16. This last sentence appears only in the 1918 edition.

17. See p. 17–18.

18. See p. 33–34.

19. See Graham 1960:79–80.

20. See p. 16.

21. See Graham 1960:35.

22. See p. 23–26.

Chapter 1: The Historical Question

1. In Berlin's *Die Gegenwart* (December 23, 1911), Julius Bab writes, "One cannot thank Martin Buber enough for the work that he has done with the beautiful selection, the fine and pure translation, the clever commentary on this document of high culture." In Bern's *Der Bund* (November 10, 1912), discussing the translations by both Buber and Richard Wilhelm, Hermann Hesse writes, "Of all the books of Chinese thought that I know, this has the most charm and clarity." Perhaps the most critical response came more than ten years later from Arthur Bonus, who writes, "It thus appears to me that Martin Buber's afterword to his very handsomely and richly translated 'Talks and Parables of Chuang Tzu' serves to bring us considerably deeper into this mental world, though I cannot agree with the particular terminology" (source unknown). Other reviewers included Julius Hart, Carl Dallago, Hans Kohn, Paul Tausig, Moritz Heimann, Alfred Frhr. v. Mensi, and Max Brod. JNUL, Arc. Ms. Var. 350/48.

2. One indication of the impact of *Reden und Gleichnisse* is the August 1918 edition of the short-lived periodical *Freideutsche Jugend*, which

opens with an excerpt (section XXXV, "The Ways of the World") printed in its entirety on the title page. Walter Laqueur writes, "What did Chinese philosophy and Indian mysticism mean to the generation of 1918–19? Strictly speaking, nothing at all; but they liked the parables; the fact that these were not at all applicable at a time of political and social crisis to people with an entirely different cultural tradition in the heart of Europe, was a secondary consideration." In addition, Chaim Schatzker lists *Die Rede, die Lehre und das Lied* among two-dozen of Buber's works most frequently cited in Youth Movement publications. Interestingly, *Ich und Du* was quoted less often and in a narrower range of periodicals. See Laqueur 1984:116; Schatzker 1978:154.

3. There are a number of cases where scholars examine this material only for the purpose of making other aspects of Buber's philosophy more intelligible. Maurice Friedman: "We cannot understand Buber's central work to which his thought led, and from which the rest came, namely, *Ich und Du, I and Thou*, unless we understand the Taoist concept of *wu wei*." James Moran: "Buber, echoing Chuang Tzu, asserts that society passes to each of us the accumulated habits of mind and behavior which constitute the objective world of It, the world of function and use." Robert Wood: "There are at least six interlocked Taoist notions that became important for Buber: (1) *Tao* itself as a way, discovered and traversed by (2) *nonaction*, that involves (3) the *coincidence of opposites*, and (4) the *realization* of what one already knows, terminating in (5) the *unity of one's life* as a whole, which establishes (6) the *unity of the world*." See Friedman 1986:115–116; Moran 1972:100; Wood 1984:332.

4. The brief essay, "China and Us," which actually deals more with Taoism than with Confucianism, is a translation of an address delivered in 1928 at the China Institute at the University of Frankfurt, in response to a lecture by Richard Wilhelm. The original (*China und Wir*) appears in Buber 1929–30; an English translation appears along with "The Teaching of the Tao" in Buber 1957. Incidentally, the original manuscript of Maurice Friedman's translation indicates that the title was to be rendered, with greater fidelity to the German text, as "China and We." "The Place of Hasidism in the History of Religion" originally appeared in Buber 1943; the English translation appears in Buber 1960.

5. The references to "perennial philosophy" or "perennialism" refer to the universalist theories and methodologies put forth by Aldous Huxley, Frithjof Schuon, Huston Smith, and others. See Smith 1976.

6. Until I brought it to his attention in a telephone conversation during the fall of 1989, Park had not been aware that Buber worked mainly from English sources.

7. Hellmut Wilhelm, in an appendix to Victor Mair's influential book of essays on *Chuang Tzu*, nevertheless includes Buber's work in a list of complete translations and important partial translations. See Wilhelm 1983:158–159.

8. Personal correspondence from Eber, April 15, 1990.

9. Personal correspondence from Eber, April 15, 1990. Following up on this issue, Eber has called to my attention a recent journal article where R. J. Zwi Werblowsky writes, "Buber would hardly have engaged in a technical discussion with Buddhologists and Sinologists (though he sought their advice); he was too well aware of the difference between solid scholarship and romantic impressionism." Werblowsky 1988:93.

10. Perhaps the most salient example is that of non-sinologist Herbert Fingarette, whose book, *Confucius—The Secular as Sacred*, as well as a series of essays published over the next decade, continue to make a powerful impact. Herrlee G. Creel writes, "In the fifty years in which I have been studying Confucius, I cannot recall that I have found the work of another scholar more stimulating than that of Professor Fingarette." See Fingarette 1972, 1979; Creel 1979:414.

11. For example, more than a quarter of Buber's selections are cited or invoked in Ssu-ma Ch'eng-chen's eighth century *Tso-wang lun (Treatise on Sitting and Forgetting)*. See Kohn 1987.

12. Buber's preface to *Chinesische Geister- und Liebesgeschichten* (translated almost in its entirety for the introduction to Rose Quong's English version), though cited by Eber as evidence that Wang introduced Buber to P'u Sung-ling's stories, is ambiguous at best on this point. "During my studies in the myths of demons and spirits, I became familiar, first through translations, and later under the friendly instruction of Mr. Chingdao Wang, with the Chinese collections of ghost stories, and particularly with the classic *Liao Chai Chih Yi*." While the Buber Archive contains numerous documents (including a contract signed by both men) specifically linking Wang to Buber's translation of this work, there is no material specifically mentioning the translation of *Chuang Tzu*. Eber appears surprised that Buber "corrected" some of Giles's errors, assuming that he must have had help from a qualified sinologist, when he in fact simply consulted Legge's translation in certain places. See P'u 1946:9; JNUL, Arc. Ms. Var. 350/855:1–8.

13. For example, feminist theologian Mary Daly implicitly adds an intriguing corollary to Thomas Kuhn's often cited theory of paradigms, that an established community or loose association of scholars actually determines which subjects are appropriate for study, what range of

methodologies is acceptable for those inquiries, what conclusions can be drawn from the assembled data, and what is the cumulative significance of the conclusions. Daly argues that the guardians of paradigms in any patriarchally dominated field are invariably guilty of "methodolatry," the elevating of established method to exalted status, and thereby subordinating content to it. Daly writes, "The tyranny of methodolatry hinders new discoveries. It prevents us from raising questions never asked before and from being illumined by ideas that do not fit into pre-established boxes and forms. The worshippers of Method have an effective way of handling data that does not fit into the Respectable Categories of Questions and Answers. They simply classify it as nondata, thereby rendering it invisible." See Kuhn 1962; Daly:1973:11.

14. In his commentary on the text, von Strauss writes, "This term holds the key to moving on," adding that Lao Tzu "places all value on the overcoming might of the exemplary personality, which engenders and transfers the teaching as living stuff." In a letter to Buber just after the publication of *Reden und Gleichnisse,* sociologist Georg Simmel writes, "With the concept of the "teaching," you have actually differentiated out a very significant and autonomous category that until now has been conceptually blurred amid clamorous other tendencies. What you have communicated out of Chinese philosophy is of extraordinary significance and, like the theses of Meister Eckhart, has the urgency of something breaking forth from the depth." Carl Kerenyi writes, "From the moment when Buber begins to define the 'teaching' . . . the reader holds his breath, even when as an Occidental he is not especially inclined toward this 'basic force': then it strikes, like lightning, then it *hits*—in content and in language." See von Strauss 1870:14; Buber 1972:287; Kerenyi 1967:629–630. The concept of *Lehre* would remain an important one in Buber's later writings, though its meaning and usage would change with each philosophical context. One interesting example is "Die Lehre und die Tat," in Buber 1936, translated as "Teaching and Deed" in Buber 1948:137–145. For an involuted, but interesting discussion of the role of *Lehre* in Buber's dialogical philosophy, see Wood 1984:336–344.

15. This notion is echoed by Benjamin Schwartz, who describes mystical gnosis as "a kind of higher direct knowledge of the ineffable source of all that which lends existence meaning." See Schwartz 1985:193.

16. Buber's claim that the teaching has no subject (or, no subject other than itself) calls to mind a fragment of the current debate over methodology in the comparative study of mysticism. In an unpublished paper entitled "Remarks on the Future of the Study of Mysticism," ostensively a review of Robert K. C. Forman's *The Problem of Pure Conscious-*

ness, Robert Gimello notes that "[Pure consciousness experiences] are to be understood as events in which one is conscious or awake but in which one's consciousness or awareness has no content. There is, of course, much to say from a philosophical perspective about such curious vacuities. How, I wonder, does contentless consciousness differ from a two-sided triangle, from directionless movement, or from a pain of which the sufferer is unaware?" (1990:5).

17. Eber also gives a mild suggestion that Buber may have been predisposed to finding and perhaps exaggerating this theme, given that he had already discerned it to be a crucial element in Hasidic texts, one that provided a creative stimulus for reconciling contradictions in his own Jewish identity. See Eber 1991:xii–xiii.

18. The 1912 date places this essay just after Buber's two volumes of translations from the Chinese. While Buber's use of the terms "Orient" and "the East" (*das Morgenland*) is ambiguous in *Reden und Gleichnisse,* in this essay he is explicitly referring to the entire area stretching from East Asia through the Indian subcontinent all the way to Egypt and the Middle East. Thus, Buber is claiming that the modern Jewish psyche is more closely identified with the Oriental spirit than with that of Europe. See Buber 1967:56–78. The essay was delivered in 1912, but first appeared in print as "Der Geist des Orient und das Judentum," in Buber 1915 and Buber 1916.

19. This is contrasted with the European "sensory-type man" for whom cognition is a "centripetal" process, as "an impression is made on his soul and becomes an image."

20. Here, one may detect considerable resemblance between the positions of Buber and Wilfred Cantwell Smith. Both grant low status to "religion" as a compartmentalized entity, a reification of something that cannot be separated from the lived human life. Like Buber, Smith argues that there is a "critical difference between a religion and a transmitted tradition." As such, both develop a "personalist" view of truth statements. Where Buber states that "there is no truth in concepts" (89), Smith echoes this with his suggestion that "the locus of truth and knowledge . . . is persons." See Smith 1962:69, 119–192; 1979:148.

21. The phrase, "obliterating unity," is here chosen quite intentionally. In one instance, Giles had translated *t'ien ni* as "the obliterating unity of God," rendered by Buber as "the all-quenching oneness of Heaven" (20). Phrases like this certainly informed Buber's reading of the text. See Giles 1889:31.

22. Buber 1957:ix–x. In a review of this collection of essays, Reinhold Niebuhr, unaware of Buber's repudiation of the "The Teaching of the Tao" that appears in the Prologue, notes that "his appreciation of Taoism reveals how much of the original mysticism remains." Maurice Friedman recounts a humorous story, told originally to him by Ursula Niebuhr, of how Buber accosted Niebuhr at a social gathering, in order to admonish him for this oversight. See Niebuhr:1958:36–37; Friedman 1970:67.

23. This above-described position of "pure monism" is to be distinguished from what Buber characterizes as "modern monism" (75), a type of perennialism that formulates its position as a doctrinal proposition on the unity of God or of existence.

24. The German here is *Relation,* which, unlike *Beziehung,* suggests separation and opposition.

25. In the strict sense, this cannot actually be considered a "developmental" scheme, given Buber's claim that the teaching "cannot develop after it has found its fulfillment in the central man" (94). Rather, it is a sequence depicting the literary products of the human fulfillment of the teaching as it occurs in different existential contexts.

26. Buber does not specifically employ this term, "liminality," but it is appropriate for what he is describing. It was originally coined by anthropologist Arnold van Gennep in *The Rites of Passage,* and further elaborated in several works by Victor Turner. It describes the threshold phase that occurs at the moment or moments of interface between two more clearly demarcated stages of a transition, "a cultural realm that has few or none of the attributes of the past or coming state." See van Gennep 1909; Turner 1966:94.

27. It is interesting to note that the only appearance of *Beziehungen* in the commentary is tied in to a proto-dialogical formulation.

28. Eber appears not to attach much significance to Buber's point that the texts of Lao Tzu and Chuang Tzu have different ontological relationships to the teaching. She instead notes that Buber "assigned to Zhuangzi the subordinate position of 'apostle' in the essay" and tended "to ignore significant differences between the two philosophical works" (1991:xv).

29. A fortuitous ambiguity of the English verb *to realize* is that it can mean both "to make real" and "to discover." Both connotations apply in this case, as the process of making the oneness an actuality is simply a process of discernment. Wilfred Cantwell Smith writes, "Given the am-

bivalence, in modern English, of 'realize' (which can mean to actualize, to make real, or can mean to recognize theoretically the actuality of), one might suggest—for those for whom the concept 'God' is meaningful—that a component of faith is the realization of God in one's life" (1979:102).

30. I am indebted to James Engell for suggesting this connotation of the term.

31. See Scholem 1971:233–236, and Jacobs 1991:95–98.

32. See Lester 1985:134–143.

33. See pages 29–30, 84, 90, 91.

34. It would, of course, be pointless to try to reconstruct the last century of debate on this subject. Suffice it to say that Kuo Mo-jo and Lu Chen-yu were among those holding to the traditional date, while Fung Yu-lan and Lo Ken-tse placed the text prior to Chuang Tzu but after Confucius. Ch'ien Mu was among the most influential of those to challenge whether Lao Tzu's text was, in fact, anterior to the historic Chuang Tzu. See Kuo 1954:235; Lu 1955:53; Fung 1952:170; Lo 1958:282–312; Ch'ien Mu 1935.

35. This new translation is based on the manuscripts unearthed in 1973 at Ma-wang-tui, which, dating back to the beginning of the second century B.C.E., are the oldest extant versions.

36. Buber's historical perspective on the *Tao Te Ching* is analogous to what William Graham characterizes as a community's perception of scripture as possessing "unicity of source, content, and authority." Graham writes, "No matter what the historical origins or textual development of its constituent parts, and no matter how diverse those parts, a scriptural corpus is commonly conceived of as a unified whole, both in its ontological origin and sacred word and in its authoritativeness and internal consistency as sacred truth." See Graham 1987:141–142.

37. Buber provides a mild suggestion that his understanding of the role of "images" is inspired by a single quotation from the *Tao Te Ching* (discussed at some length by von Strauss) which he decontextualizes severely to justify this claim. In a tenuous argument that slips away from a pure monism, Buber hints that even while there may be an imperceptible essence that underlies the truthful life, the fact that "in it are the images" (83) renders it aniconic. This is further indicated in Buber's unpublished commentary on the *Tao Te Ching*, where he writes, "Three things are declared of Tao, in it are the images, the being, and the spirit. The speech is of the potential manifestation,

of the manifestation in Tao, not as world. Under images has meant the whole thus-being of things. Individuation in a narrower sense. In it are the primordial images of all things." Though the discussion of images is prominent in Buber's commentary, the term *Bild* does not appear with any consequence in the text translation. See von Strauss 1870:110–111; JNUL, Arc. Ms. Var. 350, 16.

38. In an unpublished essay (1989), an early draft for this text, LaFargue writes, "Each statement remains insular, rooted in the experienced character of the state of mind cultivated, and functioning primarily to celebrate the wonderful character of this state of mind and/or to encourage one in further cultivating it in oneself."

39. One must, of course, be wary of reducing the interpretive process to isolating information such as authorship and dating. Prefacing his critical commentary on a classical Confucian text, Tu Wei-ming writes, "I maintain, however, that although genetic problems are closely related to our quest for a broad understanding of the text, they are not to be confused with the problems of the semantic nucleus around which the symbolic articulations of the text evolve" (1976:xi).

40. The implication is that he was probably mutilated for having committed some kind of crime and is, therefore, similar to the cicada-catcher and wheelwright in low social status.

41. "Inner Chapters" 12/52; "School of Chuang Tzu" 57/22/7; LT, 2:6, 43:99.

42. This term appears in *Chuang Tzu* nearly forty times, though its uses in the "Primitivist," "Yangist," and "Syncretist" documents are almost all in the verb form and are not particularly edifying. In any case, because this chapter is concerned principally with matters of historical reconstruction, all subsequent citations are drawn from the "Inner Chapters," the "School of Chuang Tzu" section, or sections not conclusively identified with a source.

43. Moreover, the term is etymologically related to *hsiao* ("filiality"), and originally carried connotations of "conferring" something upon someone or of "fulfilling."

44. Meng Tzu 1A:3, available in Legge 1970:131–132.

45. This is actually from a passage included in Buber's text translation (section IX, "With Men,"), though Buber does not employ the term *Lehre*. He does, however, recognize that this episode depicts Yen Hui's methods in a less than flattering light.

46. *Chung Yung*, 1:1–2, available in Legge 1971:383–384.

47. While this may appear to be inappropriately reading a naturalism into this Confucian document, it is not without precedent, as Tu notes repeatedly. For example, Ch'ien Mu argues that the author may have been specifically influenced by the thought of Chuang Tzu. See Tu 1976:16; Ch'ien Mu 1955:2–8.

48. This line (74/26/37) is from a passage not attributed to a source.

49. One might be inclined to wonder why Buber did not include this passage in his text translation, given its importance to his discussion of the teaching. One possible explanation is that Giles, Buber's principal source for the first edition, translated *chiao* as "doctrine" and misread the intended analogy, thus comparing the doctrine (not the great man) to shadow and echo. Another possibility is that the short essay is buried in a chapter comprised largely of "Primitivist" and "Syncretist" documents, and that both Giles and Legge very tenuously tacked it on to the block of material right before it—which Graham believes to be garbled fragments of a "Primitivist" essay and a "School of Chuang Tzu" snippet on self-alienation—thereby rendering it virtually unintelligible and quite easy to overlook. See Giles 1889:133; Graham 1981:184–185, 216–217.

50. In his own footnote to this, Wu writes, "Martin Buber and Gabriel Marcel in the world of philosophy of the modern West perhaps come closest to Chuang Tzu in this regard" (1990:402).

51. In an essay that is extraordinarily sensitive for the work of a non-sinologist, Wilfred Cantwell Smith suggests that the Chinese worldview is characterized by a "complement dualism." See Smith 1972:67–80.

52. Kuo Hsiang's terms, such as principle (*li*) and demarcation (*fen*) are those that would eventually be used by Chu Hsi in his formulation of Confucian orthodoxy: "Principle is singular; its demarcations are diverse." For an accessible translation and discussion of *Chu Tzu Yü-lei (Classified Conversations of Chu Hsi)*, see Gardner 1990.

53. This topic is addressed in greater detail in the next chapter, though a definitive resolution is not likely to be forthcoming here or elsewhere. Historically, interpretations of *Chuang Tzu* have sometimes been so discordant with one another that they hardly appear to be addressing the same text; Kam Louie even reports that at a symposium during the Mao Tse-tung era, Chinese scholars nearly came to blows during arguments over the text's philosophical stance and the likely social positions of its authors. See Louie 1986:118–119.

54. They are "hard relativism," "soft relativism," "neither relativism nor non-relativism," "both relativism and non-relativism," and "asymmetrical relativism (either relativism or non-relativism)." Allinson 1989:111–126.

Chapter 2: The Hermeneutic Question

1. Abe 1971:30–36; Kodera 1977:273–276. I am grateful to Masatoshi Nagatomi for calling to my attention an article (Shaw 1985) which directed me to these two essays. Incidentally, the *Maha-Parinibbana Sutta,* the original Sanskrit of which is no longer extant (English translations are taken from the Chinese), is the one Buddhist document cited in Buber's afterword (79).

2. Buber reported having had a sudden enlightenment experience, a conversion to Hasidism in 1904, at the age of twenty-six. He published *Die Geschichten des Rabbi Nachman* in 1906 and *Die Legende des Baal Schem* in 1908, only three years before *Reden und Gleichnisse.* See Buber 1958b:60–63.

3. The fact that one case has inspired decades of debate while the other has been met with relative unconcern does not imply a qualitative difference between the two. Throughout his life, Buber remained involved in the question of how best to revitalize the Jewish spirit, and he never abandoned his Hasidic studies; thus, it has been incumbent upon the Jewish community to find an appropriate scholastic and aesthetic place for his work. On the other hand, though he wrote and spoke sporadically of Taoism even in his later years, he clearly addressed it to a Western audience with his agenda for Jewish renewal at the forefront; the sinological community had minimal opportunity or impetus to consider his work.

4. In particular, Scholem is referring to Buber's disregard for the magical and communal elements of the tradition and his emphasis on the narrative rather than theoretical material.

5. Not coincidentally, Katz holds an important position in the current debate on methodology in the comparative study of mysticism. As the editor of two influential volumes—*Mysticism and Philosophical Analysis* and *Mysticism and Religious Traditions*—Katz is identified with a particularistic approach sometimes called "constructivism," the view that all mystical experiences are in some way "constructed" by the historical and cultural contexts in which they occur. The most important ramifications of this methodology are that mysticism does not exist as a sui generis category, that all instances of it are historically bound and tradition-specific, and that the very enterprise of a

"comparative mysticism" is somewhat suspect. Katz himself dislikes this term because of its implication that the experience is somehow not genuine, preferring instead terms like "mediated," "contextual," or "particularistic." The "constructivist" label is used extensively in Forman 1990 and Forman 1994, the former of which was the topic of a provocative panel at the 1990 annual meeting of the American Academy of Religion.

6. Kepnes cites Leopold Zunz and Moritz Steinschneider as principal figures in the movement. See Kepnes 1987:88.

7. Actually, Schleiermacher contrasts "grammatical interpretation with "psychological interpretation" (also called "technical interpretation"), which spans the "divinatory" and "comparative" methods as complementary components: "By leading the interpreter to transform himself, so to speak, into the author, the divinatory method seeks to gain an immediate comprehension of the author as an individual. The comparative method proceeds by subsuming the author under a general type. It then tries to find his distinctive traits by comparing him with the others of the same general type. Divinatory knowledge is the feminine strength in knowing people; comparative knowledge the masculine. Each method refers back to the other." See Schleiermacher 1977:150.

8. The issue of whether or not there is such a thing as a "mystical propensity" that one may possess independent of cultural or linguistic particulars is a hotly debated topic among scholars of mysticism.

9. Buber had originally studied with Dilthey just before the turn of century, but he later attended lectures in the period from 1906 to 1911. See Kepnes 1988:195.

10. Ironically, in an intriguing experimental essay, one modern sinologist writes, "Specifically, I use Hans-Georg Gadamer's analysis of 'play' in *Truth and Method* as a hermeneutical tool for understanding Chuang-tzu's vision of life in the *Inner Chapters*." See Kepnes 1987:92–98; Kepnes 1988:206–213; Crandell 1983:102.

11. To date, Irene Eber's introduction to Alex Page's translation is the only published work to discuss Buber's text translation in any detail, though her comments on this topic are comparably brief. See Eber 1991:xiii–xiv.

12. It should also be recalled that when the essay stood alone in later compilations, it was retitled "The Teaching of the Tao."

13. This is nearly identical to a footnote that Buber provides at the first appearance of Tao in the body of his text. See p. 19 n. 3.

14. This definition recalls the "Primitivist" author's expression, "the essentials of nature and destiny." See p. 40 n. 2.

15. It is this subject of non-being that establishes the most continuity between Buber's interest in Chuang Tzu and his earlier interest in Jacob Boehme, whom Maurice Friedman identifies as among the first of Buber's "mystical" influences. In his *Erklarung über das Erste Buch Mosis*, Boehme writes, "God is a nothing even to himself." And in *Von 177 Theosophischen Fragen*, he writes, "God is called the seeing and the finding of the nothing (though it is God Himself) because it is inconceivable and inexpressible." See Stoudt 1968:199; Friedman 1970:44–47.

16. It should be parenthetically noted that this bears some resemblance to Kuo Hsiang's insistence that Chuang Tzu's "non-being" should not be understood as an entity. See Robinet 1983:75–79.

17. See p. 86, n. 47; p. 87, n. 54.

18. It should be noted that Buber evidently recognizes this reference as an allusion to Tao, even though this is not made explicit in the original Chinese, which, in fact, makes no mention even of a "primordial" one. In numerous other places, Buber assumes that Tao is the implicit subject, a practice that has considerable precedent in sinological circles. Since this chapter is concerned with the integrity of Buber's interpretive process rather than the reconstructive "objectivity" of his conclusions, the original Chinese is not provided here for each example (though in cases of extreme or interesting glosses, annotations to the text translation demonstrate the extent of the departure by juxtaposing Buber's German with the original). Recently, Chad Hansen has suggested that the tendency to assume Tao as subject simply reflects the erroneous predisposition of interpreters to find the text concerned with a unitary metaphysical concept of "the tao." See Hansen 1983a:25–26.

19. The other creation-myth fragment is in the chapter entitled "The Boring" ("Senses," before the 1951 edition), where Buber in his footnote identifies Hun-tun as "chaos, undifferentiated primordial being." See p. 39.

20. The notion of Chinese cosmogony as ongoing process is one that has been given much currency in recent years. Frederick W. Mote writes, "The genuine Chinese cosmogony is that of organismic process, meaning that all of the parts of entire cosmos belong to one organic whole and that they all interact as participants in one spontaneously self-generating life process." Tu Wei-ming writes, "The organismic process . . . exhibits three basic motifs: continuity, wholeness, and dynamism. All modalities of being . . . are integral parts of a continuum which is often referred to as the 'great trans-

formation.' " The phrase placed in quotation marks by Tu appears originally in the Confucian text *Hsün Tzu* in a reference to *yin yang ta hua,* "the great transformations of yin and yang." See Mote 1971:19; Tu 1985.

21. In recent years, the "Inner Chapters" have received more scholarly attention than has the remainder of the text, and the second of these chapters has certainly been the most popular, if often troublesome, point of focus. Indicative of the disparate approaches to the material are the various translations of the three-character title, *ch'i wu lun,* which was in any event appended by a redactor. Watson renders it as "Discussion on Making All things Equal," Graham as "The Sorting Which Evens Things Out," Mair as "On the Equality of Things," and Michael Saso as "Abstaining from Discourse on the World of Multiplicity." Watson, Graham, and Mair agree with the standard interpretation of pairing *ch'i* and *wu* into the dyad *ch'i-wu,* while Saso's translation pairs *wu* and *lun* into *wu-lun,* reflecting the tradition of a particular monastic Taoist sect and unintentionally echoing the suggestions of Wang An-shih, Chiao Hung, and others. Nevertheless, all appear at least to agree that the chapter addresses the relationship between unity and multiplicity. See Watson 1968:36; Graham 1981:48; Mair 1994:10; Saso 1983:143; Ch'ien 1975:284–286.

22. Interestingly, the final line of "The Four Friends," in reflecting on death, also employs the imagery of slumber to represent fluid transition: "I will go where I am sent, to awaken peacefully as a man wakes out of dreamless sleep" (35).

23. John E. Smith correctly observes that Chuang Tzu's skepticism anticipates the vertigo expressed by John Addington Symonds in the account quoted by William James in his "Mysticism" lectures from *The Varieties of Religious Experience.* "Often have I asked myself with anguish, on waking from that formless state of denuded, keenly sentient being, Which is the unreality—the trance of fiery, vacant, apprehensive, skeptical Self from which I issue, or these surrounding phenomena and habits which veil that inner Self and build a self of flesh-and-blood conventionality? Again, are men the factors of some dream, the dream-like unsubstantiality of which they comprehend at such eventful moments?" See James 1961:304; Smith 1983:253.

24. It is interesting that Eber does not recognize the pivotal role that this topic plays in Buber's commentary, as she notes briefly that "a number of selections from (the text translation) discuss the notion of transformation, yet this is not a major theme in Buber's essay." See Eber 1991:xiv.

25. The sporadic mention of Taoism in Buber's later writings would continue to echo this sentiment. In an essay originally delivered as a lecture to American universities in late 1951, Buber writes, "Similarly, the

Chinese Tao, the 'path' in which the world moves, is the cosmic primal
meaning. But because man conforms this his life to it and practices 'imi-
tation of Tao,' it is at the same time the perfection of the soul." Buber
1952:33.

26. Buber writes, "To surrender oneself to Tao means to renew creation" (91). At this point, one may notice a more than passing resemblance
between this particular understanding of Tao and Mircea Eliade's concepts
of the sacred and "archaic ontology." In brief, Eliade's fundamental premise
is that "the religious moment implies the cosmogonic moment," that religious man "must . . . create his own world and assume the responsibility of
maintaining and renewing it." See Eliade 1959:30, 56. In recent years,
some sinologists have drawn explicit connections between Chuang Tzu and
Eliade. For an engaging if highly technical discussion, see Girardot 1983:77–
133.

27. This concept of actively taking part in an ongoing creation is also
developed in *I and Thou*: "Creation happens to us, burns itself into us,
recasts us in burning—we tremble and are faint, we submit. We take part
in creation, meet the Creator, reach out to Him, helpers and companions."
See Buber 1958:82.

28. Note that this echoes the discussion from the previous chapter,
where it was discussed how the transformative power of the parable allows
one to realize his or her actuality: "For indeed the teaching brings nothing
to man, but it says to each person that he has the oneness when he
discovers it and animates it in himself" (82).

29. It is also relevant to this discussion that Victor Mair, in his
translation of the *Tao Te Ching*, chooses to translate the second character
of the title—a crucial virtue of the Taoist sage—as "integrity." See Lao Tzu
1990.

30. Interestingly, the German text reads *Relation*, not *Beziehung*.
For whatever reasons, even at this early stage Buber is not claiming that
Beziehungen collapse in the face of unity.

31. It should be noted that even in Buber's most monistic passages,
he still employs language that foreshadows the dialogical principle. As
pointed out in the commentary portion, the "wholeness of being" phrase
anticipates the first page of *I and Thou*. Moreover, Buber seems to suggest
that such a unified knowledge affirms the integrity of the individual things
that are encountered, a formulation that also resonates with the later
philosophy: "Because (this cognition) possesses all things in its oneness, it
never stands against them; and when it regards them, it regards them

from themselves out, each thing from itself out; but not from its manifestation, rather from the being of this thing, from the oneness of this thing
that it possesses in its oneness. This cognition is each thing that it regards; and so it elevates each thing that it regards out of manifestation to
existence" (89–90).

32. Of course, it should be remembered that for Buber's argument as
presented in the afterword, conceptual categories like "ethics" or "epistemology" represent nothing more than artificial superimpositions. Despite
the discursive language employed here, one should not lose sight of Buber's
crucial point that the teaching is not really reducible to objectivity and
imperative, that matters of being, salvation, knowledge, and action are
fundamentally inseparable.

33. As noted in the previous chapter, several scholars (for example,
Wood, Friedman, and Moran) interested in tracing Buber's debt to Taoism
have suggested that non-doing may be the single most important and
evident theme carried over into *I and Thou*. This is discussed in greater
detail in the next chapter.

34. Admittedly, there are not many instances in the "Inner Chapters" of *Chuang Tzu* that Buber could find as illustration. A. C. Graham
writes, "For the Syncretist editor, (ideal kingship) would be the greatest of
themes, but it is plain that to find anything remotely relevant in Chuang-
tzu's literary remains he had to scrape the bottom of the barrel." See A. C.
Graham 1981:94.

Chapter 3: The Further Hermeneutic Question

1. The purely monistic strain of the commentary was at first more
evident to Buber's readers than to Buber himself. As late as 1953, more
than forty years and two revisions after the original edition of *Reden und
Gleichnisse*, Buber's introduction to *Hinweise* begins, "I have compiled in
this volume a selection of my essays springing from the years 1909 to
1953. Of the oldest, I have taken up only those which in the main I stand
by even today; where I can no longer represent the basic view of an essay,
I have forgone it without regard for its philosophical or literary worth."
For the 1957 translation appearing in *Pointing the Way*, Buber amended
this prologue only after Maurice Friedman suggested to him that the
pantheistic strand in "The Teaching of the Tao" required some conditional
repudiation. (In a letter to Friedman dated August 22, 1956, Buber writes,
". . . you are right that the essay is too 'mystical.' ") It is also Friedman who

characterized Buber's more mature position not as "pantheism," but as "panentheism," since the former "proclaims that the world *is* already holy if only it be recognized as such," while the latter echoes "the Hasidic affirmation that everything *can* be hallowed." See Buber 1953; "Vorwort"; Friedman 1970:66–68.

2. Obviously, there is some textual basis for Buber's reading, and many modern scholars do put forth similar interpretations. To some extent, the question here is merely one of degree, as Chuang Tzu's appreciation for an experience of unity does not necessitate a total unconcern for worldly matters. A. C. Graham describes Chuang Tzu as a "Heaven-intoxicated man," but quickly adds that he "does not in practice expect to live in a permanent ecstasy moving like a sleepwalker guided by Heaven." See Graham 1981:15–16.

3. Examples such as these provide some context for a few of Buber's own metaphors that may otherwise seem a bit puzzling when they appear in the commentary. In some cases, Buber appears to be emulating Chuang Tzu's imagery, while at the same time employing the earthier images that he obviously prefers: "The unified man is like a child who, from the harmony of his powers, cries the whole day and does not become hoarse, out of collected virtue keeps his fist shut the whole day, out of undetached attentiveness stares the whole day at one thing, moves himself, rests, adapts himself without knowing, and lives beyond all trouble in a heavenly light" (91).

4. Similarly, the very first passage in the text translation portrays a "spirit-like man" (*geistergleicher Mann*), who displays invulnerability and other magical powers: "(He) feeds on air and dew; and riding the clouds, flying dragons his team, he wanders beyond the four seas." The passage concludes: "The world of things cannot wear on him. In a flood that reached to Heaven, he would not even be moistened. In a fire that melted the metals of the Earth and scorched the mountains, he would not become hot" (16).

5. This passage includes translations of two interesting coinages. The word translated by Smith as "make . . . into functions of the soul" is *verseelen,* rendered by Kaufmann as "psychologize." The word translated as "illusion about the soul" is *Seelenwahn,* rendered by Kaufmann as "psychical delusion." See Buber 1970:141.

6. In a second essay, published six years after the one cited just above, Friedman quoted this passage as illustrating "unmistakably the mysticism of the particular and the concrete," and he again notes it as "a

clear presentiment of Buber's mature philosophy of dialogue." See Friedman 1976:415–416.

7. Buber would later write, "I become through my relation to the Thou; as I become I, I say Thou." In both cases, actualization does not occur within an isolated entity. See Buber 1958:11.

8. The tension between these two perspectives is one of the issues at the heart of the controversy surrounding Buber's interpretations of Hasidic tales. Representing the traditional Hasidic view, Louis Jacobs writes: "Engagement in worldly things in the here and now is basic to Hasidism but only as the unavoidable means for meeting the divine sparks which reside there waiting to be reclaimed by holy living. The end of the meeting is, as it were, its total transcendence." Jacobs further notes that Buber reads these worldly engagements, such as those of a cobbler repairing shoes or a coachman admiring the beauty of a passing girl, as ends in themselves, as the actual loci of transcendence. See Jacobs 1985:96–97.

9. Several other passages from the original, not included in the translation, also speak of the "use of the useless." See "Inner Chapters" 11/4/75–82, 12/4/82–91; "School of Chuang Tzu" 51/20/1–9.

10. Once again, the lack of familiarity with the text translation on the part of most Buber scholars has left a self-evident connection either undiscovered or unstated. This has occasionally given rise to some interesting, if incomplete speculation. For example, Donald L. Berry begins an otherwise well-researched study with a lengthy chapter entitled "The Tree," where he notes that Buber's interest in trees and other natural objects has left many interpreters puzzled: "Thus the connection of Buber's vision of mutuality to the natural, to the tree, has remained unidentified and undeveloped, or forgotten altogether. I hope here to correct this misfortune, and to show how Buber's contemplation of the tree points to an absolutely central dimension of his whole program." Nevertheless, Berry's project, which includes a partial concordance of "zoological entities, at the threshold of mutuality," "botanical entities, at the pre-threshold of mutuality," and "the elements, at the subthreshold of mutuality" appearing in Buber's writings, makes no mention of Chuang Tzu or *Reden und Gleichnisse*, though it does refer to Lao Tzu once in passing and note that "The Teaching of the Tao" essay includes references to "butterfly," "cricket," and "mushrooms." Berry traces Buber's earliest fascination with trees to the very beginning of the century; in "Über Jakob Boehme" (1901), Buber writes, "And sometimes there comes to us the desire to put our arms around a young tree, and to feel the same surge of life as in ourselves, or to read the secret of our own life in the eyes of a dumb animal. We experience the

travels and fading of the most distant stars as something which happens to us. There are even moments in which our organism is quite completely another piece of nature." Most importantly, Berry notes Buber's depictions of trees in *Daniel*, whose 1913 publication date places it just a few years after the original edition of the Taoist volume and only a few years before the first draft of *I and Thou*. In particular, the depiction of a stone pine is recognizable as a transitional piece between the two, and an account of a personal encounter with an oak tree may even explain the motivation behind a superficial correction in later editions of *Reden und Gleichnisse*, where the subject of "The Holy Tree" was changed from simply a "holy tree" to a "holy oak tree." Interestingly, James Moran cites Chuang Tzu's story of the useless tree (from the impressionistic translation by Thomas Merton) as a parallel with Buber's philosophy, but he makes no mention of the most relevant passage from *I and Thou*. See Berry 1985:1, 7, 17–18, 77, 99–101; Moran 1972:100.

11. Hideki Yukawa writes, "The day will come, I believe, when we shall know the heart of the elementary particle, even though that will not be achieved with the ease with which Chuangtse knew the heart of the fish." See Yukawa 1983:61.

12. As discussed previously, the German represents a most unusual and creative gloss of Buber's. This is the most important instance where Alex Page's impressionistic translation of the text bleaches out some absolutely crucial language. Unaware of either Buber's intention or the ramifications of the passage for dialogical philosophy, Page badly mistranslates the key phrase—"he beheld being, his I, countenance to countenance"—as "he looked from moment to moment as though he had transcended his very self." See Buber 1991:29.

13. "The It is the eternal chrysalis, the Thou the eternal butterfly" (Buber 1958:17).

14. While I know of no one else who has made a similar claim about *I and Thou*, there have been occasional suggestions that the text does, in fact, function as more than just a personal religious address. For example, Buber's handwritten outline extant in the Buber Archive (and reprinted in Buber 1970:49–50) points out that the text was originally intended to serve as a largely methodological work in the phenomenology of religion, which would isolate universal patterns in the development of human religiosity.

15. The applicability of Eliade's theories to cosmogonic and ritual motifs appearing in *Chuang Tzu* is considered in depth in Girardot 1983:77–133.

16. The impartiality of the cosmic processes is a recurring theme throughout the text. For example, "Heaven covers without partiality, earth carries without partiality" ("Inner Chapters" 19/6/96–97).

17. This latter phrase is a translation of the troublesome tetrad, *pu tao chih tao*, which forces the reader to adopt a suitable meaning for Tao as a verb. Graham translates this as "an untold Way," Watson as "the Way that is not a way," Mair as "the Way that cannot be walked up," and Wu as "Tao of not Taoing." Perhaps here, Chad Hansen's experimental definition of Tao may be applicable: "A tao is a way of *shih*ing and *fei*ing of performances of conventionally or socially defined actions. . . . A tao is a scheme of classifications (names) which generates a pattern of behavior via its influence on affective attitudes—desires and aversions. To have learned how to use a name is to classify or divide things in the way one's linguistic community does and to have to appropriate pro and con attitudes." See Graham 1981:57; Watson 1968:45; Mair 1994:20; Wu 1990:147; Hansen 1983a:36.

18. "If you follow your completed heart-mind and make it your guide, then who alone is without a guide? . . . affirming or negating without having completed one's heart-mind, that is like going to Yüeh today and arriving yesterday" ("Inner Chapters" 4/2/21–22).

19. While this emerging orthodoxy may be traced to Kantian epistemology, it was Susanne Langer who made the most eloquent statement of the position: "For if the material of thought is symbolism, then the thinking organism must be forever furnishing symbolic versions of its experiences, in order to let thinking proceed. As a matter of fact, it is not the essential act of thought that is symbolization, but an act *essential to thought*, and prior to it. Symbolization is the essential act of mind; and mind takes in more than what is commonly called thought." This position has also been used to justify the particularistic approach to mysticism held by Steven Katz and others contributing to his two volumes of essays. Robert Gimello: ". . . what is perhaps mislabelled 'interpretation' is actually ingredient in and constitutive of . . . experience." Hans Penner (quoting Maurice Godelier): ". . . there are no direct experiences of the world, or between individuals except *through* the social relations which 'mediate' them." John E. Smith: "We must rid ourselves of the illusion that there is 'raw' experience and recognize the unavailability of any experience which is not in some way expressed and interpreted." See Langer 1942:41; Gimello 1983:62; Penner 1983:89; J. Smith 1983:248.

20. Smith renders *unmittelbar* as "direct," Kaufmann as "unmediated." See Buber 1958:11; Buber 1970:62.

21. This citation (63/23/42) is from one of the heterogeneous miscellaneous chapters; Graham believes that this fragment is thematically and linguistically related to the "Inner Chapters."

22. An interesting corollary is that "evil" does not have ontological status in Chuang Tzu's vision of the cosmos. Because the hierarchical poles of right and wrong, good and evil, are not legitimate manifestations of Tao, evil emerges only as an existential problem, a condition of inequality produced within the human realm. It must also be noted that "good" is not an adequate existential solution, as the continuation of the dichotomy serves only to sustain the conditioned hierarchy; the true answer must lie outside of this orientation. And while Buber does not dispense with the concepts of good and evil, he too maintains that the appropriate response to evil is not simply a reversal of the undesirable ethic, but a movement to a new way of being in the world. For Buber, evil occurs in the realm of I-It; good is attained not in speaking more I-It combinations, but in the qualitative breakthrough to saying I-Thou. "One cannot do evil with his whole soul, one can do good only with the whole soul." See Buber 1961:130.

23. This is an intentional reversal of the language used by Langer in her discussion of symbolic transformation, though the "transmitter" portrayed here is an active, attentive one. See Langer 1942:42–43.

24. For example, Julia Ching writes: "Looking into the mirror stands for looking into one's own depths, finding one's real self. In the case of the Confucian, the truth is both beautiful and ugly, so that one might choose to promote the desirable and correct the faulty. In the case of the Taoist, the 'real self' is the universe. To speak of detachment here is thus actually to speak of the continuum of subject and object, of conscious self and unconscious 'nucleus,' of man and nature. This is not necessarily ontological monism. It represents a transformed consciousness, achieved by cultivation and purification—as a mirror is cleaned and dusted." Lee Yearley writes: "A mirror accepts whatever is presented to it without interpretation, judgment, or desire. A mirror makes no judgments on rightness or wrongness; it impartially reflects a child killed or a child saved. A mirror possesses no desire to pursue or to grasp what passes before it; it just lets desirable objects come before it and then pass away. Mirrors accept; they do not evaluate or cling or seek." Harold Oshima writes: "Reflections make no real impression on the mirror—images only dance and play on its surface and never damage the mirror itself. Similarly the world's most catastrophic events can never make a permanent or even lasting impression on the sage. If only he can keep his mirror free from dust, clear of all the concerns that stick to the ordinary man's *hsin*, he can enjoy perfect freedom and detachment." See Ching 1983:242; Yearley 1983:133; Oshima 1983:77–78.

25. This latter phrase is a translation of *liang hsing*, rendered by Watson as "walking two roads," by Graham as "letting both alternatives proceed," by Mair as "dual procession," and by Wu as "double-walk." Moreover, Wu puts forth his own scheme as to how the "double-walk" mediates between poles. "To such interrelatedness of things and thinking, we can respond with three attitudes. We can either neglect it and become *dogmatic* or be obsessed with it and become *relativistic* (namely, indifferent and withdrawn), or we can *participate* in it and allow ourselves to freely [*sic*] respond to it. Only the last is the correct way." Wu also refers to "living participation in the ontological mutualities" as "crucial for making up the world." See Watson 1968:41; Graham 1981:54; Mair 1994:17; Wu 1990:142, 174–175.

26. Livia (Knaul) Kohn writes: "This means one should fully realize that whatever happens is part of the Tao and therefore good and cannot be changed. All value judgments and emotional reactions are erroneous and ultimately meaningless. There is no need to feel separate from life and the Tao or to evaluate it in any way, because one is always part of it. The Tao is the *now* that is right here to be participated in absolutely." See Kohn 1991:13.

27. Buber, in fact, makes reference to "the primally simple fact of encounter." See Buber 1970:126

28. Of the latter variety, Yearley writes: "The two key elements are an immutable transcendent reality and a contingent but real world. One reality gives itself its own eternal existence, and it must be—it is necessary. The other reality receives its existence from elsewhere, can change, and need not necessarily exist—it is contingent. In the mysticism of union these two separate realities meet but are preserved: a union but not a unity exists between the unchanging Real and the changing but still real particular individual." Of the former: "It rests on a monistic base; only one reality exists, and no particular is fully real. Anything that is, insofar as it is, is one; therefore any individual is a mere negative limitation on the universal. The union is as complete as that of salt and water or of a drop of water and the ocean." This bears some resemblance to the typology established by Ninian Smart between Rudolf Otto's concept of "numinous" experience and a more quietistic "mystical" experience." See Yearley 1983:13; Smart 1978:13.

29. In particular, Yearley says that Chuang Tzu at his most radical is putting forth a vision that affirms the aesthetic to the exclusion of the human: "All life should be viewed as an esthetic panorama. We are not fulfilled through the interactions between human beings as most think.

Rather we are fulfilled when we see all that we encounter as esthetic objects. Life is a series of esthetically pleasing new beginnings, and all such beginnings should be grasped and then surrendered as change proceeds." However, even this is in fundamental agreement with Buber's position that human relationship is not the exclusive locus of meaningful encounter and that the actual meaning is not found within the ordinary parameters of human emotions and value systems. In a telephone conversation (May 1992), Yearley acknowledged that the "encounter with esthetic objects" described above more closely resembles "meeting" than it does "objectification," though he did question exactly what kind of interpersonal relations, what observable semblance of "ethics," would follow from this aesthetic perspective. See Yearley 1983:136.

30. The conference was held in San Diego, California, in October 1991. Papers included Christine Downing's "Feminism's Rediscovery of the Dialogical," Maurice Friedman and Tamar Kron's "Problems of Confirmation in Psychotherapy," Joy T. De Sensi's "The Implications of Martin Buber's Dialogue-Mutuality and Its Relevance in Society in the Forms of Music, Sport, and Dance Performance," Pat Boni's "Buber and Shakespeare's *King Lear*," and Virginia Shabatay's "Strangers in Relation: Intimacy, Privacy, Secrecy, Deception." "A Workshop on Buber and the Twelve Step Program" was moderated by Daniel Escher and Angela Spencer. Several of the papers from this conference, including my own "I and Tao: Buber's *Chuang Tzu* and the Comparative Study of Mysticism," make up the forthcoming volume, *Martin Buber and the Human Sciences*. See Friedman 1996.

31. "Chuang Tzu talked about sense-knowledge versus spirit, chipping-breaking versus entering, instead of the I-It versus the I-Thou. (Gabriel) Marcel's description (of dialogical philosophy) has as uncanny affinity with Chuang Tzu, who predates both Marcel and Buber by almost twenty-four centuries" (Wu 1990:344).

Chapter 4: Conclusion

1. "In other words, I should like to restrict the term [Taoism] to the Way of the Celestial Master and the organizations that grew out of it. . . . Yet I recognize that for many others in the English-speaking world—which has a profusion of translations of the *Lao-tzu* and *Chuang-tzu*, but, so far, none of any major Taoist religious text—such a view may be difficult to comprehend. Still, whether or not my own criteria are accepted, I maintain that utter and disgraceful confusion will flourish in Sinology as long as

scholars try to define Taoism without reference to the contents of the Taoist Canon, and without taking into account the complexities of Chinese social history" (Strickmann 1979:165–166).

2. Smith makes this point in a number of his works, but the best statement of it is to be found in Smith 1981:1–44.

❧-BIBLIOGRAPHY-❧

Abe, Masao. 1971. "Dogen on Buddha Nature." *The Eastern Buddhist* 4, no. 71:30–36.

Allinson, Robert. 1988. "Zen in the Light of Taoism: An Exercise in Inter-Cultural Hermeneutics." *Zen Buddhism Today* 6:23–38.

———. 1989. *Chuang–Tzu for Spiritual Transformation*. Albany: State University of New York Press.

Balfour, Frederick Henry. 1881. *The Divine Classic of Nan–hua, Being the Works of Chuang Tsze, Taoist Philosopher*. Shanghai and Hong Kong: Kelly and Walsh.

———. 1887. *Leaves from my Scrapbook*. London: Trübner's Oriental Series.

Berry, Donald L. 1985. *Mutuality: The Vision of Martin Buber*. Albany: State University of New York Press.

Bloch, Jochanan, and Gordon, Haim, eds. 1984. *Martin Buber: A Centenary Volume*. Negev: Ktav.

Buber, Martin. 1906. *Die Geschichten des Rabbi Nachman*. Frankfort: Rütten & Loening.

———. 1908. *Die Legend des Baal Shem*. Frankfort: Rütten & Loening.

———. 1910. *Reden und Gleichnisse des Tschuang–tse*. Leipzig: Insel–Verlag.

———. 1911. *Chinesische Geister- und Liebesgeschichten*. Frankfort: Rütten & Loening.

———. 1915. "Der Geist des Orient und das Judentum." In *Der Neue Merkur* 2, no. 3 (June 1915): 353–357.

———. 1916. *Vom Geist des Judentums*. Leipzig: Kurt Wolff Verlag.

———. 1917. *Die Rede, Die Lehre, und Das Lied: Drei Beispiele*. Leipzig: Insel–Verlag.

———. 1918. *Reden und Gleichnisse des Tschuang–tse*. Leipzig: Insel–Verlag.

———. 1924. "Besprechungen mit Martin Buber in Ascona, August 1924 über *Lao–tse's Tao–te–king*." (Unpublished manuscript). Jewish National and University Library, Arc. Ms. Var. 350.

———. 1929–30. "China und Wir." *Chinesich–Deutscher Almanach für das Jahr Gi Si*, 40–43.

————. 1936. *Die Stunde und die Erkenntnis. Reden und Aufsatze, 1933–1935*. Berlin: Schocken Verlag.

————. 1943. *Die Chassidische Botschaft*. Heidelberg: Verlag Lambert Schneider.

————. 1947. *Tales of the Hasidim, The Early Masters*. Olga Marx, trans. New York: Schocken.

————. 1948. *Israel and the World: Essays in a Time of Crisis*. New York: Schocken Books.

————. 1951. *Reden und Gleichnisse des Tschuang–tse*. Zürich: Manesse Verlag.

————. 1952. *Eclipse of God*. New York: Harper & Row.

————. 1953. *Hinweise*. Zürich: Manesse Verlag.

————. 1956. "Dem Gemeinschaftlichen folgen." *Die Neue Rundschau* 67, no. 4:582–600.

————. 1956a. *The Tales of Rabbi Nachman*. Maurice Friedman, trans. New York: Horizon.

————. 1957. *Pointing the Way*. Maurice Friedman, trans. New York: Harper & Brothers.

————. 1958. *I and Thou*. Ronald Gregor Smith, trans. New York: Charles Scribner's Sons.

————. 1958a. "What Is Common to All." Maurice Friedman, trans. *Review of Metaphysics* 2:359–379.

————. 1958b. *Hasidism and Modern Man*. Maurice Friedman, trans. New York: Harper & Row.

————. 1960. *The Origin and Meaning of Hasidism*. Maurice Friedman, trans. New York: Horizon.

————. 1961. *Good and Evil: Two Interpretations*. New York: Charles Scribner's Sons.

————. 1963. "Interpreting Hasidism." *Commentary* 36, no. 3:218–225.

————. 1967. *On Judaism*. Nahum N. Glatzer, trans. New York: Schocken.

————. 1967. *A Believing Humanism*. Maurice Friedman, trans. New York: Simon & Schuster.

————. 1970. *I and Thou*. Walter Kaufmann, trans. New York: Charles Scribner's Sons.

————. 1972. *Briefwechsel aus sieben Jahrzehnten, Band I*. Heidelberg: Verlag Lambert Schneider.

————. 1991. *Chinese Tales*. Alex Page, trans. Atlantic Highlands: Humanities Press International.

Burneko, Guy C. 1986. "Chuang Tzu's Existential Hermeneutics." *Journal of Chinese Philosophy* 13:393–410.

Carus, Paul. 1896. "Lau–tsze's Tau–teh–king. The Old Philosopher's Classic on Reason and Virtue." *The Monist* 7, no. 4:571–601.

————. 1898. *Lao–tse's Tao–te–king*. Chicago: Open Court.

Chan, Wing–tsit. 1964. *A Source Book in Chinese Philosophy*. Princeton: Princeton University Press.

Chang Chung–yuan. 1963. *Creativity and Taoism*. New York: Harper & Row.

Ch'ien, Edward T. 1975. "Chiao Hung and Revolt against Ch'eng–Chu Orthodoxy." In de Bary 1975:271–304.

Ch'ien Mu. 1935. *Hsien–Ch'in chu–tzu hsi–nien k'ao*. Hong Kong: Hong Kong University Press.

————. 1951 *Chuang Tzu Tsuan–ch'ien*. Hong Kong: Tung–nan Yin–wu Ch'u–pan–she.

————. 1955. "Chung–yung hsin–i." *Min–chu p'ing lun* 6, no. 16:2–8.

Ching, Julia. 1983. "The Mirror Symbol Revisited: Confucian and Taoist Mysticism." In Katz 1983:226–246.

Chuang Tzu. 1956. *Harvard–Yenching Institute Sinological Index Series*, no. 20. Cambridge: Harvard University Press.

Cohen, Ralph, ed. 1974. *New Directions in Literary History*. Baltimore: Johns Hopkins University Press.

Crandell, Michael. 1983. "On Walking Without Touching the Ground: 'Play' in the *Inner Chapters* of the *Chuang–tzu*." In Mair 1983:101–124.

Creel, Herrlee G. 1979. "Discussion of Professor Fingarette on Confucius." In *Studies in Classical Chinese Thought* (Journal of the American Academy of Religion Thematic Issue) 47, no. 3S:407–416.

Cua, Anthony. 1977. "Forgetting Morality: Reflections on a Theme in *Chuang Tzu*." In *Journal of Chinese Philosophy* 4:305–328.

Daly, Mary. 1973. *Beyond God the Father—Toward a Philosophy of Women's Liberation*. Boston: Beacon.

de Bary, Wm. Theodore, ed. 1975. *The Unfolding of Neo–Confucianism*. New York: Columbia University Press.

de Harlez, Charles. 1891. "Texts Taoistes Traduits des Originaux Chinois et Commentés." In *Annales du Musée Guimet* 20:283–339.

Denny, Frederick M., and Taylor, Rodney L., eds. 1985. *The Holy Book in Comparative Perspective*. Columbia: University of South Carolina Press.

Eber, Irene. 1991. "Introduction." In Buber 1991.

————. 1994. "Martin Buber and Taoism." *Monumenta Serica* 42 (1994):445–464.

Eliade, Mircea. 1959. *The Sacred and the Profane*. Willard Trask, trans. Orlando: Harcourt Brace Jovanovich.

————, ed. 1987. *Encyclopedia of Religion*. New York: Macmillan.

Faber, Ernst. 1877. *Der Naturalismus bei den alten Chinesen sowohl nach der Seite des Pantheismus als des Sensualismus oder die sämtlichen Werke des Philosophen Licius*. Eberfeld: Verlag von R. L. Friderichs.

Fingarette, Herbert. 1972. *Confucius—The Secular as Sacred*. New York: Harper Torchbooks.

———. 1979. "Following the 'One Thread' of the *Analects*." *Studies in Classical Chinese Thought* (Journal of the American Academy of Religion Thematic Issue) 47, no. 3S:373–406.

Forman, Robert K. C., ed. 1990. *The Problem of Pure Consciousness*. Oxford: Oxford University Press.

———. 1994. "Mystical Knowledge: Knowledge by Identity." *Journal of the American Academy of Religion* 61, no. 4 (Winter 1993): 705–738.

Freideutsche Jugend, 4:8 (August 1918).

Friedman, Maurice. 1955. *Martin Buber—The Life of Dialogue*. New York: Harper & Row.

———. 1970. "Martin Buber's Encounter With Mysticism." *Review of Existential Psychology and Psychiatry* 10:43–81.

———. 1976. "Martin Buber and Asia." *Philosophy East and West* 26: 411–426.

———. 1986. *Martin Buber and the Eternal*. New York: Human Sciences Press.

———. 1988. *Martin Buber's Life and Work*. Detroit: Wayne State University Press.

———. 1988a. "Interpreting Hasidism: The Buber–Scholem Controversy." *Leo Baeck Institute Year Book* 33:449–467.

———. 1989. Book review of Lawrence [sic] J. Silberstein, *Martin Buber's Social and Religious Thought: Alienation and the Quest for Meaning* (New York: New York University Press, 1989). *Journal of the American Academy of Religion* 59, no. 1:197–199.

———, ed. 1996. *Martin Buber and the Human Sciences*. Albany: SUNY Press.

Friedman, Maurice, and Schilpp, Paul Arthur. 1967. *The Philosophy of Martin Buber*. La Salle, IL: Open Court.

Fung Yu–lan. 1952. *A History of Chinese Philosophy*, vol. 1. Derk Bodde, trans. Princeton: Princeton University Press.

Daniel K. Gardner. 1990. *Chu Hsi: Learning to Be a Sage*. Berkeley: University of California Press.

Giles, Herbert A. 1889. *Chuang Tzu: Mystic, Moralist, and Social Reformer*. London: Bernard Quaritch.

Gimello, Robert. 1983. "Mysticism in Its Contexts." In Katz 1983:61–88.

———. 1990. "Remarks on the Future of the Study of Mysticism." Unpublished manuscript, presented at the Annual Meeting of the American Academy of Religion; New Orleans; November 18, 1990.

Girardot, N. J. 1983. *Myth and Meaning in Early Taoism*. Berkeley: University of California Press.

Gordon, Haim, and Bloch, Jochanan, eds. 1984. *Martin Buber: A Centenary Volume*. Negev: Ktav.

Graham, A. C. 1960. *The Book of Lieh Tzu*. New York: Columbia University Press.

———. 1969–70. "Chuang–tzu's Essay on Seeing Things as Equal." *History of Religions* 9, nos. 2–3:137–159.

———. 1979. "How Much of *Chuang–tzu* Did Chuang–tzu Write?" *Studies in Classical Chinese Thought* (Journal of the American Academy of Religion Thematic Issue) 47, no. 3:459–501.

———. 1981. *Chuang Tzu: The Inner Chapters*. London: George Allen & Unwin.

———. 1983. "Taoist Spontaneity and the Dichotomy of 'Is' and 'Ought'." In Mair 1983:3–23.

Graham, William A. 1987. "Scripture." In Eliade 1987, vol. 13:133–145.

Green, Arthur. 1979. *Tormented Master: A Life of Rabbi Nahman of Bratslav*. Alabama: University of Alabama Press.

Hansen, Chad. 1983. *Language and Logic in Ancient China*. Ann Arbor: University of Michigan Press.

———. 1983a. "A Tao of Tao in Chuang–tzu." In Mair 1983:24–55.

———. 1991. "Should the Ancient Masters Value Reason?" In Rosemont, 1991:179–208.

———. 1992. *A Daoist Theory of Chinese Thought*. New York: Oxford University Press.

Henderson, John B. 1991. *Scripture, Canon, and Commentary*. Princeton: Princeton University Press.

Herman, Jonathan R. 1985. "On Chuang Tzu: Toward a Statement of Human Project." Unpublished manuscript, January 4, 1985.

———. 1986. "On Martin Buber and I–Thou Mysticism: Toward an Expansive Interpretation." Unpublished manuscript, May 1, 1986.

Hirsch, E. D., Jr. 1967. *Validity in Interpretation*. New Haven: Yale University Press.

Iser, Wolfgang. 1974. "The Reading Process: A Phenomenological Approach." In Cohen 1974:125–46.

Jacobs, Louis. 1985. "Aspects of Scholem's Study of Hasidism." *Modern Judaism* 5 no. 1:95–104.

James, William. 1961. *The Varieties of Religious Experience*. New York: Macmillan.

Jauss, Hans Robert. 1982. *Toward an Aesthetic of Reception*. Timothy Bahti, trans. Minneapolis: University of Minnesota Press.

Katz, Steven T. 1978. *Mysticism and Philosophical Analysis*. New York: Oxford University Press.

———. 1983. *Mysticism and Religious Traditions*. New York: Oxford University Press.

———. 1985. *Post–Holocaust Dialogues*. New York: New York University Press.

Kepnes Steven D. 1987. "A Hermeneutic Approach to the Buber–Scholem Controversy." *Journal of Jewish Studies* 38, no. 1:81–98.

———. 1988. "Buber as Hermeneutic: Relations to Dilthey and Gadamer." *Harvard Theological Review* 81, no. 2:193–213

Kerenyi, Carl. 1967. "Martin Buber as Classical Author." In Schilpp and Friedman 1967:629–638.

Kodera, Takashi J. 1977. "The Buddha–Nature in Dogen's *Shobogenzo*." *Japanese Journal of Religious Studies* 4, no. 4:273–276.

Kohn, Livia (Knaul). 1982. "Lost *Chuang–tzu* Passages." *Journal of Chinese Religions* 10:53–79.

———. 1985. "Kuo Hsiang and the *Chuang Tzu*." *Journal of Chinese Philosophy* 12:429–447.

———. 1985a. "The Habit of Perfection: A Summary of Fukunaga Mitsuji's Studies on the *Chuang Tzu* Tradition." *Cahiers d'Extrême–Asie* 1:71–85.

———. 1986. "Chuang–Tzu and the Chinese Ancestry of Ch'an Buddhism." *Journal of Chinese Philosophy* 13:411–428.

———. 1987. *Seven Steps to the Tao: Sima Chengzhen's Zuowanglun*. Netteta: Steyler.

———. 1991. *Taoist Mystical Philosophy*. Albany: State University of New York Press.

———. 1992. *Early Chinese Mysticism*. Princeton: Princeton University Press.

Kuhn, Thomas. 1962. *The Structure of Scientific Revolutions*. Chicago: University of Chicago, Press.

Kuo Mo–jo. 1954. "Lao Tan, Kuan Yin, Huan Yüan." In *Ch'ing–t'ung Shih–tai*. Beijing: Jen–min ch'u–pan–she.

LaFargue, Michael. "Sayings About Tao in the *Tao Te Ching*: Foundations or Celebrations?" Unpublished manuscript, delivered at the New England American Academy of Religion meeting, March 31, 1989.

———. 1992. *The Tao of the Tao Te Ching*. Albany: State University of New York Press.

Langer, Susanne K. 1942. *Philosophy in a New Key*. Cambridge: Harvard University Press.

Lao Tzu. 1963. *Tao Te Ching*. D. C. Lau, trans. Middlesex: Penguin.

———. 1990. *Tao Te Ching*. Victor H. Mair, trans. New York: Bantam.

Laqueur, Walter. 1984. *Young Germany: A History of the German Youth Movement*. New Brunswick: Transaction.

Legge, James. 1891. "The Writings of Kwang–tze." In *The Sacred Books of China, the Texts of Taoism*. London: Humphrey Milford.

———. 1970. *The Works of Mencius*. New York: Dover.

———. 1971. *Confucian Analects, The Great Learning, and The Doctrine of the Mean*. New York: Dover.

Lester, Robert C. 1985. "Hinduism: Veda and Sacred Texts." In Denny and Taylor 1985:126–147.

Levering, Miriam. 1984. "Reading *Chuang–tzu*: One Way or Many?" *Religious Studies Review* 10, no. 3:228–237.

———. 1989. *Rethinking Scripture*. Albany: State University of New York Press.

Liu Xiaogan. 1994. *Classifying the* Zhuangzi *Chapters*. Ann Arbor: University of Michigan Press.

Lo Ken–tze. 1958. "Chuang Tzu che–hsueh 'wai' 'tsa' p'ien t'an–yuan." In *Chu–tzu K'ao–yin*, 282–312. Beijing: Jen–min ch'u–pan she.

Louie, Kam. 1986. *Inheriting Tradition, Interpretations of the Classical Philosophers in Communist China*. Oxford: Oxford University Press.

Lu Chen–yu. 1955. *Chung–kuo Cheng–chih Ssu–hsiang–shih*. Beijing: San–lien Shu–tien.

Lynn, Richard John. 1970. "Orthodoxy and Enlightenment: Wang Shih-chen's Theory of Poetry and Its Antecedents." In de Bary 1975:217–270.

Mair, Victor H., ed. 1983. *Experimental Essays on Chuang–tzu*. Honolulu: University of Hawaii Press.

———. 1990. "Afterword." In Lao Tzu 1990:119–153.

———. 1994. *Wandering On The Way: Early Taoist Tales and Parables of Chuang Tzu*. New York: Bantam.

Mori, Makisaburo. 1972. "Chuang Tzu and Buddhism." *The Eastern Buddhist* 5, no. 2:44–69.

Moran, James A. 1972. "Martin Buber and Taoism." *Judaism* 21:98–103.

Mote, Frederick W. 1971. *Intellectual Foundations of China*. New York: Alfred A. Knopf.

Munro, Donald J. 1969. *The Concept of Man in Early China*. Stanford: Stanford University Press.

Neumann, Carl Friederich. 1836. *Lehrsaal des Mittelreiches*. Munchen: Dr. Carl Wolf'sche Buchdruckerei.

Niebuhr, Reinhold. 1958. "Essays on Man." *New York Times Book Review*, April 13, 1958:36–37.

Oshima, Harold H. 1983. "A Metaphorical Analysis of the Concept of Mind in the *Chuang–tzu*." In Mair 1983:63–84.

Park, O'Hyun. 1975. "Chinese Religions and the Religions of China." *Perspectives in Religious Studies* 2:160–190.

Penner, Hans. 1983. "The Mystical Illusion." In Katz 1983:89–116.

P'u Sung–ling. 1946. *Chinese Ghost and Love Stories*. Rose Quong, trans. New York: Pantheon.

Ricoeur, Paul. 1981. *Hermeneutics and the Human Sciences*. John B. Thompson, trans. Cambridge: Cambridge University Press.

Robinet, Isabelle. 1983. "Kouo Siang Ou Le Monde Comme Absolu." *T'oung–pao* 69:73–107.

Rosemont, Henry, Jr., ed. 1991 *Chinese Texts and Philosophical Contexts*. La Salle, IL: Open Court.

Roth, Harold D. 1991. "Who Compiled the *Chuang Tzu?*" In Rosemont 1991:79–128.

Saso, Michael. 1983. "The *Chuang–tzu nei–p'ien*: A Taoist Meditation." In Mair 1983:140–157.

Schatzker, Chaim. 1978. "Martin Buber's Influence on the Jewish Youth Movement in Germany." *Leo Baeck Institute Year Book* 23:151–171.

Schilpp, Paul Arthur, and Friedman, Maurice, eds. 1967. *The Philosophy of Martin Buber*. La Salle, IL: Open Court.

Schleiermacher, Friedrich. 1977. *Hermeneutics: The Handwritten Manuscripts*. Heinz Kimmerle, ed.; James Duke and Jack Forstman, trans. Missoula: Scholars Press.

Scholem, Gershom. 1941. *Major Trends in Jewish Mysticism*. New York: Schocken.

———. 1971. *The Messianic Idea in Judaism*. New York: Schocken.

Schwartz, Benjamin. 1985. *The World of Thought In Ancient China*. Cambridge: Belknap.

Seidel, Anna, and Welch, Holmes, eds. 1979. *Facets of Taoism*. New Haven: Yale University Press.

Shaw, Miranda. 1985. "Nature in Dogen's Philosophy and Poetry." *The Journal of the International Association of Buddhist Studies* 7, no. 2:111–132.

———. 1988. "Buddhist and Taoist Influences on Chinese Landscape Painting." *Journal of the History of Ideas* 49, no. 2:183–206.

Silberstein, Laurence. 1987. "Martin Buber." In Eliade 1987, vol. 2:316–318.

Smart, Ninian. 1978. "Understanding Religious Experience." In Katz 1978:10–21.

Smith, Huston. 1976. *Forgotten Truth*. New York: Harper & Row.

Smith, John E. 1983. "William James's Account of Mysticism; A Critical Appraisal." In Katz 1983:247–279.

Smith, Wilfred Cantwell. 1962. *The Meaning and End of Religion*. New York: Harper & Row.

———. 1972. *The Faith of Other Men*. New York: Harper & Row.

———. 1979. *Faith and Belief*. Princeton: Princeton University Press.

———. 1981. *Towards a World Theology*. Philadelphia: Westminster Press.

———. 1989. "Scripture as Form and Concept: Their Emergence for the Western World." In Levering 1989:29–57.

Stoudt, John Joseph. 1968. *Jacob Boehme: His Life and Thought*. New York: Seabury.

Strickmann, Michel. 1979. "On the Alchemy of T'ao Hung–ching." In Welch and Seidel 1979:123–192.

Taylor, Rodney L., and Denny, Frederick M., eds. 1985. *The Holy Book in Comparative Perspective*. Columbia: University of South Carolina Press.

Tu Wei–ming. 1976. *Centrality and Commonality: An Essay on Chung–yung*. Honolulu: The University Press of Hawaii.

———. 1985. *Confucian Thought: Selfhood as Creative Transformation*. Albany: State University of New York Press.

Turner, Victor. 1966. *The Ritual Process*. Ithaca: Cornell University Press.

van Gennep, Arnold. 1909. *The Rites of Passage*. London: Routledge & Kegan Paul.

von Strauss, Victor. 1870. *Lao Tse's Tao Te King*. Leipzig: Verlag von Friedrich Fleischer.

Wang Chingdao. 1912. *Confucius and New China: Confucius' Idea of the State and its Relation to Constitutional Government*. Shanghai: Commercial Press.

———. 1913. "Die Staatsidee des Konfuzius and ihre Beziehung zur konstitutionellen Verfassung." *Mitteilungen des Seminars für Orientalische Sprachen. Abt. 1: Ostasiatische Studien* 16:1–49.

Watson, Burton. 1968. *The Complete Works of Chuang Tzu*. New York: Columbia University Press.

Welch, Holmes, and Seidel, Anna, eds. 1979. *Facets of Taoism*. New Haven: Yale University Press.

Werblowsky, R. J. Zwi. 1988. "Reflections on Martin Buber's *Two Types of Faith*." *Journal of Jewish Studies* 39, no. 1:92–101.

Wilhelm, Hellmut. 1983. "Chuang–tzu Translations: A Bibliographical Appendix." In Mair 1983:158–161.

Wilhelm, Richard. 1979. *Lectures on the I Ching*. Irene Eber, trans. Princeton: Princeton University Press.

Wood, Robert. 1984. "Oriental Themes in Buber's Work." In Gordon and Bloch 1984.

Wu Kuang–ming. 1982. *Chuang Tzu: World Philosopher at Play*. New York: Scholars Press.

———. 1986. "Dream in Nietzsche and Chuang Tzu." *Journal of Chinese Philosophy* 13, no. 4:371–382.

———. 1990. *The Butterfly as Companion*. Albany: State University of New York Press.

Yearley, Lee. 1983. "The Perfected Person in the Radical Chuang–tzu." In Mair 1983:125–139.

Yukawa, Hideki. 1983. "Chuangtse: The Happy Fish." In Mair 1983:56–62.

❀-INDEX-❀

Allinson, Robert, 125–126, 189–191, 250 n. 54

Bab, Julius, 241 n. 1
Balfour, Frederick Henry, 4, 10
Berry, Donald, 257–258 n. 10
Boehme, Jacob, 252 n. 15
Boni, Pat, 262 n. 30
Bonus, Arthur, 241 n. 1
borders, 170–174
Burneko, Guy, 125

Campbell, Joseph, 198
Ch'ien Mu, 237 n. 34, 249 n. 47
Chan, Wing-tsit, 10
Ching, Julia, 260 n. 24
community, 152–154
cosmogony, 139–145, 154, 234–235
  n. 33, 252–253 nn. 19–20, 254
  n. 26, 258 n. 15
Crandell, Michael, 251 n. 10
Creel, Herrlee, 243 n. 10

Daly, Mary, 243–244 n. 13
De Sensi, Joy, 262 n. 30
death, 141–142, 160, 166, 195, 253
  n. 22
de Lubac, Henri, 198
dialogical hermeneutics, 135, 154
dialogical philosophy, ix–x, 11,
  104, 188, 211 n. 8, 227
  nn. 11–12, 244 n. 14, 254–255
  n. 31, 257 n. 7, 258 n. 12;
  applied to *Chuang Tzu*, xi,
  157, 168–185, 187, 192–198,

216 n. 3, 262 n. 31; contrasted
  with monism and pantheism,
  111–112, 131–132, 148,
  157–158, 161, 254 n. 30,
  256–257 n. 6; eternal Thou,
  162, 167, 181, 185; proto-
  dialogical thought, 112–115,
  117, 125–126, 137, 157,
  162–167, 183–184, 196, 216
  n. 3, 246 n. 27
Dilthey, Wilhelm, 133–134, 251
  n. 9
Dogen, 130
Downing, Christine, 262 n. 30
dream, 113, 142, 253 nn. 22–23

Eber, Irene, xi, 105–107, 111, 129,
  205 n. 7, 206 n. 11, 243 n. 12,
  245 n. 17, 246 n. 28, 251 n. 11,
  253 n. 24
Eliade, Mircea, 170, 254 n. 26, 258
  n. 15
equality, 140–141, 170–175, 184,
  253 n. 21, 260 n. 22
Escher, Daniel, 262 n. 30
eternal Thou. *See* dialogical
  philosophy

fasting, 194–196
Fingarette, Herbert, 243 n. 10
forgetting, 174, 195
Forman, Robert, 244–245 n. 16,
  251 n. 5
freedom, 2, 159, 164, 180–183,
  185, 260 n. 24

275